2020

THE END

let us live again

KARANVIR GUPTA

BlueRose
Publishers
NewDelhi • London

First Published in October 2021

ISBN: 978-93-5472-421-3

BLUEROSE PUBLISHERS

www.bluerosepublishers.com

info@bluerosepublishers.com

+91 8882 898 898

Cover Design:

Karanvir Gupta

Nischayata Mishra

Typographic Design:

Ilma Mirza

Distributed by: BlueRose, Amazon, Flipkart

Dedication

Dedicated to
entire human generation that lived
before, during and after the pandemic

I owe them
All of me

Ishani Mengi *(Wife)*
for being my undeterred life support
and pillar of strength

Ritambhara Vir Gupta (Sister)
for being my infinite bundle of love
and a forever friend

Ruchi (Ritu) ***Gupta*** (Mama)
Yudhvir Gupta (Papa)
for being my philosophers, guide,
refuge and my home

Table of Content

Acknowledgements

It took me 18 years, 2 half-manuscripts, a pandemic and eventually 15 months to complete - what was destined to be my first book. This book is a labour of love, immense patience, a long drawn battle between profession and passion. It was a rejig of many priorities and responsibilities. In the end, I have come to make peace with the fact that it was just a matter of time. As the book sees the light of the day, the long wait finally comes to an end. But it would be absolutely selfish of me to take the entire credit for the completion of this project. There are so many people behind the accomplishment of this feat.

My family has been phenomenal in extending their support to fulfil my dream of becoming an author. I am thankful to Dad for spending time with me in sharing his ideas and thoughts from time to time. There are no words to express my feelings for all what Mom has done for me always. Her immense love, belief in me, and a humanistic perspective, (and feeding me with yum food) has always softened the harsh edges in my life as well in my book. Dad's practicality and Mom's empathetic attitude have played a great role in how this book has shaped up. Thanks to my sister, for always being there for me and keeping me in her prayers. She has also been my strongest critic who has helped me keep a reality check on my emotions and my words. My immense love and gratitude to my wife for being an unwavering pillar of strength and my support ecosystem all the while. It is only with her bearing with my tantrums, having an undying belief in my ability to write a book, listening in to my half-baked stories the whole of night(s) and her poise that this book has been possible. Thank you Mama-Papa, Ritambhara and Ishani.

I would also like to extend my gratitude to all my teachers in Little Flower School and Army School Ratnuchak for laying the foundation of our character in the initial years of our life. A huge thanks to VIT, Vellore and its chancellor Dr. G. Vishwanathan for nurturing me and inspiring me through his annual batch addresses. Thanks to IIM Shillong for infusing courage and belief in myself. A heartfelt gratitude to Dr. A.P.J. Abdul Kalam Sir for always inspiring me through his work. I was amazed to see his energy while he was a visiting faculty at IIM Shillong and that has kept me going during the toughest of times. A loud shout out to all my friends in my alma-maters for accepting me the way I am. This is priceless.

I would also like to thank places - in order of their epiphany into my life - Jammu, Vellore, Chennai, Shillong and Bangalore for being perfect in their nature to nurture my dream.

In a world that lives and breathes over social media, it would be unfair on my part to not thank those folks enough who have inspired me through their work. Thank you. Thanks to those folks who have constantly appreciated my work or left constructive feedback on my work.

My gratitude and thanks to all my friends, extended family, relatives who have shown encouragement and shared their happiness with me from time to time along the journey of publishing this book.

My obeisances to Sh. Ram Chand Gupta (Dadaji), Smt. Raj (Dadiji), and Sh. Mahesh Das Gupta (Naanujaan) for bestowing their blessings upon me from their heavenly abode, and lots of love to Smt. Shakuntla Devi (Naanijaan) in whom I seek the affection of all grandparents. I bow to all of you. I am proud and humbled that I am your progeny.

Last but not the least, I am extremely thankful to the Almighty for making this possible. It is only with God's will that I have been able to successfully complete and publish the book. I cannot be more thankful to the Gods and Goddesses for blessing me with the right thoughts, right words and the skill to capture those words into an impactful story for generations to consume.

Thank you, team BlueRose publishers, my editors, illustrators, web-developer, music composers for augmenting the experience of consuming the book for readers.

Love

Karanvir

Prologue

There comes a time in the history of civilizations when everything is put to a grinding halt. The current and existing order of things goes topsy-turvy. All the knowledge and information which is accumulated over a period of time seems futile and of no use. All the learnings gathered over experiments and research; interaction with million other creatures on the planet; study of human anatomy and of hundreds of other animals; and the zeal to understand beyond just the realms of earth extending to the universe - all our effort seems to be wasted. One is not able to figure out where we faltered as a race and how we arrived at the current *State of Chaos.*

Once in every 100 years, *Homo Sapiens* are thrown out of their comfort zones putting all their knowledge and beliefs to question. So much so, that we are forced to question our *existence* and our position in the larger schema. We are coerced to look inside-out and vice-versa. We are made to believe that being indomitable and an indomitable spirit are two very different things. *And we humans are NOT* indomitable - just indomitable spirits. That is where our glory lies. We are forced to ask ourselves the question if there really is a superpower esoteric to human understanding and reach. Once in every 100 years, Humans of Earth are given a reality check to correct their future course of action.

2020 happened to be one such year in the history of Planet Earth. This is not the first time, nature took the reins of the earth in its own hands. Last it happened at such a large scale was in the year 1918-1920, when the infamous Spanish Flu infected the lives of 500 million people across the globe. There have been other instances as well, before and after that, but with a less rampant infection and resulting deaths. These pandemics include Asian Flu (1957-58), Flu pandemic (1889-1890) and the Russian Plague (1770-1772).

The first ever recorded epidemic has been in China known by the name of Circa (3000 BC) followed by the Plague of Athens (430 BC). The mysterious thing to note is the extent to which these epidemics affected the civilizations while travel was not so common and air travel didn't even exist. The most recent pandemics include AIDs (1981-present), H1N1 Swine Flu (2009-2010), Ebola (2014-2016) with the latest being Zika virus (2015-present) before the Corona pandemic (referred to as COVID-19).

The interesting thing to consider here is the increasing frequency of these pandemics in the last few years. However, we(humans collectively) have not been moved by these pandemics and their increasing frequencies. Why so? Is it because of their restricted reach and impact? Is it because they affected the geographies that are not mainstream in today's demographics? Or because these human lives "supposedly" have a little lesser role to play in the equation of politics and economics? The reality is we all have been in a State of Apathy because no recent pandemic has affected and touched each one of us like COVID-19 did.

COVID-19 showed up like a dragon spewing the fire of fear and death looming over the entirety of humanity. It just toppled the world order putting all human and economic activities to a complete halt. The most startling thing that sprung out of this pandemic was our inability to prevent the world from getting affected by the pandemic. It highlighted our unpreparedness as a species to prevent something of this scale to affect All of Us.

However, we humans were under the delusion that nothing could deter our trajectory of unprecedented growth, development and accomplishments. And why would we not believe so? After all, the last three decades have been a master stroke by humanity in winning over the mysteries of the world and the universe. The last 30 years have a different story to tell.

From Hubble Space Telescope (in 1990) to International Space Station(1998); from discovering 358 extrasolar planets to 2700 exoplanets and being able to see the shadows of black holes to landing on Mars - not only Earth, we have been on our path to fathom the Universe. Spaceships are being tested and life on other planets is being explored. We found out how matter gathers mass - the famous Higgs Boson particle discovered under the CERN's Large Hadron Collider experiment. And unraveling the first hybrid human, 90000 years old bone of a teenage girl, whose mother was a Neanderthal and father a Denisovan.

All the inventions and discoveries have been turbocharged by the advent of technology in the recent decades. The world wide web (www.) that we access so ubiquitously came to existence only in 1990. Google, the "know-it-all" came into being in 1996. And it's been just 21 years since Wi-Fi was invented. The devices such as iPhone, Android phones, iPad and the journey from desktop to tablets and smartphones has only been recent starting 2007. The internet and smartphones together have made the sharing and exchange of information really fast and super simple - available at a few clicks and taps on the touchscreens.

From being able to send the first SMS in 1992 to 65billion messages being sent over a day (via Whatsapp, an instant messaging app, with 2billion active users in 2020), we surely have come a long way in our ability to stay connected with fellow humans across the world. The world has shrunk literally. Our ability to connect, communicate and share has grown exponentially. We can start a global revolution while being in one remote corner of the world - of which the Arab Spring of 2010 will remain the first anecdote in the history of mankind. Many followed.

And while all this development has taken place, the average human life span has increased from 65.2 years in 1989 to 72.5 years in 2018. There has been tremendous advancement being done in the field of medical sciences to ensure the longevity of us humans to experience the most we can in a single lifetime.

One can only wonder then why despite so much advancement, growth and evolution - we could not predict a pandemic. And even if we could not, how all our intelligence fell flat and the only option the humans were left with was to stay indoors under a world wide lockdown. Quite contrary to the quantum of development we had fathomed in the last few years and decades. All we could be was to feel surprised and shocked!

We are then only left with questions. Where did we go wrong? What is it that we could have done better to be more prepared as a species? Were the preceding pandemics a hint to be ready for something as devastating and disturbing as COVID-19? Were we - all this while - just fooling ourselves with inventions and discoveries that didn't matter really? Was there something - a variable - in the equation of our being that we were constantly giving a miss?

In our pursuit of extraterrestrial intelligence, the digital revolution and the scientific advancements - the desire to carve an intelligent world and unfathomable human species - did we gravely miss paying attention to something that mattered the most

This book The End is a reflection onto all such things and emotions. It is a take on not being able to find answers to everything around but also to be intelligent enough to ask the right questions at the right time. The book is an observation of how we had shaped our lives in the last few decades and how we were living when the pandemic hit the world in 2020.

This book takes a stroll through some pressing challenges mankind faced during the times of pandemic. It hits hard on some of the great realizations that we had otherwise very conveniently ignored or deliberately chose to neglect. The book goes on to share the experiences of people across the countries in the world and how humans reacted to the pandemic. And also how nature reacted to the pandemic and took the reins back in its hands.

This book however is not just about the pandemic times but a reflection on the society and the civilization as a whole. It makes you ask some pertinent questions at an individual as well as at a community level. It is an attempt to invigorate a debate inside you and all of us. And how it took a pandemic for us to revisit and rethink what we had built over a century. It surely does question moral values and conscience and how far fetched is an idea of the ideal world. And what would it take to break all hell loose?

2020 was a pause button played by the pandemic, COVID-19, in the era of human excellence only for us to reflect on what we have become and where we wish to go from here. It dawned upon us to tell us that coexistence with nature in and as an ecosystem cannot be an afterthought but has to be our way of living. The only question that will remain is if the pandemic happened for us to reflect upon our doings and course-correct or just take a break for a while and continue as is or if it was here to prepare us for a larger war that remained to be fought. Only time will tell.

The book The End is a reminder to all of us to believe in our indomitable spirit and uncanny ability to adapt but also to stay grounded and humble at the same time. This book will be your and mine watchdog! This book is for you, me, and each one of us to share with our future generations. This book will act as a reminder for the entire humanity - for years to come - to not commit the same mistakes again. And remember that after each end, there is a new beginning - there is a new normal towards which all of us will have to work together.

Chapters

1. The Last Outing

(The entire world was partying, absolutely immersed in themselves when the storm hit. All we needed were a few shots to rant out, feel light and have some meaningful conversation but in the normal course, we had forgotten to do so. Not knowing that soon our outrage for partying was going to be curtailed and the need to have a heart-full of conversation would be more than ever. We need to converse more)

2. A Month Back

(While all the clamouring kept happening, things were not so much even a few months ago. People were ready to slit open the throats of each other - only in the name of religion. This State of Apathy was not something new but we could not survive if we continued to behave likewise in the days to come - We need to get out of our State of Apathy)

3. Taj Mahal, 1989

(Times had changed considerably over the years. We were dwelling in a fancier yet a lonelier world. While we were more connected by technology, we had never been more disconnected in reality. And the pandemic was our chance to establish those connections and to bring back the dash of simplicity that sailed us through till here.)

4. The Canceled Bachelors

(It was a crazy world out there where everyone was traveling or wanted to travel. In this pursuit of wanderlust, we had forgotten that there is a seeking that happens from within. Technology and the rampant money flow pushed the world to pick up this rage. Only to find that this was going to get truncated too. Our international trips got canceled. We still couldn't realise that we were up for something disastrous.)

5. Work From Home

(From our foreign travels being truncated, our local travel was halted as well. Our world was shrinking rapidly with work from home orders being passed everywhere. It was not until then we had realized if something had impacted all of us globally. WFH was the first hit we took to realise that the pandemic is here. We were caged to the four walls of our house - The Pandemic happened)

6. Lockdown 1.0 - The Beginning

(And then country after country started announcing complete lockdown with no economic activity or human activity taking place. The world was shutting down. This marked the onset of the new normal - How did the world lock itself down?)

7. Will I do it?

(The time had come when our morals and values would be put to test. We will have to make choices between the right and the wrong. These times would need us to be more empathetic towards our fellow beings. Our moral compass would be put to test. Will we pass the test?)

8. The Survival

(What is Survival? Does it mean different things to different people? The times now were to remind us that survival actually does mean the same for each one of us. In today's world - Internet was a plus besides *Roti*, *Kapada*, and *Makaan*)

9. The Drug Called Content

(In the last few years, we have revolutionised the way we consume content. From newspapers to libraries, matinees to prime time - all of these have been replaced by digital media. There is so much content available for us to consume, breaking the chain of human interaction and killing our ability to create. Will we let this drug dumb us forever?)

10. The Big Boss Arrives

(Amidst all the chaos and confusion, there was an attempt to establish collective strength. If there were any biggest takeaways for all of us from these turbulent times, it was that there is immense power and magic in living as one collective group of individuals. Together we could move mountains. Did we know that yet?)

11. Mothers Without Instagram

(Days, weeks and months passed. People have gotten to broom, sweep and cook and the social media was abuzz with all these posts, stories and soon to arrive reels. The display and sharing was endless, putting into question the years of hard work our Mothers put into taking care of us and families without posting any of it. Social media was at its peak!)

12. The Joy of Doing Nothing

(We had crafted our lives to be extremely busy and occupied. The pandemic and the lockdown was an opportune moment to take a pause from that hectic routine and find time to relax and breathe. This joy of not doing anything left us to ask the right questions, demand answers and think in the right direction. Did everyone find nirvana or did we have symptoms of withdrawal?)

13. Basics Gone Wrong

(A personal reflection. I found myself thinking deeply into how distorted we had evolved as a society. The human race had tried hard to vanquish eternal nature and its laws only to find our own self at the receiving end. Had it not been for the pandemic, we might have continued in the wrong direction.)

14. The Lockdown Continues!

(Heavy curtailment of activities and a complete lockdown - yet all was not over yet. The lockdown continued in various parts of the country in varying measures and enforcement. The daily workers, the businessmen, the ones in unorganized sectors were left lurking waiting for this to end soon. It was a long drawn battle.)

15. Ambush

(Amidst all this pandemonium, there was someone who walked all over the world with a shining armour. Like someone who had got back the reins of what truly belonged to it. Was it enough a hint or was there more we needed to heed to realise what got to be changed?)

16. The Irresponsible Ones

(The confusion was just growing with each passing day. And you come across these idiots who fuel this ruckus by defying all safety standards. They put their guard down to enjoy their right to freedom. The challenge was would you save lives or their right to live? One could only ponder.)

17. Did we think we are indomitable?

(There was no doubt that mankind had begun to think of themselves as larger than life. Our decades of evolution as a species and advancement in science and technology had catapulted our growth story. But was that growth enough? Will that growth alone be enough for the times to come, for us to survive?)

18. Our Anticipation of The End

(If you have watched movies like Titanic, The Wave, Kedarnath - the general idea about the end of the world is drastic, catastrophic, traumatic and extremely painful. The pandemic shook us to reality to make us realise that the end can be slow, gradual and not so horrendous yet extremely painful.)

19. Unlock - Business as usual

(After 3 months of strict lockdown, being homebound and eating home cooked food - the captivity seemed to be our normal state of mind.

Everyone was looking forward to rushing outdoors and rampaging the cities again. Unlocking was yet but a small ray of hope towards going back to the normal.)

20. Ghar Waapsi

(Everybody went home. Daily workers, cab drivers, home helpers, nannies, IT employees, software engineers, the actors and the dancers, painters and the poets - all of them went to the recluse of their hometowns - the very place they had left to shine bright. So did we!)

21. Of Families

(After years away from home, coming back felt different. Everything was the same yet everything was different. It took some time to fit into the social fabric that many of us had very conveniently plugged ourselves out from. The family get-togethers, tambola nights, house parties minus booze felt good. How long were they to continue? How long could we survive them?)

22. Yaar Anmulle

(There is no emotion in this world that you cannot enjoy with your friends. During such times, when everyone was going through an emotional outburst, being with friends would have made life easier. It is during such times, one misses the good old days spent with friends. Let's hold those friendships forever.)

23. Tested Positive

(Everything was hearsay till we survived Covid.)

24. To Seeking of our self

(When everything goes for a toss, when the world turns upside down, we are left with no other option but to take refuge within ourselves. That is the safest place to be in. But do we know that place well enough to spend some of the toughest times of our lives? One needs to break the shackles of our own facade about ourselves and it would be tough.)

25. Come 2021, Come Hope!

(The country looked forward to the new year and the hope it will bring with it. The cases saw a massive decline since the pandemic hit the country. The medical system seemed stable, the recovery rate was higher, people were rejoicing welcoming the new year with all the fanfare. We were back. Were we?)

26. The Anticlimax

(They say happiness is limited and sorrow seems forever. If that was to be believed, our happiness with the new year was limited, and the country was hit by the second wave of the pandemic, much deadlier and much more devastating. The horrors of the past came manifold.)

— The Sceptic Me —

27. The Seeking of the Truth

(The two years of captivity built a lot of frustration amongst the people across the world. We had lost many loved ones , many of us became depressed with nothing to look forward to. Amidst all the despair, everybody was equally moved by the curiosity to know who pushed the world to a state of misery. Who's accused and guilty?)

28. In a state of Oblivion

(Will the desire of people to get back to normal make them forget the miseries of the recent years? Will it make them forget about the pandemic that hit the human race once in every 100 years? Will we be more cognizant or will we choose to be in a state of oblivion?)

29. Khichdi

(Have you eaten khichdi to break away from the routine of eating the same food everyday? You should. There is immense happiness and a sense of fulfillment in simplicity. Simplicity - the forgotten virtue in the 21st century that needs a comeback. Will it?)

30. The World Needs to Heal

(There has been so much that COVID has taken away from us. It is unfathomable grief to simply express in words. Only those who have experienced it can feel it. Unfortunately, no one in the world has remained untouched by the tyranny of this virus. The world is in a desperate need to heal - physically and emotionally.)

31. The Dreams Get you Going

(They say when the going gets tough, the tough gets going. It is true. It is also true for those who are dreamers. They collect, ensemble their cups of positivity to illuminate the lives of everyone around them and everything that brushes them on this journey called life.)

32. Recap

(Those chapters in our book of life, which we would not want to revisit. We only have great realizations, some stark - both beautiful and ugliest - memories from these times. All of which would go to grave with us, leaving behind a legacy of a pandemic that the human generation survived, hopefully so!)

33. The Lost Track

(How often have you lost track of day, date and time? The pandemic was no less than a hallucination leaving us clueless of what day and date we were living in. The times were a reminder to live in the present - in the moment and fight for survival. *Aankh hati, durghatna ghati.*)

34. The End, is it?

(Given the circumstances, it was not foolish or uncommon to ask each other if we were nearing our end. The entire state of affairs across the world was so grim and sad that doubts like these were obvious and all of us - the human race - had started to believe that the world is nearing its end. If not today, but very soon.)

35. The Beginning

(It is tough to stay positive, and hopeful in such distressed times. In precarious times like these, it is impossible to imagine a silver lining amongst the clouds. What we forget is that everytime we feel that the end is near, there is a new beginning - there is a new normal towards which all of us will have to work together. A new chapter in life awaits us , always.)

--- The Optimistic Me ---

Chapter1: The Last Outing

We were living in strange times if I think of it today. Consumed in ourselves and our busy lifestyles, nothing else mattered. Our eyes glued to the mobile screens always, thumbs actively scrolling up and down. Our feet tapped towards the malls and PVRs and our calendars booked for one vacation after the other. We lived our life weekend to weekend. And sloshed! And it was a matter of shame if we traveled, ate, or partied without making check-ins and uploading some "kewl" (read cool) pictures of our own on social media. Not all of us were consumed by this lifestyle, but most of us!

Strange because despite being thoroughly engrossed in ourselves, living (or pretending to live) our lives to the fullest, yet we had unhappy eyes and depressed souls everywhere. All we were left with was *abundant* food, *unlimited* content, *24x7* entertainment, a lot of sleep debt, and a disconnected human race. We had picked milestones after milestones to fulfill our sense of accomplishment. Eat, Work, Party, Sleep (actually no sleep, only sleep debt) was our usual mode of living.

To say or feel the least, those were the best and yet the worst times to be in. We were living in one of the most highly aware social set-ups but filled with consciously dead beings. And I must confess that we (three of us) were no different than the rest of the world!

It had been months and months of tireless work. The last we had dressed up, decked up, and even got out for a dinner together was probably before Diwali 2019. Once we were back from home (Jammu) after all the festivities were over, it was non-stop catching up with the work pace, meeting the year-end targets, and setting up the goals for the new year. Were you going through the same grind? The year 2020 was about to arrive. Time had just flown by, without even us realising the fact that the three of us had rarely eaten a single meal together in a long time. But somewhere all of us were excited and were looking forward to the year that was soon going to dawn upon us.

My sister generally had an early start to the day while my wife had a hectic routine to follow and I had been busier during the later part of the day. This meant the three of us were never present at any given moment together. It was either two of us or just one of us. It looked pretty normal or mostly, we had gotten used to it.

Weekends were neither special to say. We all had our plans. We would catch a glimpse of each other in between moving in and out of the house. Once in a while, we would order our favorite Mani's Dum Biryani for dinner which can be best described closest to our time together. December came and went by in this frenzy and so did January and hence February. We were just running by the clock or "need" of the hour. Or also maybe we have started feeling too tired of the infamous Bangalore traffic. Those bumper-to-bumper rides, non-stop scrolling up and down on the mobile screen, or attending to the relentless calls of the sales agents of various policies and investment plans - all of this defined how we spent time in between the home to office ride. Amidst all this hullabaloo, the only breather was the call from Maa who has always been equally relentless in showering us with her love, mending our ways, and asking us if "naashta achche se kiya?" (Did you have breakfast satisfactorily?). And if you happen to be a bachelor, there would always be this one addition "Shaadi kab karni hai, koi hai to bta de - log mujhse poochhna shuru ho gaye hain ab" (When are you going to get married, if you have someone of your choice - let me know - folks here have started pestering me).

Today, when I think in retrospect - it seems weird, perhaps strange because that person who is stuck in that 9 to 5 rut - is not who we were, that is not who we are. That is not the real us. There have been times when I couldn't relate to that version of mine. And I am sure this happened with many others around me. But we chose denial over acceptance.

Aren't we someone beyond daily catchup, monthly metrics, scrum meetings, and Jira tasks? Well, there have been times when we headed to hitch-hiking, or found a quick escape on a Sunday morning for a sumptuous breakfast, or just found ourselves a table for a lunch buffet - of which you have countless options to choose from in the thrilling Bangalore culinary scenes. That is how many of our friends, colleagues, and peers have been spending their weekends as well and so were we following the same. Not only our friends in Bangalore, but also Mumbai, Delhi, Pune in India, and friends in London, New Jersey, Colorado, Perth, and Singapore across the globe.

But this time we have just been too caught up, when one fine day over another Biryani night, we realised that the three of us have not treated each other for quite some time. Not even the weekends have been kind to us. Our shopping spree has seen a pause, our binge eating sessions have not happened for long and there has been no slurping and slouching after a night full of insane drinking. What we were actually seeking was - jumping from one meta state to another.

Those have been crazy nights when we would start drinking at the pub or a bar finding our way back home over an Uber or Ola ride. Get home, jugaad some instant-chakhna and have another full round of drinks that would last till midnight. All of us laughed it out at the very thought of it. But that random conversation over dinner got us thinking. When did we get so busy?

The next morning, to my surprise, all of us were there at the breakfast table together talking about an outing. Aah! It made me realise that all we needed was a heart-full of conversation to get us on the same page. The day was chosen, the place was finalised and the entire itinerary was planned. Splurge!

This outing was in fact the opening ceremony to the week-long celebrations of me turning 31. Over the banter of how less we had gone out to eat, shop, and drink in the last few months - the following week was supposedly a compensation for all of it, which also meant a big hole in my pocket (laughs out loud). Judge me if you want but that's true. Plus it was me who had got an appraisal recently and hence by all means it was me who was treating everyone. But trust me I didn't mind any expense if it got all of us together.

Well, the day was here! Uber had just launched a new feature of pre-booking a cab called Uber-Schedule. The cab arrived at the doorstep at 11:45 AM. In our spring look, we splashed and hopped around shops in the mall. It was 7 March 2020. With our hands full of shopping bags, our stomachs were roaring empty . We found a nice cafe near the mall that offered some mouth-watering sandwiches and sliders, and a cup of kadak chai to go with. We headed back home, took a nap, and got up again because tonight was the night!

Breaking from the monotony of the work and being dumped on our beds like forever for the previous few months - it was time to look our best because we were headed to Sarjapur Social. The place, all three of us were looking to go for a long time, all three of us mutually agreed upon. Lest we knew, that this was the last time we would be stepping outside our homes before the world came crashing upon all of us.

But that night will always remain special, now that I think of it. Despite the peak-hours, we secured a prime place for ourselves. The guy who was serving took extra care of us. We ate like wolves, drank like horses. While we were all sober, I remember the guy asking "Sir, are you sure I should get more shots for all of you?" And we said "Yes! Yes!" We opened our hearts out and talked about random stuff from our colleagues at workplaces (who we thought were absolutely jack*** and ones who were absolutely amazing), aunties back home and questions they keep pestering our parents with, to how life was before when we were kids and how things have changed since we have grown to be adults. We delved into more serious topics, about our aspirations and life-goals. Well, the shots had started playing their magic spell on us. We finally talked about something that was just more than what we had confined ourselves to. We were having real conversations.

And then we let loose on the dance floor. It got to the point where we removed our shoes and danced naked-feet. I can still feel the coldness of the cemented floor that I felt then - it is a strong memory indeed. It was the last touch we had with the ground, literally. The ecstasy was esoteric. I have faded memories of hands swirling high in the air, bodies swinging left and right, there was darkness around with shimmers of light coming touching upon us once in a few seconds, and some of them outbursting to tears of joy or sorrow - I am not sure why, but they were overwhelmed by some emotion, I am aware.

Probably that is what happens when you let go of what is caged inside you for so long or you set yourself free from what has abducted you forever. Something which - all of us - as humanity was to witness in the days and times to come. That night will be etched in the epochs of our history till our last breaths because of so many reasons. It was a warm, fuzzy, and frizzy evening. Our souls danced wild and free, and our hearts were on a ranting spree. We all were hallucinating (yet more connected to reality) and wondered why each day and each moment was not lived and felt like it felt that day. After so many days, we had sensed and felt our existence (which was soon going to be questioned)

What bothers me the most is why we do not feel our existence each day, each moment we spend on this earth. What got us so busy that we lost touch with ourselves? Why does it take people like you and me and everyone one or another form of ecstasy to open up and have heartfelt conversations? When and why did we grow so delusional about everyone and everything around us while deep down being aware of the reality. Why does the world pretend to be what it is not?

That night left me intrigued with all these questions hovering in my head only to be reinforced with the days and months to come.

That night marked the onset of a new world we were getting into. It was The Last Outing we had before we were pushed behind the four walls of our house.

Chapter2: A Month Back

We did not sense it now, and we had not sensed it a month back as well. We were as ignorant today as we were a few days ago. At times I fail to understand if ignorance is an inherent characteristic of us humans or we deliberately choose ignorance to ward off unwanted situations and circumstances.

Amidst our busy day-to-day lives, there were news headlines making noise about some virus outbreak in the Republic of China and other southeast Asian countries such as Thailand. How did that happen, if you may ask? Because a hungry human had eaten an infected bat in the town called Wuhan in China.

Did we pay any heed to the news? No.

It seemed to everyone as if something had gone wrong somewhere but it didn't move any of us. But now we know how we humans are, don't we? Until and unless something hits us directly, something causes us direct trouble - we do not care. We cannot relate to the very pain and suffering that comes at scale to the larger society and humanity. We tend to be in this constant state of denial and apathy.

We are instead more moved by things like neighbors parking their car in front of our house, their pet peeing on the electricity pole adjacent to the wall, a tree from across the wall peeking into our house, Who has got a bigger car, Who receives more visitors, more gifts, who is making more foreign trips, who is hooking up with whom, whose daughter/son scored what marks in their latest exams. These seem to be more important concerns to us - concerns that move us! For all other matters, we choose apathy to be our state of mind.

A similar state of apathy could be seen and found in India (North East Delhi) during January, February, and March - the onward journey that started towards the end of December 2019. Just around the time when that hungry man had eaten the bat.

All this started in the form of the Anti-CAA (Anti-Citizenship Amendment Act) protests. This bill was passed in the parliament on Dec 11, 2019. This bill conferred citizenship upon various migrants who had moved to India till 31st Dec 2014 (from the neighboring countries of India) and had faced religious persecution or fear of religious persecution in the respective countries. These protests that started against this amendment on 14th December 2019 came to be known as Shaheen Bagh protests. It has been reported that supposedly these protests were against the CAA-NPR-NRC and came to be known for its famous slogan called Kaagaz nahi dikhayenge (won't show documents), where NPR is National Population Register and NRC stands for National Register of Citizens. The fear that gripped these protestors was that India will find illegal migrants and deport them to their respective countries.

Our apathy puts the larger fear looming over society and humanity at the backburner.

Well, these protests went on to become a brutal bloodbath in the State Capital of Delhi on 23 February 2020. And this is where my concern begins and the State of Apathy rings in full-blown once again in the annals of Indian history. What happened over those 2-3 months makes me question so many facts, claims, and information presented at the face of it both by the media and the social jury available on Facebook, Twitter, and many other social forums. Let's try to go through the sequence of events in chronological order.

If the Bill Amendment was announced on 11th Dec, how is it possible that such large-scale protests were organized in various cities across India just after two days (14th Dec 2019)? Until and unless programmed. Let's assume that these protests were prima facie. Despite there being so much opposition and unwillingness to bring the amendment to life by the public, what were the representatives of these sections of people doing all the while? They should have been able to prevent the bill from being passed in the assembly.

Let's say, yes there had been a miscalculation and the representatives could not judge the mood of their public on-ground and the verdict went wrong in both the assemblies. Wasn't it their responsibility to calm the public and walk them through the amendment instruction by instruction? Or were their intentions otherwise to incite the public and masses and drive more furor over the ruling party which ultimately was responsible for bringing this amendment then?

We all know that the Delhi elections were due in the first two weeks of February 2020. Was this entire thing - loot, destruction, killings - pre-planned and chalked out to cause disturbance in the state to affect the legislative assembly elections? In that case, either of the parties could stand beneficiary because of this orchestrated ruckus. Who knows!?

Why was Jamia Millia Islamia University the epicenter of the anti-CAA protests? Are we still stuck in an era where we want to paint everything orange versus green that ultimately turns red?

If the CAA-NPR-NRC combo affects the impoverished, poor, and the other migrants in India, why would the students of Jamia Millia Islamia and other colleges protest against it? How and why are they concerned? Are they directly affected or are they more empathetic than the rest of India?

And if they are more educated and empathetic than the rest of us, why would they ever indulge in the kind of protests that destroy property and loss of human lives? Then in the first place - if they can't differentiate between right and wrong - should their protests and demands be considered? Or maybe the students of Jamia Millia were not even privy to this entire orchestration of events and the entire story was just concocted?

But before I jump to my final question - is it legitimate for these people at the Shaheen Bagh to protest for a social cause? Yes, Obviously yes! Isn't that what democracy is for? To let people and citizens of a country question the decisions their representatives and the government takes on behalf of them. And it is the government's responsibility as well as those who represent these people at the state or center level to explain to them the bill and its consequences.

Kaagaz nahi dikhaayenge, however, can never be the solution. Because, if you are to be a part of a country and a sovereign nation, as a citizen it is upon you to abide by the orders. After all, no one is forced to leave the country. But this kind of sense can prevail only when there is mutual trust between the system and its public. Had we come to the point where the trust had gone missing or was this part of a well-orchestrated plan?

Coming to what happened on 23 February - was that legitimate? No, Not even a cent. You can count 36 dead bodies of Muslims and 15 dead bodies of Hindus or vice-versa - no count ever justifies the loss of human life caused by other humans. It is a horrendous and sorry state of affairs. We have been living in it since time immemorial. And let me tell you, we all are equally responsible for this.

Politicians have been busy in this dirty game of using the public as a tool to fulfill their agenda and ulterior motives. If we are not learning from the history and tyranny of the times, we are doomed to learn it the hard way. People who are responsible for such a pogrom are you and me. The world no doubt has grown into a much more opinionated place, but we all need to shield ourselves from the overdose of this opium called opinion. In our sheer desire to reflect our ideologies and stand by our principles, we forget how we are used as a decoy to attack our fellow brethren.

During all this time that followed during the protests, many of us went on to share the anti-Muslim and anti-Hindu posts on our social media feed - vehemently - without bothering how it makes our friends feel.

Let me ask you - in your lifetime - how many evil Muslim have you met personally (if you are a Hindu) and how many evil Hindus have you met (if you are a Muslim). Not even one and even if you have, you can't recall either his face or his name. Then who do you post this anti-Muslim, anti-Hindu posts for? You have fallen for the sheer propaganda. You just shared one post and let it hang on your newsfeed forever but in the schema of the overall system it is an avalanche of hatred that trickles from post to post that is shared over and over again.

During all these months, I felt quite agitated by how many of the people I knew - belonging to well-educated families and backgrounds - went on to share such hatred posts. Their hatred - sudden spurt of hatred - seemed unfathomable and uncalled for. It made me feel uncomfortable. And it broke my heart to witness many amazing beings and friends going missing from the social scene because of the fear of being dragged into this vicious chain of things, dialogues and discussions just because their names represented a sect, a religion, and an ethnicity.

We can go on to blame the politicians for brewing this hatred in the hearts of the public and masses but let's not forget that we are equally responsible for invigorating the flames of the hatred. We are no different. To have an opinion is different, to side with an ideology is different but to take a stance that can put the lives of fellow beings at risk is disgusting. To create an atmosphere of hatred and lit up the fire that is already flaring up is outright irresponsible.

But this apathy is not new. We have been there and done that but we always fall for the trap. Because the ones flaring it up are not the ones who bear the brunt of the hatred that spews over debate hours and media propaganda. Intellectuals have this hatred served hot as their breakfast and evening snack. The Common Man might have a digestion problem though.

The forgetfulness about the fact that we all are no different from each other is going to cost us a fortune and an opportunity to live peacefully in the best of times. Religion - is a matter of practice of faith that we have chosen for ourselves and in most cases, inherited. Given to nature, we are all born human beings. Nature doesn't differentiate between any of us ever. Nothing is partial - nor its love nor its qayamat. The wrath of nature is never going to ask you, "Arey child, tell me what race, religion, or ethnicity you belong to? I will perish you accordingly."

In the eyes of nature and its court of law, we all are born equal. No single soul can defy that fact. But ignorant as we are or choose to be, we couldn't see this coming. Only if we could have guessed that nature was going to show her might and put our state of apathy into question in just a few days to come, we might have stopped. The very abodes of these faiths were locked with gates shut for all of us - the pseudo bearers of the glory, we breathe, die and kill for - leaving us lurking to find the faith, purpose, and peace inside our own houses and inside ourselves.

When you see so much hatred around, your hearts and minds fail to register that there could ever be times where one would read "Jama Masjid remains closed for Eid and Sehri and Iftari being prepared and distributed in the Vaishno Devi temple" But such times come! These times came. We were to witness such times only to show us that the power of nature is over and above any other power in the world. Well, isn't that India we all would love to take pride in, dream to live for, and want to be a part of?

The India we saw and witnessed a month back was not for real. The previous month had been sad and dismal. It was gut-wrenching to see humans kill humans. Nothing could get worse than that! Only if humans had a hint of what lies ahead in their way, and where they were headed in just a few days from now. Only if they had known that it would take a virus to dispel protestors at the Shaheen Bagh, all the ruckus could have been avoided.

I always wonder if all this hatred that we carry in our hearts exists for real or is it just a cup of venom shoved down our throat as a part of growing up? The answer to that is probably a yes to the latter. When I think of it and compare it to the bygone years and decades, not much has changed since then. The State of Apathy prevails today as much (or maybe more) it did back then. The only difference is today, it is wrapped in the garb of pseudo-wisdom and irrational logic.

Chapter3:
Taj Mahal, 1989

It is harshly cold across India during January and February. You cannot bear the winters with a cold-blooded heart. But despite all the coldness, I have always loved this feeling of winter. I find the silence on the roads captivating. There is this constant wave of cold air that stirs you deep inside, at times tears you apart, and gives you enough time to reflect on your life. There is this constant need to stay warm. While there is haze all around, winter is that time of the year that gives you a sense of clarity. But who gives a dime about what winters make you feel or think?

For most of us, winter is the time to snuggle inside our quilts, repeat chai orders, feed ourselves some more good hot food, and binge-watch. But only if your work gives you enough free time. My heart yearns for something else, however. I have this intense desire during winters to cozy myself with some good stories that keep me warm with a character sketch lingering in my head for days and months to come.

In the winter of 2020, I chanced upon Taj Mahal, 1989 streaming on Netflix, exactly the kind of story my heart was craving for. Something that was not fast-paced to give me an adrenaline rush, something not too slow to bore me to find yet another story or web series. I wanted a story I could live through, pause and reflect upon - a story that would be an apt mix of nostalgia and yet brings with itself freshness. Taj Mahal, 1989 happened to be just one such story.

I might not fall under the strict definition of a marathon watcher but I am sure one of those sprint viewers who love to watch their content fast and in one go. Hey! So I am not sure if you can call me a "binge watcher". Maybe binge-watcher would be a hybrid of both (Laughs). But that is how I love watching stuff - pick one, focus on that and not rush from one series to another too fast.

I found this Taj Mahal, 1989 just like my chai, to be enjoyed in sips. A warm fuzzy series that strolls you through the lanes of love from various angles and perspectives. The youthful love, the strained love, the eternal love, and the amateur love! Four love stories intertwined with each other but not really in a complicated way. Simple like our ways of living used to be back in 1989. Set in the backdrop of the pre-90s era, with a flavor of socialist regimes and blurred lines between socialism and communism ideologies - it doesn't get into the complexities of those ideologies. But it simply wades its way through how life used to be at those times without the internet and technology. A simple right or left swipe couldn't decide the future of your relationship or a one-night stand. You would have to earn them both - either a fling or a serious commitment wala relationship. Mobile phones were not available either. It was an era of landlines that used to be a privileged possession too.

Being a 90s kid, I still reminisce about us going out to play in the parks and the fields. If not that, gully cricket is not something you would miss. Each gully had its Sachin-in-making. It is no secret that India has been a cricket-crazy country. But what more these cricket tournaments and friendly matches did was build a network of friends that you could count on, call upon whenever you needed them - in mischief, joy, or sorrow. I miss that camaraderie.

It is not easy to find such bonds in today's virtual network. Our camaraderie is limited to pokes, like, love and comments but all of this - sadly though - cannot replace that charm of being physically present in front of each other when they need you or when you need them. A virtual hi cannot replace a physical hug, after all!

I am sure we would be the last generation to have such friends but that intensity of friendship is depreciating at a faster rate than you and I can think of.

Today we can play ludo, cricket, baseball, or football in the virtual fields connecting with homies from across the world - who you will ever meet or never meet again. The bond breaks once the game is over. The last three decades have changed the way we play, engage, converse or build relationships. While all of it is organic for me, I still find all this very stifling when I think about how conversations have evolved.

I cannot miss those Sundays enough when the entire family would glue to the screen to watch Ramayana, Mahabharata, Shaktiman, or Chandrakanta. Lassi ka glass after that poori chana was to kill for. And if you were brought up in the northern part of India, Rajma-Chawal was your de-facto Sunday lunch. It still is. Post which, all the cousins would join for a game of carrom or board games or even Santolia, which can be called your physical Jenga game where you join hands with everyone to hit the person with a cosco ball who breaks your pile of stones.

As the evening would approach, you could see a whole bunch of folks ready with their cycle to race in the lane. You would not find a kid who didn't have a cycle. And then there was another set of kids who would be cartoon fans and would watch Popeye, Scooby-Doo, Duck Tales, or Mowgli.

None of this is gone really from our current set-up either but the medium and the way we consume all of this has changed drastically. I cannot fathom the fact that all of this can be done without a single human touch-point or conversation. I can watch all of this at my convenience, at my own sweet time. I can play games. I can watch my favorite series. I can talk to people across any part of the world. I can make or break relationships while I am seated miles apart from another person. All at a single click, a few ticks, and a few blinks of eyes. All you gotta do is Subscribe to the channel or the app for a few bucks.

You and I don't need to be talking to each other in a room looking eye-to-eye and meaning each word we say. You and I don't need to be there at all to do any of the above. We have made the physical presence mean nothing. How sad! But does physical presence mean anything? Surely, it does. And it means a lot. It is an emotion, a feeling, and a need we humans were going to crave desperately, a few months from now.

In this entire race to be more "connected", I think we never realized when we got so disconnected as a race, more than ever before. And the irony is "Connectivity" is touted to be the biggest achievement of humanity in the 21st century! If I were to give the 21st century a tagline, I would probably say '100% connected, 0% connection'.

I remember how it used to be mandatory for each one of us to have dinner together because not every family member used to be at home during the lunch hour. Those study sessions were fun where all cousins were found pranking each other. But today they are lost in our secluded lifestyles. And let's not forget the 'who will drink milk first' competition. We all had that one younger sibling who would throw tantrums because they hated milk. Those memories have gone missing.

The picnics where Aloo Parathas were packed in abundance but would still fall short. The car would stink of the fruit that was packed for the journey. And there were always two (and sometimes more - 4 in my case) children who were asked to sit in the boot, especially if you had an Omni Van. Those picnics have gone for a toss. The singing of an old melody and joining each other to sing in unison while playing Antakshari has gone missing somewhere. In a world full of discoveries, some wonderful pleasant memories and anecdotes are lost forever.

You have to believe that all the romance could happen by counting the number of times your lover rings the landline at your house or the shop outside your house. The clandestine, coy yet unabashed love.

That defined the intensity of the love. That romance has gone missing. Pushing yourself to seek romance for a lifetime has gone missing. I still find that persuasive love intimate. It is a challenge to find such love in today's times.

Those times were intimate, cozy and so full of love and life. Those times were beautiful in their simple ways. That simplicity has gone missing.

Do you remember the house birthday parties and get-togethers? I do. They used to be a madhouse. Friends and family would meet, gather, "talk", eat and share their life stories, their day-to-day cliched incidents. And probably that is what kept them connected because they knew each others' troubles, pain, sorrow, and joy and they could relate to each other. We all knew we had something in common. Our lives were not a secret but a shared resource - and that I believe was the secret sauce to have happier faces, lit eyes, and at-peace souls around.

Clicking pictures was mandatory but you only got one shot at it. Unlike today where you have gazillion shots in the same pose at the same spot. And by the way, clicking pictures of food and decor was not mandatory back then. Maybe that is why conversations were healthier and relationships stayed longer.

I look around and ask myself, "Why are there so many sad eyes around me today?" The only answer that comes to my mind is, "we have lost connection with everyone and everything around us. We are too busy and aloof in our small world. The only being that matters to us is us. On the contrary, nature is designed to let all living beings - All of Us - live in harmony with each other in and as an ecosystem. Not adhering and obeying to that law of nature has got us here and has brought all the suffering."

We can do all the chest-thumping and sing songs of our laurels out loud but there is something wrong that we have brewed in the last few years and decades. It brought us where we were going to be in a few months/days from now.

Have you ever wondered how our parents sailed through troubled times? Surely, they didn't have it easy, and very likely they had it tougher than us. Then what kept them going? Having their support system - in the form of their friends and family - intact. Leading a simpler life made everything less complicated. That is what made them sail through smoothly, even if tides were rough.

Those were simple times if you ask me. My favorite memories to date belong to that era. Today, when I am too consumed in my busy life, and stress takes a toll on my mind and body, I fall asleep to the nostalgia of those times. They induce this magical calm in my mind. I miss the bedtime stories my grandfather used to narrate to me. I miss those relatives dropping by at home without letting us know. Surprise! I miss the festival celebration with a crazy bunch of cousins. I miss my days in school and catching up with friends outside the school. I miss leaving the school in a gang after the lunch break, walking 2kms to the matador spot only to halt in between to eat samosas. The gang you could rely on for almost everything you would want and need in your life. I even miss those churan sticks and ice lollies. I miss that simplicity and the warmth of my loved ones that would keep me warm during the cold nights of the winters. And warmth, as I say, is all you need to survive the winters of life.

I do not know why, but the world surely became a fancier yet lonelier place to live in. And the only thing that I see missing in the equation today is people. People who we truly love and want to spend our lives with - they went missing in our lives!

We became nuclear from joint families. The family set-up changed. All of us became more obsessed with tera-mera, kiske hisse mein kitna aayega (who will own how much), and building a unit of our own. Welcome to the individualistic mindset and the world of capitalism! Not all of the fault was that of our families or a result of greed. We had just opened as an economy in 1991, the effect of which started building up in the late 90s. It brought a gigantic revolution in terms of how our family units were set up and how we interacted and transacted with each other. And with this revolution came the thought of accumulating more and belief in our capacity to accumulate more. This led to one of the most pressing problems of today - rampant consumerism and ample depression.

But I cannot blame our families and our cultural evolution for this change. After having shared the resources and living lives of constraints, this was a change that was bound to happen. What we couldn't realize in this evolution was how to find a balance between being individualistic and the need for us to be a cohesive society. What we could not realize is the importance of simplicity in our lives. What we could not fathom is the importance of our loved ones and the need for them to be in our close proximity. What we failed to accomplish was to establish a balance between us and the rest of nature.

Taj Mahal, 1989 brought all those memories of the bygone era! It brought back the warm winters. It turned out to be a reflection of all that the 90s stood for. It reinforced my dormant belief that less could be more. It emphasized the importance of finding the yin to our yang and how those little things - coterie, conversations, compassion, concern - mattered the most.

While we were witnessing the State of Apathy in India and the unrest prevailing in the state capital of

Delhi - this series made me realize that each era has its challenges and troubles. The only trouble I was facing at this point was this State of Apathy which was prevalent in the 1990s and today. Why didn't this change over the last three decades when so much else changed and drastically?

But humans, the lesser mortals, can only see and think about the results of the ongoing or heuristic events. Not beyond that. Our vision is limited both in terms of what to expect in times to come. But it does not go beyond the recent past. But I didn't know that by fretting over the simplicity and beauty of the 90s, I would be sending omens to the universe of bringing back those times. And buoy, they did!

Strange it may sound! But the 90s era was to make a comeback. Ramayana and Mahabharata were to be broadcasted on DD National again. Families would be put under house arrest by nature. The helpers will not be allowed to enter homes. This would mean all the cleaning and cooking was to be done by yourself, bringing back the memories of sharing all the household chores amongst the family members. The shops would be shut too, the malls will be closed down and so will be PVRs and Cinema Halls. Playgrounds and fields would be asked to remain closed till further notice. Board games would be back and so would be teaming up and ganging up against each other.

It seemed as if nature conspired to make us compensate for the lost time and find our lost love and connection with our dear ones and everything around us. We were soon going to be back in 1989. The nostalgia and fear were impending - ready to hit us hard. We just didn't know it yet. We were not ready either.

Chapter4: The Canceled Bachelors

We had just come back from a short trip home (Jammu). And those 4 days with the family went too fast, too soon! It was an engagement ceremony for my brother. The days were packed with some endless dancing, binging upon delicious food, and abysmal Gupshup. The only thing that was missing was alcohol. But I believe we were still high enough! The photographs came and we didn't look any sober.

Indian weddings can be ultimate fun, costly though. They are an ostentatious display of everything you can think of - money, food, jewelry, clothes, accessories, and mood swings. They are no less than a local Cannes affair and a well-orchestrated drama. Now, we also have choreographers stationed in the bride and the groom's houses constantly training fufajis (husbands of father's sisters) and mamajis (mother's brothers) on their dance moves with their pot-shaped bellies ready to churn and videographers 24x7 in-the-house to capture all the background fun. The output of which would be a 6-minute video called Wedding Highlights. Don't get disappointed. Despite all the ruckus, we still look forward to these weddings. In today's busy lifestyle, weddings have turned out to be one such occasion where families get together at the expense of somebody else. And so were we, waiting for the marriage to happen in August that year.

Preparations were on. Dress codes were being finalized. The chariot guy had been booked and so were the drum rollers, and the band. The venues were finalized. Bookings were done. Token money was paid to book the vendors. The women were having an intense discussion about the quality of mehendi (Heena) that was put on their hands a day before the engagement. The poor mehendi guy had no damn clue that while he was putting mehendi on ladies' hands, the lines of wealth on his palm had already started disappearing. That guy had just lost business worth thousands (actually lakhs, not forgetting referrals) because the thickness and finesse of the mehendi were not up to the mark. There were better kaarigars (artists) in the city available at a cheaper price, the ladies believed.

Amidst all this wedding preparation and frenzy, this constant bickering and jokes were doing the round regarding the honeymoon destination. Bhai could not blush less to hide his embarrassment and we could not laugh less at his plight. After all, why does deciding on a honeymoon destination have to be a public and a democratic affair? We all wondered.

After all these discussions and embarrassing moments, all of us - cousins - got into one room for that clandestine drinking and bitching session. That is when the topic of bachelors came up. They say never make a decision when you are high, but we did! Because, #YOLO!

A few minutes and pegs later, Phew! the destination was finalized, the month and time of the year were locked. It may sound audacious, but on the night of 30th January, we booked the trip for 6th March to Krabi, Thailand. That was the only free time we all had in common. We had a dress code planned for this as well. The customized t-shirts were to be printed with #GroomSquad to be written over them in BIG and BOLD. The groom's t-shirt however was decided to be red and everyone else would spot a white t-shirt. The groom got to be the showstopper! Before the itinerary, a list of beachwear and accessories was packed. It included beer-shaped sunglasses, bunny rabbit headbands, flip-flops, a brooch for the main night, and LED t-shirts as well. The one that would make you glow in the night. Wow! We all were super thrilled about this one.

And why not! An International bachelors trip, are you kidding me that we should not be super thrilled? This has been the latest fad, to do an international family trip before the wedding. And just tag it, bachelors, all over social media. Does it even matter what you did over the trip? Changing diapers, ended up in a brawl with your cousins itself, couples taking up separate rooms over a fight, lost in a busy street, or maybe arrested. Who cares?

What matters is the International Bachelors trip that we took, the one we were going to take. Well we are not alone in this. Out of 38.90 Mn tourists arriving in Thailand in 2019, 2 Mn were just Indians. Clearly, we got a gang! But it is not only about the Thailand tourism growth story, the travel-bug infected a complete generation in the last few decades.

According to UNWTO (United Nations World Tourism Organisation), there were 440 Mn international arrivals across the world in 1990. This number has increased to 1.4bn as of 2018 (per the last census). Leisure being the largest segment in tourism, contributed 4,715bn U.S. dollars in 2019 of the total 9.25tr $US contribution of travel to the World GDP. But what has got the world moving?

Why this Kolaveri Di? As far as Indians are concerned, it all started with a lot of Software and IT professionals opportuning an onsite experience and then finally taking a plunge to settle there forever. Better education, better civic amenities, better quality of life, and a better lifestyle - all this attracted Gen X of India to move abroad in the 2000s when the Internet boom happened. India hit a bullseye with skilled and cheap labor. India had got talent and in abundance, when the Y2K movement sprung in 2000. India might not have been a perfect place to live back then but today we are competing with the most developed nations of the world (both in terms of infrastructure and avenues) and many of those who left India are making a comeback.

But if you look beyond Gen-X, at the Baby Boomers, they moved abroad by the share sheen of settling abroad. They wanted to stand out from the mass chaos prevalent in the country. They might as well have wanted to grow and make money, but more importantly, craft a world that didn't have to hustle through India's red tape and dysfunctional system back then. Moving abroad was like the ultimate dream for some.

This is how we came to identify our relatives as London waale Mamaji, Australia waale Chachaji, and Canada waali Buaji. Meet the Chittapa settled in Singapore or the Chinnappa who founded a company in SF.

But the last few years - a decade to say - have been startling in terms of how the intent behind traveling changed across the world. There are so many who fly to India now for cost-effective and par-excellent medical treatment. Then some love to explore different cultures and ethnicities - India being culturally rich and diverse. Traveling is a passion for them. Many across the globe are gung-ho about the Indian concept of Yoga. Thanks to our Prime Minister, Mr. Narendra Modi - he revived the Yoga culture across the world. Many now come to India to learn the art at designated Yoga Centres and take that talent and expertise back home to their countries - to open Namaste Yoga centers.

However, people from India fly primarily for social status. A trip to Vegas or Euro backpack trip, the desire to watch the Northern lights, or London eye wheel - we Indians are fascinated by these symbolic representations of these places. There is another set of the breed for whom Dubai and Singapore are like extended shopping malls aka streets. For them, it is like an alley extending from Promenade in Delhi or Orion in Bangalore. And Thailand and Indonesia are stopover places to where you go when you feel like partying. That is exactly how we thought while planning our bachelor trip. Just that, for us it indeed was a special occasion to travel to Thailand.

And then some decide to travel to break from the monotony, leave behind them what is containing or stifling them, find their inner peace, or land up at a place while trying to seek themselves. We all surely have our reasons to board that plane to our next vacay destination. Don't we?

What amuses me is what has changed in these last few years that there is so much influx and outflux of tourists all over the world. Travel-bugs which used to be most recognized as the hippie culture in the past and considered a trait of the Western civilization - became a living style across the world. How and why did this rage catch fire? There must be something conducive happening across the globe that we are producing Wanderlust-filled souls at an unprecedented rate.

Moolah! The first and foremost has been the increasing paying capacity of the individuals. Technically speaking, increasing per capita income. Much of the population has moved from poor to middle class and from middle class to upper-middle class strata. It is no hidden fact that the middle of the pyramid is swelling. However, this in itself is a cause and effect of the wave of capitalism and endless consumerism.

Another factor that has played a pivotal role in bringing this revolution is the advent of technology. The convenience of making purchases online at any hour of the day or while being over a video call with friends/family has fastened our decision-making. Let us agree that our impulsive buying has just got wings. There are numerous websites and apps such as Skyscanner, makemytrip.com, booking.com, etc that allow us to compare the prices of the tickets and make a purchase at the best price suited to our budget.

The Internet has also made it possible for all kinds of travelers to leave their reviews, write blogs, and create vlogs where people can leave their experiences for other travelers to read and see. This entire culture of reading, following, and sharing reviews with larger audiences through sites such as travel triangle or tripoto has caused an avalanche effect in more and more people traveling. It is now convenient for people to trust fellow travelers rather than believing the travel agents.

To top that there are constant discounts and offers being run, holiday packages ranging from Economy, Value for Money to Premium catering to the financial status of each one of us. Sometimes I feel, our problems with the middlemen existed only till they were humans. We as a race seem to be quite happy if the middleman comes wearing the cape of technology! We do trust technology more than we trust humans! I am not sure if we are supposed to be happy or sad about this fact.

Well, the ease of travel is not only limited to picking a destination and buying cheaper and value-for-money packages. The technology companies have also taken away the hassle of planning the itinerary and doing that meticulous research about the places before we would travel to those places. Companies are running on the business model of the likes of Airbnb or Headout which curate the kind of stay or nature of experiences you or I would want to enjoy while traveling.

You might like an adventure sports affair and your friend might want to head for skinny dipping or scuba diving. There are chances that your Dad wants to explore museums but your siblings want to enjoy that pub crawl while your mom wants to go shopping in that high-end fashion street or the local mart buying souvenirs. These sites curate all such experiences and club them in a lucrative combo offer, which is worth it considering all your time and effort is saved - first researching about these minutest details and then convincing your family towards a common choice. Now all of us can enjoy the kind of experiences we would want to have. What else does one need?

And if money is the tiniest of your concern, you always have those EMI options! Damn devta clad asurs, these credit cards! I guess money spent is a lot about perception rather than how much you spend.

This revolution is multiplying each second. Our ability to plan a Bachelor's trip to Thailand was maybe a result of all these factors combined -

subconsciously. On 2nd February when we were headed back to our destinations, there was not even a single sign of remorse for leaving the hometown. Rather we beamed with happiness and our souls were elated because all of us awaited the Trip of the Year. We knew we were soon going to gang up again at the much-talked-about Thailand's Suvarnabhumi airport where some of our cousins would be arriving from Delhi and three of us would be traveling from Bangalore. We didn't know God had different plans for us though. We didn't know that the wings of these wanderlust souls were to be clipped soon and for long.

It was not long before we were back in our cities that the news of the spread of a virus in parts of China and South-Asian countries started catching rage. Thailand being one of them! Oh darn! Our WhatsApp group called Bhai ka Bachelors was supercharged with what-ifs, but-ifs, and what to do, and how much to wait to take a call.

We would come back from the office and get glued to the news channels. Some people were still posting their arrival pics at their dream destination on Instagram. And we thought we should carry on with our trip too. But when we would switch to the news channels, things didn't look good. And we thought we should drop our idea. We were shilly-shallied.

We kept procrastinating our decision by 2days, 3 days. But we needed to make a decision fast. We had to initiate the cancelation of the bookings. And then we read the news of 2 cases being identified in Hyderabad, India as well. Somehow the entire scenario gave a sense that traveling was unsafe and also if we traveled, there were high chances that we would unlikely be traveling outdoors. We might have to stay inside the hotel all the time, which is not exactly what we were going for. At the back of my mind, there was also this thought that the wedding was just ahead of us in a few months. None of us could afford to get ill. It would unnecessarily make everyone uncomfortable and create hysteria. The health could not be compromised. We finally made the decision. Within a month of booking our tickets and just 10 days before the date of departure, the trip was called off. A refund was initiated.

But we all wondered, "What the heck was happening across the world? Is this the first time there has been a virus outrage? Are we not competent enough to already have a cure for the virus or is it too lethal to be cured?

Remember State of Apathy? Until and unless something hits us directly, we are not really bothered or moved by it.

Our hearts could not fathom the pain of it. All we had in our mind was The Canceled Bachelors instead of the fun and adventure we had imagined. Incidents like these reinforce the saying "Man proposes and God disposes of". Alas! Our trip was on God's disposal list. The only thing we didn't know was that this time the disposal list God had prepared was going to be endless.

The D Day arrived. It was the 6th of March. We were supposed to fly that day. We called each other to console, comfort, and cheer up. It was decided that we would go out partying in our respective cities to compensate for what we had lost and video-call everyone! It would be a virtual get-together - unaware that virtual was going to be the new norm within a few days for the entire world.

While here in Bangalore, the three of us were already making plans to go out to break from the monotony and busy schedules. We have not been spending much time with each other lately. All the conversation was reduced to a hi-bye while heading to the office or entering the house. We talked each other into an outing to reignite the sparks of conversation and let our hearts roar free. We wanted to feel normal before we boarded the plane for the Bachelors's trip, which was canceled now. Instead what happened was The Last Outing.

And like us, many other travel junkies saw their plans getting canceled. We were stopped from traveling outdoors. The entire world was put to a state of halt. The worst part is not only the international borders, we were soon going to be stopped from stepping outside the fours walls of our house. Our incessant desire to chase beauty, find relaxed-peaceful times, and seek ourselves outside was questioned and we were left to chase all the beauty, happiness, peace, relaxation inside our homes. The homes that we treated as a halt over in between our work and party hours would become our 24x7 station centers. Homes became the epicenter of all our thoughts and actions. The world entropy reduced considerably. Homes soon became our entire world. Instead of discovering beautiful-pacifying locations in the outlandish world, we were left with no option other than to create such beautiful-fulfilling places in our not-so-familiar homes.

Chapter5:
Work from Home

We woke up to a beautiful Saturday morning after the outing last night. Home felt a little different, a little better, as if someone had lifted the weight off the air and lit up the entire house. I, still in my bed, looked out through the curtains swirling in front of the window. The sky shone blue - crystal clear with a hot ball of fire seeming calm - with the sunlight finding its way through crevices of the window passing through our small balcony. Well, that is the most you get to interact with the sun in the metro cities. It must have been 11 already by the time we woke up. There were usual noises around - of the drilling machine in the adjacent plot, of the chimneys and exhausts in the office building at the back, of the kids crying on the upper floor, of the Bengali couple fighting in the adjacent building, and of the vendors hooting on the road trying to sell flowers and onions. Amidst all this, there was only one unusual thing: that we all woke up with a cheerful heart and a lighter soul.

It is strange though that it takes a few shots to play its magic on us. I wondered, "*Does it happen to me alone or does it happen to others as well?*" I wonder, "*Why do we need a dash of ecstasy to bring out a dash of us?*" It takes a lot to live in the moment forgetting the vagaries of the past and fancies of the future. It is tough, to say the least, to be yourself.

None of us would have ever thought when we were kids, that being yourself and keeping your heart on the table slay open would be one of the most courageous things to do in the 21st century. And that we would be caught up in the pretentious trap, that we would live our life from one weekend to another.

We all have been so busy in our day-to-day life that we have forgotten to let go of ourselves, vent out our hearts and let loose. And days kept passing by with us succumbing to the miseries of the world very much fabricated and designed by us. We have been infected by the same bug which got the better side of us last night, setting ourselves free.

There is this one promise we had been muttering to each other for the last couple of months but not heeding to fulfill it. The promise of keeping ourselves - health and family - first before anything else. But we have been failing at it miserably. There were days of insane work that passed without calling up our parents, even for a few minutes. There seemed to be an eternal disconnect between friends and families. And then there have been those sleepless nights - spent completing the unfinished work - taking a toll on our health just because we had a thrashing from our boss the previous day.

To be honest, we have not been able to draw a fine line between work and life. Neither have we been able to merge them well to have a balanced outlook. I am not sure which way we are headed and how long we will be able to sustain this kind of lifestyle! The work-life balance remains a myth.

Amidst all this, we forgot to have food on time, drink enough water, or get up and stretch a bit only to find our bones frozen in the same position. At times we stood defeated to our virtual vices of scrolling up and down our mobile screen, swiping left only to find none "worthy" of swiping right or being a couch potato binging upon the show that remained there in the Watch-list for ages. Somebody has rightly said, "we are the choices we make." And all of us have chosen to become *dehydrated, sore bodies and restless souls!*

Our sedentary lifestyle has become more of a concern rather than a mere habit. But this time, three of us solemnly took the pledge of fulfilling our long forlorn promise and abiding by to the tee of it.

The new morning brought that promise out in us with fresh fervor. “The fresh us” began feeding ourselves to our favorite eggs-in-blanket brunch following which we got engaged in our own set of activities. My sister had a plan with her friends, my wife resorted to checking out the latest fashion and makeup bloggers over IG TV. And I got back to my usual reading. I was hooked on this book called *Kashmir: Land of Regrets*, which I had started a few weeks ago but have not been able to complete yet. Saturday was spent like that. It was a Sunday, and we talked to our parents. I called up some of my friends I had not talked to in a while. They seemed happy and busy in their life. The highlight of any Sunday for that matter is *Rajma-Chawal* for lunch. Yes, this is one ritual we have not let go even being away from home for 14 years now. This keeps us connected to our roots and keeps reminding us of our homes and our mothers. After all, who minds Rajma Chawal and a hint of nostalgia on a Sunday afternoon.

The weekend was gone but we were pepped up to take the week(s) by storm - fueled by our motivational speeches to each other and the promise we had made to ourselves. Monday came and went by. So did Tuesday. We had already reached the mid-week. The work continued in full steam.

Each one of us was occupied in the office. A few of us were brainstorming in the smaller meeting room. A large bunch of folks were in the conference room doing their sprint planning. Then suddenly all of us were called to the announcement bay. We had no idea what it was but the ping on the slack channel said *Urgent Announcement*. The entire office gathered there in a jiffy. Our management had declared *Work From Home* for the next week to run an experiment if we would be able to pull off a show. The reason was the COVID-19 pandemic. This was the first time many of us took the word - the word that was pouring in our ears for quite some time now - seriously.

I remember we had a bunch of folks who flew from the US the previous week and they were not allowed inside the office citing safety and health concerns for the rest of the employees. Then a few days before 2 positive cases were reported in Hyderabad. I believe that is when everyone started behaving cautiously and started taking the spread of COVID-19 seriously. The COVID-19 virus had entered India. Despite all this, we were in a state of anticipation that this will be gone in a few weeks, in a month - at the most from now. Not knowing that this is going to be a long battle to fight for all of us and the entire world.

There was this mixed feeling in the atmosphere. We were confused. After all, it was not the kind of announcement we were used to. Work From Home was a break from the routine and not the routine itself. Work from home as a means to establish a sense of liberty and freedom in our very much tied-up world. The announcement seemed to take that feeling away from us as well. The management meanwhile, had released a set of guidelines on travel and safety. Travel was not advisable but many people did travel. They also had drafted and shared WFH etiquettes defining the SLA for replying to the pings and responding for better coordination with each other. I thought that not so much of this could happen in a day. There must have been a lot of thought and discussion that would have gone into detailing the same.

However, there was a big challenge that remained ahead for the companies and their workforce. Many of the working folks did not have proper amenities at home, many of us had huge family setup which was not so conducive for work, some of us suffered a poor internet connection, some of us had more dependencies on other teams which meant a tough task at hand working remotely. But all of this was thought to be solvable with time.

The office was abuzz with rumors about the WFH extension. Many of my colleagues were already making plans to travel back to their hometown. Some fighter folks planned to travel to nearby hill stations such as Ooty, Kodaikanal, Hampi,

Chikmagalur, Conoor, Coorg, etc. till the time WFH was called off.

I, on the other hand, took a cab and traveled home 2kms away from the office - in an anxious and amused state. In a while, we got to know that my sister's workplace had announced WFH as well starting the following Monday. My wife decided to work from home as well starting Monday while the official mail was yet to come from her HR department. The entire private sector was beginning to announce work from home for their employees here in Bangalore. Partly due to government restrictions and partly due to the fear of what if employees felt sick. The companies needed to run if they had to survive.

On Thursday however, my wife came home early looking worried. They got to know that one person who had traveled from Hyderabad to Bangalore last week in their office was detected Covid positive and the entire cafeteria, where he was last spotted, was sealed. But the management was yet to release an official work from home order. Her decision to work from home was reinforced. The next day my sister came early again petrified. Her cafeteria was being sealed because another person was detected covid positive. Luckily her office had already announced work from home. This got us scared. The fear of the virus having manifested in humans, humans roaming around us. The fear of being infected seemed to loom over us. The pandemic was for real.

How does this spread? How do we protect ourselves? Are only those people affected who have a recent history of travel? Or are travelers from specific countries getting infected and carrying the infection along with them? Or is the virus targeted towards a specific genome? What are the symptoms? How will we be sure about the differences between the symptoms of normal flu and COVID-19? Is there any medication yet? How severe is it? How to fight this out? There were umpteen questions that remain unanswered.

WFH under such suspicious circumstances seemed to be the obvious option. It is so strange that we never thought it would come to this despite work from home being announced for a cousin in Singapore in the month of February itself. And now within a few days WFH was announced for my sister-in-law who was then settled in Amsterdam, Netherlands. The Work From Home announcements came like a wave traveling west from far east forcing companies to let their employees work from home to avoid public transport and travel.

Twitter made working from home for employees mandatory across the world on 12 march 2020, just a day after the World Health organisation declared

COVID-19 a world pandemic as the global death toll crossed 4000 (at 4291) of 1,18,000 positive cases reported in 114 countries. "*When did all these cases of infection happen*", I thought to myself. "*Where were we when the infection was spreading around the globe?*", I wondered. But I told you, that we humans do not really care about something until and unless it directly hits us. We have learned to live in the State of Apathy. And now that cases had started to mushroom in India across neighborhoods, localities and cities - we suddenly took notice of each minute detail regarding the Coronavirus.

Google along with many other major tech giants such as Amazon, Apple, Facebook and Microsoft recommended their employees in Seattle to work from home considering the increase in coronavirus cases in Washington.

As on date, there were a total of 5523 cases reported in Europe , 987 cases in the USA and the first death in India was reported in the State of Karnataka (of total 73 cases reported). While China, the epicentre and origin of the virus was witnessing 80,793 positive cases and 3169 deaths of overall 4600 approx. deaths in the world.

Meanwhile, we here in Bangalore canceled our plan of going out for a movie on Wednesday night. The thought that if it is not advisable to meet and work with a handful of colleagues who we know - then how advisable it is to head out to a theatre to watch a movie with strangers seated nearby. If you remember,it was my birthday week, the celebrations for which we had kickstarted the previous Friday. Not knowing that the day of my birthday would be spent at home, but that is how I ended up celebrating my birthday - in a state of frenzy, fear, and confusion. But yet unaware of what followed next.

4 days went by when another mail came from HR extending the work from home for another week. This got us thinking that something was not right and the situation seems to be far worse than we had initially anticipated or not even guessed, to be honest.

The last I remember I did work from home was when I had a bad stomach. Work From Home was parked for occasions where you could work but did not feel comfortable enough to dress up and go out to the office. WFH was parked for those delivery-at-home days. WFH was for those days when our pets used to be cranky and needed attention. WFH was kept for those doctors' appointments and family functions where you could work but you needed to be at home as well. WFH for me personally used to be those days when I had too much work to do and wanted to isolate myself from the office noise. WFH meant to take a break from the monotony and treat me to me-time. Work From Home was never the norm. It was a break from the norm. Work from home used to be an attempt to maintain a work-life balance.

"But who can work from home for each consecutive day", we all thought! But here we were juggling between finding the hot spot for a stronger internet connection, trying to speak in hush-hush voices so that each one of us could take up calls without disturbing each other. And buoy, there was no whiteboard in the house - how and where would I do my storyboarding exercises. We all had our troubles getting tuned to this work-from-home culture.

Today I feel so ignorant and naive thinking of these little troubles considering what all we had to go through in the coming months and times. It's been more than a year and work from home continues.

I am not sure how effective WFH was for the corporate world and did it impact productivity and revenue positively. But I am quite sure work from home gave everyone a chance to look beyond just their work. It gave wings to many dreams and passions which were finally fuelled by some time at hand. It lets people have some time parked for their hobbies which in this period eventually turned out into some successful and some not-so-successful business ideas. But everyone did finally get a chance to let their wings of dreams take a flight. Only till companies worked out a plan to extract the most from the employees while they were working from home.

It had been only 9 days since we started working from home. We have not even got used to that, when the Prime Minister Mr. Narendra Modi himself called for a countrywide *Junta Curfew* via a televised message on 22 March from 7 am to 9 pm. He advised all of the public to avoid going out of their houses. He emphasized that "..this will prepare us for the forthcoming days." He asked the state and central governments to work in unison to handle and tackle the situation. He asked all of us to follow self-control so that we can be prepared for future challenges. Only those who were a part of the essential services such as healthcare, grocery, security personnel were permitted to go out serving the nation. Rest all of us were strictly advised to follow "*social distancing*" norms and not congregate in gatherings in *chawls*, societies, community halls or parks, or any other public place for any religious ceremony, wedding, or other forms of celebration.

The Prime Minister of India - Republic of 138 crore people - came on television to personally request its citizens to cooperate for the safety and health of each other. Nothing else could emphasize the gravity of the situation more. There were hints in his speech and his words that the pandemic was here to stay for longer than we could think of. *Work From Home* was just the opening up of Pandora's box. Work From Home was the least we could do to break the chain of the virus.

Chapter6: Lockdown1.0 - The Beginning

Work From Home! Junta Curfew! We were just trying to make peace with one announcement after the other. But it looked like there was no end to it. The world was hit by a storm - everyone was going to grapple with it. Come 24 Mar, a day after the Junta Curfew, and the Prime Minister of India - was there on the television again - announcing a 21-day (3 weeks) countrywide lockdown across states and Union Territories. What did this mean?

This meant the entire country would undergo sleep mode. From malls to theatres, from playgrounds, restaurants, and cafes, pubs and bars, salons and spas, retail outlets to online delivery - everything will see a complete shutdown. Public transport, cab facilities, road, rail and air travel would be put to a halt. The only few services that remained operational were medical shops, grocery stores, hospitals, petrol pumps, and defense services. All these put together were classified as "essential services" for the nation.

Today when I think of it, it seems as if a villain had made an unprecedented entry in a romantic relationship - between humans and life like in a Bollywood movie. But it remained to be seen *who would be our hero who would walk us out of the situation.*

I was listening to the live announcement of the PM with his hands joined and requesting our support - the support of each citizen - in all his earnestness. I can remember how he emphasized the importance of '*Social Distancing*'. He highlighted that social distancing was the key to prevent the spread of the coronavirus. Social distancing was to be followed not only from the one who is detected COVID19 positive but also from all others because it took a few days for a COVID positive person to start showing symptoms. This meant an undetected infected person could be infecting other people he or she came in touch with without either of them being aware of it.

According to WHO data, it took 61 days to reach 100,000 infection cases, another 11 days to 200,000, and just 4 days to reach 300,000 in number. The coronavirus spread like fire. If social distancing was not followed, humans will not be able to break the chain of infection. The virus would gobble the world with bones and flesh served on a platter, thereafter lying unattended on the ground.

In his speech, the Prime Minister talked about the strictness with which we all needed to follow the lockdown. He told all of us to imagine a *Lakshmana Rekha* drawn outside our house. This symbolized the protection we could give to ourselves and our family members. And once you cross this Lakshmana Rekha, it would mean letting coronavirus in. Unusual for a Head of State but he was absolutely clear and explicit in his instructions, guidelines, and a word of caution to the public.

Some details could be avoided but he went on to highlight that more medical arrangements are being done. In terms of safety kits, PPE (Personal Protective Equipment) kits, and more tests are being conducted across the country. We are not there yet but his government has allotted 15,000 crores for preparing the nation to face this world pandemic. And then you know that honesty has its flavor. It catches you right in the eyes, arm-twists you but deep down makes you believe that you will - we all will - get over this. Honesty instills that confidence and courage inside you. More importantly, it is the will that drives our actions.

He consoled the public by communicating that all arrangements were in place so that each citizen can get easy access to the essential services. This could prevent people from panic buying and hoarding stuff leaving no stock for the rest of the people. His heart went out for the poor and daily wagers who would face the brunt of this lockdown the most and pointed out that we should do all we can to help the poor sail through these strange and tough times.

I feel no one would have ever believed the gravity of the situation if all this was made a part of the news headlines or part of the social media campaign or an aggravated forward from the Whatsapp University. No one would have believed even if it came from the respective head of state either. The fact that the PM took upon himself to convey the sad and grave news to the nation highlighting the intensity of the situation made people doubly aware and cognizant of the prevailing times.

I will never forget those words and the intensity of those words when he said if we do not follow this nationwide lockdown for 21 days, we will go back 21 years in time as a nation. I had goosebumps listening to those words then and I have goosebumps today as I recall those inauspicious words. These lines sent a shockwave across the nation and the public. This reflected the severity of the damage and crisis this virus could create in cities, states, and countries. This could have resulted in hysteria and paranoia but the fact that the PM himself came in front of the nation to communicate this crucial message held the people by strength and courage to face it all and together. A few hours from now the entire nation went under a state of curfew.

Curfew has not been a new word for me. I have grown up reading this word more than any other word in the Headlines on the first page of my state daily for most of my life. At times because of a bomb that blew off on the border, sometimes because of the surge in an insurgency in the northwest frontier province of Kashmir. Sometimes the curfews were a way of demonstrating the unease and unhappiness about the center always neglecting Jammu over Kashmir. Sometimes these curfews were public led, sometimes political parties led, and then there were days when these curfews were declared by the Army or CRPF as a safety measure.

As a kid, I used to feel happy about these days of curfews because the schools would declare a holiday and I would not know why the cities go to sleep and the roads are flooded with those yellow-colored barricades. But as I grew up, I started seeing and feeling the restlessness and motto behind these curfews. And what bothered and grieved me more was the fragmented thoughts and ideologies people fought over during these curfews. But this countrywide lockdown (read curfew) was different from those curfews back in time. Sigh!

The entire nation stood together in solidarity for the safety of every individual. The safety and healthcare above all - any ideology or school of thought. This was the only silver lining in the dark times we were going through. Entire India came to stand united in those unprecedented times. It made it a bit easier than we could have thought.

Well, we were not alone. At the time (24 March), when India went under lockdown, many countries in the world had already started announcing lockdown. In most parts of the US, the lockdown started coming into effect by 19 March. Argentina and Brazil had announced countrywide lockdowns starting 19 March and 17 March. In France, the lockdown was announced on 17 March followed by Germany on 23 March. Italy, owing to the rapid rise in the COVID19 positive cases and the first nation to be affected severely outside China, decided to announce the lockdown starting 9 March.

Australia supposedly had the longest lockdown amongst all the nations in the world starting 23 March and not giving any hint of opening up even in June 2020. New Zealand had the most controlled and effective way of curbing the spread of the coronavirus where they announced the lockdown on 26 March and started shifting towards opening up on 14 May.

Interestingly, there has been no update on the lockdown in China except for the 73 Day lockdown that was imposed in the city of Wuhan, Hubei province which was the epicenter of this worldwide pandemic.

By 26 March 1.7 billion people were under stay-at-home orders which increased to 3.9 billion (more than half of the world's population) in the first week of April. The world was shutting down. All the commotion that became our way of living was turned off in a jiffy. The entire world was coming to a state of halt. It seemed as if someone had clipped our wings of freedom and played the pause button. Statue!

One could not move out of their house. No one could come to visit you. There was no going out for partying or clubbing. The morning gym routine or heading to the park for that 5km run had to stop for a while. Hanging out with friends after office hours was not an option anymore. The birthday bash was homebound. The Kitty parties and *housie* continued though but were confined to virtual mediums. Online gaming took over the ruggedness of the sports on the playgrounds and the fields. Our cricket gullies turned abandoned. The evening cycle marathons were stopped. All modes of entertainment and transport were grounded. The world turned indoors. And we didn't know how long this was going to last!

The sight of people walking on the road felt necessary, the hum of the cars, honking of the horns, and roaring of the bikes suddenly felt fulfilling. Not that the sky was our favorite sight of the day, but only when we were asked to stay indoors - the sun and the sky suddenly seemed so much more important. There was this piercing silence that reflected how used to we had become to so much noise.

For stepping out for a pity thing such as fetching groceries and essentials seemed a herculean task. Humans had to plan and safeguard themselves. Wearing a mask while heading out, washing and sanitizing hands regularly, and covering your mouth or nose if coughing or sneezing became mandatory. And most importantly distancing oneself from another by a margin of 2 meter. *Social distancing*, as we the humans embraced it.

While many of us were struggling to figure out a way to live this new normal and how to stay indoors with minimum interaction with anyone outside, there were these machismos planning their travel back home. In between the work from home and the day of the complete lockdown being announced, many people flew back or traveled back to their hometown. One among these was our helper whose family also happened to be the security guard of our building. All 4 of them traveled back to their village - somewhere between Karnataka and Andhra Pradesh state border. We also had to tell our cook to stop coming. This turned out to be a pressing challenge in the days to come.

For now, the doors remain locked. The roads remained abandoned. The silence became deafening. The corridors became haunting. The only thing we could hear was the whisper of our neighbors and the shout-out of the police vans - patrolling every once in 2 hours - and advising everyone to stay indoors.

We had no clue what to do. After all, this is not a situation you witness now and then. We sat glued to the television, looking for correct information, to avoid falling into a trap of any misinformation and rumors. We talked to our parents who sounded worried but we tried to remain calm or at least pretended to be so. It was a long night indeed.

There was this sadness that gripped and echoed *"Where have we come?"*, *"How did we arrive here?"* *"What wrong did we do to deserve this?"*. There was this fear if all this was a conspiracy and a plan for another World War. Back then, there was also this rage pointed at China towards establishing its world supremacy by pushing the entire world to *nadir* but this sentiment faded way too soon with the change of power in the US in November 2020. The humanity stood unarmed with a BIG question looming over their heads, *"How long will this all last?"* Our hearts were filled with anxiety anticipating how we would survive this and what we were going to do next. We did not know that there was going to be more sadness and distress we would need to make peace with, in the times to come.

The first thing we did after the call with our parents that night was to audit the stock we had at home, things we needed urgently, and things we planned to stock up for just more than 15 days. I planned to go to the grocery store the next morning to fetch all I could. *Lockdown1.0 was ON!*

Chapter7:
Will I do it?

There are whirlpools and butterflies in the stomach when you have an exam the next day. The whole night was spent like that, feeling restless and anxious wondering if I would be able to make it.

Somewhere deep down, my heart believed that the times ahead were going to be challenging. Humanity had to undergo a litmus test of its morals and values. A subject that none of us took seriously as a student and now the time was going to tell if we failed or passed basis that. The most interesting thing about this subject is there are no individual results. Only collective results. You either fail or pass as a group, as a neighborhood, as a society, as a nation, and as a world. You falter at any level and the results start deprecating. I fail, you fail. You fail, I fail. Compelling, as much as it could be!

Well, for now, my list of items was ready. The list included Aashirwaad atta (flour), India Gate rice (the pink packet), a few pulses, a packet each of Parry's sugar, TATA salt and Red Label chai Patti (tea-brew), Amul butter, Britannia bread, Amul cheese slices, tetra packs of Amul milk, Parle-G biscuits, Maggi, some snacks, and vegetables. Like many other households, we also used to stock up twice in a month for 15 days once at the beginning and once somewhere in the middle of the month. But today we had decided to be prudent in stocking up and not buy stuff more than what we needed.

A little scared though, I woke up and got ready with my mask on to go buy the grocery and essentials. It must be somewhere around 9 in the morning. I was just heading out when we also added *sanitary napkins and a packet of condoms* to the list.

There was only one caveat to the list though, that each item mentioned had to be of a specific brand or make. The confident, nonchalant me marched ahead. Deep down, I was happy that we will be sorted for almost 21 days of lockdown once we have sourced this list of items. I picked up the carry bags and walked towards the shop which was around 600 meters from our house. The area was a cluster of shops scattered here and there. So it made an obvious choice to head in that direction.

But all I came back with was a loaf of bread. That is it! The shop seemed ransacked! It was empty. There were leftovers of unessential items scattered on the shelves. I enquired with the shopkeeper and he said, *"Sir, raat mein Modi ki announcement ke baad hi logo ne dhaawa bhol diya. Sab kuch khatam ho gaya hai. Ab samaan godown se aa raha hai."* I asked him, *"Phir main kab tak aaon?"* He retorted, *"Waise aap subah 7 baje aaoge to bhi samaan mil jaayega. Aaj waise bhi roads band hain, abhi pass ban raha hai toh sure nahi hai ke gaadi ko kab aane denge. Uske baad hi saamaan aayega."*

("Post announcement, people came and bought stuff in bulk. There's nothing left", that is what the shopkeeper said. He further added that I could visit the shop the next morning as he was not sure when the carriage of the goods would arrive owing to the ban on travel and the pass for the essential's vehicle was still being issued.)

My happiness was crushed. But my confidence was not gone yet. We dropped the idea of sticking to the items from specific brands, any make would do. It was time we started making compromises with our demands and wishlist. It was time we got to reality. I reaffirmed myself that there must be households such as bachelors or the ones with kids who would need more food or specific items and that is why shops went empty. To be honest, I was a bit worried though.

But the next morning I was up again ready to buy the grocery. I wore the mask and stepped out into this new world. The world that had gone clueless. I was there at the shop at 7:00 AM as suggested by the shopkeeper but all I came back with this time was a pouch of milk and a few veggies.

I grew frantic. "*Is my family going to starve because I am not able to source basic food items for them?", the thought grew stronger in my head.* Despite all the confidence and trust, the PM tried to bestow in the public and masses, the panic buying did happen. People did go out at the last minute and swept out the shops.

I came back home and switched on the TV. The same thing was being broadcast on the news channels. Not only here in Bangalore, but across other cities of India, the condition was quite similar. People had made panic purchases. There were clippings of empty shops and hypermarkets. The shelves lay there empty and abandoned. Departmental stores were shut with the messages 'Stock Out' in front of their shutters and gates. For sure, we humans were not able to contain our anxiety and fears.

On the 3rd day, I went again to the shop but this time at 6:30 AM. Not all the items on my list were available but I managed to buy quite a lot of them. I was there at the counter when 2 people jumped over my shoulder to pay for their stuff. One of them tried to snatch away the items which were there in my basket. I froze for a second. No, I didn't let go of them. I firmed my grip and looked behind from over my shoulder and nudged him back. He got my message. Meanwhile, the other guy stole the bread from the counter and ran away. I paid the bill, collected my items, stuffed the carry bags, and rushed back home.

I had never in my lifetime witnessed any such thing. I have only heard of the pick-pockets, robberies, thefts of gold and money. I had never in my entire 30 years heard about someone stealing the loaf of bread and running away. Maybe a loaf of bread was never that important. Or maybe none of us anticipated that bread alone could motivate someone to steal and run. Or maybe we had never got to witness the other side of the world - beyond the usual and granted comfort zone of our lives.

On the way back, my eyes welled with tears. I was anxious, scared, and shaking inside. Is this what we have come to? Is this all the will and character humanity has got? Just one announcement and a few days of lockdown - and we are already breaking the code of ethics and moral values. These thoughts occupied my brain for most of the day.

Then there was this thought that suddenly sparked in my head, "What if one day there is almost no stock left and I am left to choose between letting others buy or stealing away the loaf of bread. Will I do it?"

I was surprised with my answer to myself. I said to myself, *"Yes, I will do it. I will steal the loaf of bread if for the sake of my family."* If that is all it takes to keep my family alive, why not? The very thought and my response to that thought calmed me down from the shock in the morning. I realized that there is a possibility that the person genuinely needed that loaf of bread and didn't have money to pay for it. I left my trail of thoughts there convincing myself to be more empathetic and patient during the times to come. Things people do to keep their family safe and sane! There is no extent to what one can do to save their family. *"The pandemic was here and it was going to leave us with some great realizations"*, I shuddered.

I came back home and narrated the incident to my wife and my sister. We all had a whiff of laughter but I saw it in their eyes - the looming fear.

But such incidents were reported across several cities across the globe. The fruit vendors are being looted in the bright daylight. People quarreling and beating each other up to be first in the queue to pay for their list of items. There were incidents of brawls and injuries where the public had threatened and beaten up the shopkeepers because they went *Out of Stock* too soon. The hypermarkets and supermarkets were looted and rampaged. We had gone berserk.

I have always failed to understand why we grow so impatient when things go for a toss around us. Just when the ecosystem fails to deliver us, there is this fury that flares inside us. There is a rebel in all of us that wakes up all of sudden. We forget that you and I together make that ecosystem. We make - what we call society. And times we were going through were not usual - these were unprecedented times. Once in 100 years - are we hit by a pandemic. Such circumstances need us to put all our wisdom and acquired knowledge to use but interestingly and surprisingly - we tend to slip through the cracks and fall for the trap. We turn barbaric and uncivilized. We turn cold and apathetic towards our fellow beings, but how? Is that what we have made of ourselves as a society?

Unfortunately moral values, ethics stand no chance if it is a choice one has to make between saving the family and saving the moral grace. Another day and moral choices may get brutally killed if it comes to saving ourselves. Unfortunately, moral values are let go when the situation demands a collective larger good for the society. And what takes the centre stage is the selfish human instinct. We had started to witness the onset of the pandemic and the imposed lockdown.

This is the thing about morals. They can't survive in isolation. You alone can't be keeping the sanctity of the moral values. They are an avalanche reaction trickling from one layer of society to another. The only thing that differs is - "our motivation to break the chain of moral values."

For some, it can be a luxury car and for some, it can be that coveted position. For some, it can just be sumptuous food and for some, it can be mere recognition. Money, fame, or power - three things (read possessions) people get ready to stake their morals for. Or at least what we could fathom as the prime reasons why someone would not abide by the morals. Food, Air, Water, or Survival - these are not something we would ever imagine people letting go of their moral conscience for. We take them for granted.

But look deeper into the society and beyond from where you stand. You will find and realize that there still are people for whom food and survival is a daily battle to fight for. It is them who should be breaking the codes of conduct and forgetting the moral values when it comes to situations like pandemics and an atmosphere of uncertainty. Not you and I, who sit in our comfortable couches just wondering what is the next series we should be watching and what snack I would be eating while I binge and chill.

Sadly so, but the anxiety and fear gripped all of us. We were not able to maintain our calm. The Rich or the Poor; The Privileged or the Distraught - we all were equally hit by the storm called COVID-19. It brought all of us to the same ground fighting for the same air and food. The man-made barriers of society were suddenly put into question! Equality for all - Covid screamed!

But we have grown into a society where all we think of is about ourselves. *I* come first. Nobody ever taught us the importance of living in an ecosystem. Nobody ever told us that the differences and the gaps in terms of comforts, amenities are for real. Our society nurtures people belonging to different economic strata. And we all dwell in the clouds of thoughts that these are two different worlds. Alas! No. They are not.

They are a part of the same world divided by haves and have nots. But the air, food, and water - the resources that matter the most are to be shared by all of us equally. The fundamental rights and duties have to be shared equally by all of us. The right to equality is not for namesake. The right to justice and the right to enjoy life has to be equally shared by all of us. Unfortunately, that is not the case, that is not how our society is built up over years. That is not how our societies are matured and nurtured. The way we have been developing and progressing - we have resulted in making this gap wider and bigger.

That is where the entire challenge begins and the house of cards falls. If there is a fallacy in moral values in one section of the society, that trickles to breaking the moral codes and ethics in another part of the same society as well. And then it cascades - the *Bandwagon effect!* The pandemic was here to make us realize that we all needed to live as a single unit.

We can be living in absolutely stark different situations and circumstances but there has to be mutual respect. The economics of currency cannot decide how we treat each other. There has to be an understanding of each others' troubles and the troubles of society as a whole. We as a society need to be more empathetic than we have been.

Irrespective of caste, color, and creed; irrespective of the economic strata; irrespective of ethnicity and religion; irrespective of the nature of work we do - we all deserve to live a healthy and happy life. And that can happen only when we humans make each other feel valued and loved in our personal and professional capacity. It is only then when we will be able to pass the litmus test of humanity. For now - from what ruckus we had observed - it looked like we were going to fail miserably.

Moral science classes need not stop at the primary level of schooling. They need to trespass our journey of evolution as an individual and as a society. They need to continue as we graduate from school to college to our jobs. They need to be discussed and debated during those "auspicious" and "all-pervading" debate hours. They need to be discussed during our "Mann ki Baat". They need to be talked about during our RJ shows and they need to be sermoned by Bade-Chhote on 9XM. They need to be disseminated via all possible channels permeating all the sections of society. And the most important lesson that we all need to learn throughout our life - out of these moral science lessons - is that of *coexistence. Coexistence of all beings in nature.* It needs to be reinforced from time to time.

The incident in the shop made us realize that we would have to be cautious of our consumption. To keep things right and so that the day never arrives when anyone has to steal the stuff for their family - the best we can do is not buy in bulk and leave the stuff for others as well. We are going to be sure of what we need, what we want, and how much would be enough for the three of us. This way we could keep a check on what we were going to consume. And this attitude needs to stretch beyond just the days of pandemics into our normal lives. At our current consumption rate of natural resources we are borrowing (rather stealing) them from our future generations. This needs to be immediately stopped with a strong force in action. But I will keep this discussion for another day, another time.

For now, we also decided to give some extra cash to our helpers because their husbands were daily wagers and were without work now. A few days of lockdown and home delivery were in full force with all protection and safety measures. Dunzo, a home-delivery app, did a great job of providing essentials at the doorstep. Their post-delivery page on the app said "*Thank you partner*" and "*Thank you shopkeeper*" where shoppers like you and me could offer some tips. We realized that it would take some time for the delivery partner to reap those tips. So we also decided to give extra cash to these delivery boys who were staking their lives just to ensure that we have all essentials with us at the convenience of our home.

We knew these were not just 21 Days of Lockdown, these were going to be 21 Days of testing human mettle, perseverance, patience, and ability to coexist. These 21 Days had to be *21 Days of Positivity*.

We all need to create a society where if anyone has to ask this question to themselves, "Will I do it?" the answer should be an emphatic No!

Chapter8: The Survival

Isn't it strange, that when everything is going smooth, no one bothers, no one cares? We all behave unabashed and walk over the earth as ruling kings and queens - looting the earth as if it will replenish itself quickly and continue to do so till eternity. Isn't it strange that when things are smooth, we behave as if in a state of trance - totally unaffected by how our environment is changing, how our society is evolving, and how its needs are changing too?

Strangely, consuming more (content, internet, shopping, food, air, water, things we need and ones we don't) is our primary concern always rather than survival. Survival? Why should we even worry about that? Is our survival temporary or jeopardized? We are not moved by any of these thoughts - neither as individuals nor as a race. We consider ourselves indomitable.

It is only during the turbulent and stressful times, that the real side of the society - the one below the facade of daily vagaries - shows up. It is when the status quo is questioned does society feel the heat of what you and I have built together. Society is a concoction of values we have fused into it. The moral fiber and social thread that we all together have woven for ourselves - only to find ourselves entangled in the same. The society that is a rut we all made piece by piece, step by step over the years leading us here. A society that is in a state of pandemonium because of us. It is only when *Survival - something we do not care about -* is put at stake does the real side of the society surface.

A few days had passed since the lockdown had begun and I received a call from the cook at our home. We had asked her not to come till things got better. We had no clue that things are not just getting better anytime soon and we would give up sooner than we could even imagine and call her back to work. But her call that day surprised me. On talking to her, I got to know that her husband was out of work. He was a contractor (mason worker with a team of 3-4 other amateur people joining him) to say but his earnings would come from the work he would get daily and in certain cases on weekly contracts and a monthly basis for a few projects. I listened carefully. She had more to say.

She went on to explain that the new academic year for their 2 kids was going to begin and the school management had asked to deposit a total sum amount of 1 lac for their children to continue studying. She expressed her inability to do so since her husband's work would be uncertain. And since she had stopped going to work, not all the households were giving her the monthly payment. But she had no complaint in her voice.

I was at a loss for words. I didn't know how I should react. But after my confused pause, I asked her "*How can I help you, Didi?*" She replied "*Bhaiya, yeh Corona kab tak khatam hoga?*". [By when will this corona end?] From all the little knowledge I had gathered from reading or hearing stuff on the news and online, I told her that things were uncertain and it could be 3 months or 6 months or even more before all of this ends. It has been more than a year since she called and we all are still grappling with the uncertainty.

But I couldn't connect the dots behind her sequence of questions then. While in retrospect it does make sense, at that time it was not very obvious to connect the duration of corona with her husband's loss of income and the academic sessions for her kids. I asserted, "*Didi, hum aapki kaise madad kar sakte hain?*"

Her primary objective of talking to me was to gauge if depositing the school fee would make sense or not or will it be wasted money that otherwise would be used to survive during this period.

She was in a moral dilemma of withdrawing her kids from school because corona meant the kids will have to study from home. This implied 2 laptops/mobiles in-home so that children could connect virtually as well as someone at home who could babysit the kids and guide them through these virtual classrooms. Neither she had the extra money to buy these devices nor any of the parents were educated enough who could help the kids with that. I realized her dilemma existed because of her inability to let her kids continue their studies, which was one of the key reasons she had moved to city life from her village. *(The kids dropped out of school as I started writing this chapter and have been re-admitted as I finish this book).*

On further prodding, she explained to me that she and her husband have planned to use the little savings they have towards paying the monthly rent for the house they are living in. And all little of what her husband is going to earn will be used to buy the groceries and other essentials items for the house. She had her priorities set.

But I could not fathom any of it. I could not fathom that her kids were going to stop studying. I could not fathom that people decided not to pay her because of the pandemic. I could not fathom that there will be days when they might as well go to bed hungry. I could not fathom that despite all of this that has befallen her, she was so poised.

But she was not alone. It was estimated that a total of 1.6 bn informal workers globally would suffer damage to their livelihood owing to the pandemic. This number was already 122Mn in India by the end of April 2020 (one month post the onset of the pandemic). They faced an extreme financial crisis, due to which they were not able to meet their day-to-day spends let alone spend on healthcare, education, and other amenities. Sometimes, all that we think of as BASIC is not basic but comes at the cost of something else.

This led me to think about *Survival.* The big question looming over my head - does survival mean different things for different people?

It does! At least that is what we are told to believe. That is what we are grown up believing. Isn't it? For a family living in the *chawl*, being able to procure food for 2 times a day means survival. For a person leaving at the roadside, just trying to prevent himself from being overrun by a car is survival. For a middle-class family, being able to celebrate their moments means survival. For someone, ensuring the education for their kids is survival. For someone getting their children married is survival. For a family living in opulence, having a jacuzzi bath and food at their choicest restaurants or traveling to their favorite destination would mean survival. For a few, being able to breathe is survival. Something we think of as a given-forever privilege for all mankind. But it is not. Sooner than imagined, was the entire world fighting to breathe for their survival. Equality for all screamed COVID!

When the pandemic hit the world, none of this mattered. From shopping malls to cinema halls, roadside dhabas to the poshest restaurants, from salons to other entertainment zones, from parks to zoos and other tourist spots - all were shut. Clearly, they didn't stand a chance to bag the trophy for "*Things we needed for survival!*"

In fact, the travel by any means was halted as well. What remained opened was the delivery of groceries, medicine, and defense. Only these were deemed as "essential services". For all of us - irrespective of the socio-economic strata we belonged to - this is all we all could consume. If I put it bluntly, what remained open were the means to eat, the means to take care of our health and maintain our sovereignty! Probably this is what we needed the most for our survival.

I wonder why none of us ever questioned - what does survival mean for mankind?

The pandemic didn't abide by the man-made classification of survival for sure! The socio-economic divide we all love to enjoy or we all have grown up experiencing went for a toss! This divide prevents us from barging closer and deeper into the lives of these "other" sections of the society to observe, understand and realize - what survival means for each one of us! What we could not learn in our oblivion - the pandemic was here to teach us.

Clearly, what we all needed was *Roti, Kapda, and Makaan* - food, clothes, and shelter. Nothing else. In fact, I will remember this till my last breath - the uncertainty that gripped my mind when I was not able to procure food items for my family for 2 days in a row. Food took the utmost precedence for me. And for people like our cook - the shelter was an added concern as well.

It is awakening, to say the least, that she and I were concerned about similar things and now we both had the same priorities. This not only made many of us empathetic towards each other but also started eliminating the *state of* apathy we were dwelling in. We all became more considerate towards the "lesser mortals" as well. *Was the pandemic here to guide all of us - humans - towards a common goal?*

This reminds me of Charles Darwin's theory of *Survival of the fittest*! One of the most misunderstood catchphrases in our popular culture. Whenever we think of the "survival of the fittest", we tend to conclude that only those who are fitter physically will survive. The ones with physical might are going to be the last ones standing when things go awry. The rest will perish. Even worse, over the period, this has quite well translated to fitter being equivalent to the wealthier, the ones with stronger political clout and connections. This thought process has led us to believe that survival means different things for different people which is not the case. This has led us to accumulate different materialistic possessions without having any common goal to chase. This makes us believe that we all have our battle to fight without leaving any common ground for us.

We have grown (read evolve) to become a society that respects only those who are in power, or are influential, or are wealthy. But are these individuals alone or as a group the fittest to survive? Probably not! Where is the missing link between our needs and our survival?

And that is where we need to relook at the definition of "Survival of the fittest". Darwin didn't consider the process of evolution as the survival of the fittest rather survival of the fitter because the survival of existence is relative and not absolute. Darwin points out that winners concerning a species could become losers with the change of circumstances.

Darwin uses the term *Survival of the fittest* as a synonym to the word *natural selection.* Darwin says,

"It may be said that natural selection is daily and hourly scrutinizing throughout the world, every variation, even the slightest; rejecting that which is bad, preserving and adding up all that is good; silently and insensibly working, whenever and wherever opportunity offers, at the improvement of each organic being about its organic and inorganic conditions of life."

To put it simply, only those organisms or living beings - humans in this case - survived which best adjusted to the environment. Unfortunately, we humans have chosen the path to not adjust to the environment but rather consume it and twist and tweak the environment at our convenience and needs.

This way of living would rather just flourish only individuals and not the society as a whole. This lies at the helm of creating disparity and unrest at a larger level. And that is what has been happening in the last few years and decades. While we all can attempt to outshine at an individual level, we are destined to doom at a societal/community level.

Our inability to understand that our survival depends not on how much we grow and flourish as an individual but on how we maintain harmony between the society and the ecosystem and the balance between the two that nurtures us. It meant that all of mankind took a pause and reflected upon our ways of living and understood that for survival - what we need the most is a perfectly balanced ecosystem in which nature and humans can coexist. A balance in which humans of one economic stratum can coexist with humans of other economic classes as well.

Only when we can culminate this thought process will we know that Survival means chasing the same goals, protecting the same earth (and its resources), and establishing a perfect harmony between humans and nature. Survival means acknowledging the needs of each organic and inorganic life around us and let (help) them grow along with it.

I am afraid that In the hierarchy of needs if we do not learn to put the ecosystem first, we might not be deemed fit in the course of natural selection. And our survival will be at risk!

For now, we might as well thrive on food, clothing, and shelter but we need to (un)learn too fast that what got us here might not get us ahead! For survival, we need to change our game fast and now!

It amazes me to think how our cook was so adept at taking the right decisions for her family during the changing circumstances. We surely have so much to learn from each other if we keep an open mind. The call with her that day was an awakening call for me. After pondering all of this for quite some time, I shared my thoughts with my family members as well, who were amidst watching a series on Hotstar.

It was time I joined them in our daily ritual of binge-watching. For folks like me, if there was something that kept us alive beyond food and shelter (during the lockdown) was content - a lot of binge-worthy content available for streaming at much ease and nominal cost.

The survival comes in different subscription packages, I thought!

Chapter9:

The Drug Called Content

The Forgotten Army. Paatal Lok. Kaafir. Asur. Arya. Pawan and Pooja. I had just finished watching these with many more on the *watchlist.* There are countless such series ready to serve the insatiable desire of our curious minds and devil hearts. The more you dig, the more content you can find in the survival arsenal for all of us - all of humanity - worth binging and being a couch potato for. The lockdown days just passed by consuming a lot of caffeine (dalgona coffee) and content.

During the times of the pandemic and the imposed lockdown - after all - it was all we were left to do: cook, wash utensils, sweep, or binge-watch! But don't be surprised that all of us - the teens, the adults, and the ones in mid-thirties and the ones in the late forties and sexagenarians - damn all of us have been caught in the rage of online subscription viewership. This fad has not been too old to have our loyalties but surely the fastest we became loyal to anything in the recent history of mankind. Our loyalties had switched from humans-in-real to humans-on-screen.

In fact, OTT media was not even a thing six years back when I had moved to Bangalore in 2015. All one could hear was murmurs about Netflix and the rage was just catching up. *The Game of Thrones* is where it all started - a bit of sleaze, a lot of abuse, a substantial amount of skin show, and blasphemy is all that gets the nerves wrecking for the world that at times seems sex-deprived to me. This is a standard mix that can be stirred up to suit any demographics across any geography for that matter. Without undermining the quality of the content (storyline, direction, cinematography, background lyrics, and a million other factors) - but yes there are a few factors that play a bigger role in deciding what sells and what doesn't.

In the last five years, this space exploded with Amazon Prime Video, Hotstar, Alt Balaji, Zee5, MXPlayer, etc. mushrooming too fast too thick. Surprisingly with amazing quality and quantity of content being produced - better say churned month over month and days-over-days; we had more folks glued to the screen ever. In Asia-Pacific alone, Netflix has approximately 25.5Mn subscribers by January 2021. Youtube is watched by 84.2% of the digital video viewers in the US and Netflix by 67.6%. China is expected to triple its OTT revenue by 2023 to US $26 billion . Consumers in India spend 45 billion hours watching app-based video streaming services, just next to the US.

The stats are overwhelmingly reflecting an insatiable desire to consume a lot more content. These On-demand and live streaming services must be doing something right to have our attention. This is one such activity that has got us happily occupied during these lockdown times of the pandemic. Otherwise, it was tough to find something entertaining! The web content saved us from using our brains a little too much and prevented us from going insane.

We are spoiled for choices. From TV Operas to multi-starter soaps, reality shows (be it Comicstaan) to The Country X Got Talent or MasterChef, Thrillers to RomComs, Movies to Theatrics, Short Stories to Commercials, The Classics or The Contemporary - there is a buffet of options lined up from where each one of us could consume to what suits our appetite the best. And all at the meagre price of INR 500 /month (which is approximately $7/month).

Whether we are happy or sad, we are a gang or alone, party mood or melancholy, patch up or breakup, friendship or hookup vibes - we can choose the mood we want to pick our content from. Most importantly, all at just one click. The ease of choice and the sheer volume (to choose from) made it super simple for people like you and me - locked up inside our homes - to go binge and chill!

I, like most of you, spent the initial few days and months of the lockdown doing the same before I moved in with my family back in my hometown. It used to be a typical day in Bangalore. We all would get up and get ready for work. Everyone would start wrapping up by 6:30 ish or 7ish in the evening. There would be a series agreed upon mutual consent or at times to each its own. Tea, plus Maggi plus the binge watch! It would be a good kill for our so-called precious time. The biggest saving grace used to be no one would have to talk much to each other avoiding any gesture or comment that could precariously become disturbing for anyone in the short-tempered environment.

However, once we were back in our hometown, things were a little different. We looked forward to the evenings anticipating some good family time - talking about friends and relatives, knowing which kid is next in line to get married and which kid is escaping the vicious circle and flying abroad. The stories back home could capture our attention better than the *richly produced OTT content.* If not for stories, there would be a ride to the nearby market or just a drive too far out in the city. And considering all of us were back home after so many years, quite a few evenings were spent with cousins rejoicing in the distant past and reliving the days from childhood archives.

We listened in to the endless banter of who dated who for how long, contemplating the future of still-going oh-so-strong ones over a bowl of popcorn. We shared our routines, the nature of our work, what we loved doing, and what killed us daily. In between, we sneaked a peek over pings that kept buzzing. As a matter of fact, we opened up to each other. It never felt like *Once Again*. It felt like *Always before!* Our hearts enjoyed these one-to-one conversations.

Now when I recollect these evenings which were a blessing in disguise made us more cheerful and cognizant about the troubles in each other's lives. It made us realize that we all were going through almost the same cycle of pain and pleasure. Some changing circumstances through our life are bound to happen to each one of us at some point in time in the due course of time. These conversations and evenings were spent with families as if brought back life to many of us. They were like moments brought home which we were constantly missing in the world we had created outside our homes - in the noise-clad metros, in the concrete jungles that only reverberated what we produced.

It made me ponder vehemently about the futility of so much noise we make out of nothing. Our heads banging hard (and always) like empty utensils. So much content that we binge-watch ignoring the realities of life, letting go of any human connection and touch. The passive consumption of so much freely (read easily) available content at the tap of a few hits and clicks had got our brains turned passive. Weirdly, we can feel and empathize with the characters in the web series but find it hard to empathize and relate with our family and friends and co-workers and helpers. Touche! Alas! On one hand, we cannot stop *awww-ing* over those virtual characters but in real life, we have grown into harsh and cold beings who are nothing less than self-obsessed potpourris reeking of our well-being, success, and lives.

I have been forced to ask myself and many of my friends and acquaintances this question - what good does this *drug called content* bring to us? It kills time, yes! It helps us forget the realities of life, yes! It makes us avoid people we do not want to talk to, yes! It helps ignore everything, the realization of which is important for us to grow and evolve. And experiencing what could be tumultuous and excruciating.

This drug called content has come as an obstruction - an impediment - to any possible human touch and interaction. It prevents humans from talking to fellow humans and learning and realizing life. The very purpose this drug serves is to create a delusion around us of everything good or bad! This is where I find mindless consumption of so much content in whatever format or form over various digital platforms harmful. Hazardous to humans.

This content not only prevents us from letting reality hit us but also breaks the chain of any possible human communication. This leaves us with less time to discuss the challenges, experience happiness in our day-to-day lives. It stops us from sharing our experiences and learning from somebody else's experiences. Our joys are our own and our sorrows even so very much. Every emotion is caged in our hearts while our eyes are glued to a screen trying to resonate with our feelings. We prefer sticking to a digital channel rather than picking up the phone and calling a friend, a sibling, or a cousin. We have turned so passive that we would continue watching our show even if someone would call us up. If this is not an addiction, then what is! This passivity of the human brain and emotion is a dangerous consequence of this mindless consumption of umpteen content available there for us to gulp down and keep us busy forever.

Content that is available in the form of web series, infinite scrolling up and down the social media - Instagram or Facebook, social networks, swiping left and right, shopping websites, and ad-network.

Content today engulfs us in unthinkable ways and formats.

Unfortunately human interaction and not content is the key to learn, grow and most importantly evolve. But we have fabricated ourselves into wannabe unemotional uncouth beings. And that is why when we were back to the routine of evening supper sharing with our friends and family, we got so excited about it. That is the reason why we felt as if somebody brought back lives to our otherwise dead lives. This way the pandemic and the imposed lockdown have done more good to us rather than harm. It made us realize what we could do without and what we couldn't. The human touch that had gone missing came back to our life like a Midas touch making us realize the necessity of human interaction and the need for one another.

The times were tough and even tougher for those who got stuck at far-off places without any real human touch and interaction.

There is another harm that this drug called content does to us. In its existence, it creates an illusion of enough creativity being manifested in one form or the other around us. Somebody is a poet, someone is a writer, a director, or a theatre artist, composer, dancer, someone is churning blogs, and someone is a what we call a Youtuber, someone is taking potshots at others - the rest of us - on Twitter and someone is a life coach on Linkedin. While I appreciate that there are so many creative souls sprouting now and then, where it starts harming us is our complete submission to somebody else's creativity.

Our getting addicted to one series after the other, rampant scrolling up and down the screens just to watch the latest Tik Tok video, or a pep-talk - this is scarier. This endless addiction kills our creativity - our desire to create. We all are born artists, with gifted talent. The idea is to nurture that art and the talent inside us. But our passive consumption of content and sticking to this repetitive pattern prevents us from taking that step forward to learn, nurture our talent, and create something new of our own. Our limitation to create something new makes us believe in our inability to bring a positive change in society as well. This passive-aggressive production of drugs called content is a limiting factor in the success and growth of society as a whole.

While we cannot stop others from producing and creating what they wish to (and we need not) - the point I am driving is to harness our ability to create. Each one of us can be deliberately consumed in creating something as basic as a hand-knit piece, self-satiating dish, a piece of music or poetry or gardening, or maybe just engrossed in creating something that breaks this mindless-endless cycle of consuming the drug called content - all the time. For that matter, doing nothing and staring at the wall contemplating life is a much better thing to do to ourselves.

Had it not been for the pandemic that drew us back to our hometowns and gave us enough time to spend with family and friends, listen in to their experiences (the challenges and the happiness) maybe I would also not have been able to confirm my doubts about this human-numbing drug which all of us are consuming endlessly all the time.

In the last few months (been an year now), the breaking from the monotony of the back-to-back binge-watching sessions and hours of aimless screen time over mobiles has reaffirmed the need for human touch, human conversations, and the need for all of us to create something. It is the interaction of humans with fellow humans and with the self - that can prevent us from falling prey to this passivity. I could feel the change within me.

What remains is how determined and how moved we remain as a collective group of individuals - as a society - to overcome this trap.

Chapter10: The Big Boss Arrives

Abhimanyu also once entered a trap - all along. He fought the Kauravas with all valor and courage. He left many of them - on the side of Duryodhana and Dushasana - injured and defeated. But in the end, he succumbed to injuries. On the 13th day of the war he died as the final blow of Ashwathama, Drona and Karna destroyed all his weapons. Despite all the knowledge, despite all the wisdom, Abhimanyu did lose. Why did Abhimanyu lose? Ignorance. The reason behind Abhimanyu's defeat was his ignorance about the exit route from the trap. The ignorance that was bestowed upon him. He only knew how to enter the *chakravyuh*. Half-wise, like the human race, on whom the virus was bestowed like a curse.

All of us were trapped in a similar chakravyuh, the chakravyuh of the Coronavirus that surrounded all of humanity. We, however, suffered 2 challenges. One, we didn't know the exit route once infected - there was no remedy yet. Second and deadlier, we didn't even know when and where we entered the chakravyuh - where we ended up contacting the invisible virus.

Though we had our arsenal. It included three *auzaars* (read weapons) - *Social Distancing, Wearing a mask,* and *Sanitizing the hands.* But with no affirmation of these defeating the virus. Like Abhimanyu's weapons, these were to fight the virus. Not meant to defeat the virus completely.

Social distancing - avoiding contact and distance with any other human. There had to be a 6 feet distance between any two individuals in the vicinity. At home, at shops, in queues outside the shops, at medical centers or hospitals, the social distancing was to be adhered to.

It seemed everyone was playing musical chairs to the tune of the corona.

Wearing a mask - every time one had to step outside the house, wearing a mask was a must. As time went by and the corona blows severed, 2 masks were made mandatory. Not only in public but also if one was traveling alone in a car or sitting with family at home, a mask was made compulsory even then.

There was an addition to the classic monkey trio family - *bura mat bolo, bura mat suno, bura mat dekho,* and now with our mouths covered with masks - *buri hawa mat lo.*

Hand Sanitization - Every time you come home after making purchases, pick up a parcel from outside your home, touch objects outside the home whose belongings and hygiene were dubious - one had to sanitize the hands and even better wash hands with soap.

We all were now Abhimnayus stuck in a massive trap.

Chaos. Confusion. Clueless. The entire country was in a state of chaos with people left confused about what was happening around and clueless about what was going to happen next. These 1.38 bn people in India and 7 billion people across the world were all *Abhimanyus* clamorings in their helplessness looking for a way to come out of this *chakravyuh called the corona.*

No one knew the way through this pandemic, only hearsays. The scientists, doctors, research analysts, microbiologists, and anyone who was even loosely attached to the medical fraternity gave their opinion, verdict, and version of the Corona war. But no one could advise a sure-shot solution aka antidote to the virus.

WhatsApp was abuzz with hundreds of such forwards that prescribed instructions, advisories, do's, and don'ts to deal with this virus. Many of them came with *desi totke* (home remedies) such as - wrapping garlic in a handkerchief and keeping it near pillows closer to heads, increasing the intake of ginger and turmeric in the diet, consuming turmeric milk, stronger doses of *kaada* for those tested positive, burning neem leaves and fumigating the house with the smoke out of it. Then there were *babaji ki booti*, to *dudhadhari ki dawaai*. There were umpteen attempts from all possible corners to save one another.

Our local artists didn't leave a chance either. From self-made poetry to recitals shot at home, funny tik-tok videos, to recording traditional folklore songs, - we would receive a daily dosage of messages that would keep us hold the ground together. Everyone tried to create and share what they were good at or what they could do best to keep up the spirit of each other.

Not sure if creativity and humor could kill the virus, but it surely helped deal with the stress that was caused by the existence of this damn virus. In these messages and countless forwards, we found some respite from horrendous and ugly news coming from all parts of the world.

And then The Big Boss Arrives. Like an *akashwani*, like a task-master - not once but many times at regular intervals. 19 March, 24 March, 3 April, 14 April, 12 May, and so on till date to deliver those (in)auspicious sermons. Everyone sat glued to the screen in sheer exhilaration and anticipation of what he was going to share and declare about the virus.

It was a shock to see the Prime Minister of a country making attempts to connect with the people of his nation at such frequent intervals at such a personal level. There lay a subtle hint about the gravity of the situation. Did we pick the hint? I do not think so! Mr. PM left no stone unturned to step forward and pacify billions in the initial few months.

In fact, he made all his appearances interesting and intriguing by leaving the folks with something to look forward to, something to work towards together and be waiting for his next rendezvous.

The first time he addressed the nation - he asked everyone to self-isolate for a day. No stepping out of homes, observe a complete bandh - create a curfew-like state across roads, *mohallas*, cities, and states. A Self-imposed isolation which he called *Junta Curfew - by junta, for junta, of junta.* Democracy - for a right cause.

He also urged the masses to ring bells, utensils, and clap for 5minutes while standing in their respective balconies, or rooftops. This, he told people, to show gratitude and thank the medical fraternity for their endless and relentless support in these testing times. In a situation like this where no one could be sure about the lethality of the virus, where families had to abandon the infected member for that specific period - it was much more than commendable for doctors and nurses to take care of the public and masses - who were strangers to them. The doctors went on to become the real superheroes of these villainous times.

My heart filled with an unrelated hope. I cannot say with the utmost surety if we were able to convey our gratitude properly. I am not even sure if that was well-received or not. That day, at 5 PM, all everyone could hear was the echoing of utensils and claps in rhythmic intervals pouring in from one side after the other. But it didn't sound like noise. It sounded like cups of hope, empathy, and solidarity being lifted and cheered to - everywhere. It sounded like many hopes cheering up each other and flaring up in the sky. My heart was filled with momentary happiness as if everything was over and we were back to normal. But there was a long way to go.

These acts of kindness (and stupidity for some) didn't stop here.

Next time, when the Big Boss arrived, he tasked everyone with lighting up diyas (lamps) at 9 PM. He told everyone to not fuss about the availability of diyas at home. One should not step outside to procure some. That would be the last thing he would want his nation to do. Emergency lights, torch, the flashlight of mobiles would do as well.

All one had to do was turn off all the lights at 9:00 PM. Lit up the diyas (or the above devices) from the balconies. Even better, if we could club this with *Om* chants.

I do not know what got into me and the other billion people that we did as instructed. We all did it. We all got ready for the evening ritual as if it were Diwali that night. We took out the brass plate that we have kept for *Janmashtami* and *Deepawali* celebrations, put diyas - red, purple, brown, and yellow - on the plate. We filled the diyas with mustard oil. And kept the matchstick at the side of the plate. We also took out the brass diya for the main gate and kept it at the *chaukat* (the entrance of the house). At 8:58, three of us sat on the floor. At sharp 9, the chanting of Om began after lighting up the diyas.

It was dark outside and everywhere. It was equally dark inside. The world was hit by a pandemic. A pandemic of the scale that had pushed the world indoors and brought it to a complete halt. A pandemic that had brought the entire human race to its knees. A pandemic that had put to question all the collective intelligence of 7billion humans.

People were dying in numbers that were tough to comprehend. At that time - I didn't realize nobody realized that it was just the tip of the iceberg. The storm was yet to come in the form of a second wave clubbed with natural calamities across the world.

But then, lighting up diyas filled my soul with that much-needed ray of hope. That emanated from an unknown corner inside.

I wondered like many others - if this would do any good to humanity? *Thali bajao, Diya Jalao*. What are we up to? Utter nonsense and ridicule. Digressing from the main issue? Making a fool of ourselves. In the days to follow, it seemed as if all my apprehensions were right. The meme-fest had begun. The jokes and puns on utensils and lamps were in full rage. Political pundits took it to another level by debating, discussing, and opinionating about the rationale behind such acts during prime hours on the national news channels. As if this was the only thing that remained to be talked about. As if validating this act and giving a verdict on the same would help us get rid of the virus.

I was confused. Did it make sense? I asked myself this question umpteen times. On one hand, my heart did find that ray of hope, and my soul did find some respite while clapping and lighting up diyas. But my brain pesters me to believe that all this was futile and useless and maybe a sheer mockery of 1.38

bn people, their belief in that one person, and of many others who looked up to us as one powerful nation.

But is finding sense in each act so important? Or was finding sense in these acts important because they were directed by the big boss - the PM of a nation.

Every time, I find myself tussled in such contradicting thoughts and dilemmas - I push myself to take a less tough stance. I coerce myself to distance myself from the situation and any connected thoughts. This drifting away from the situation helps me look at the broader picture. It kills my biases and preconceived notions. And as my biases and prejudices move away, the clarity seeps in. I can make better sense of things.

This is what happened here as well. There was no doubt about the prevailing situation in the country. The public was aghast at what was happening. The masses were clueless about what had befallen them. For sure, clapping, and banging utensils or lighting up diyas for that matter could not help get rid of the virus. And for sure, these acts could not lessen any burden - emotional, monetarily, or of physical pain - either.

But you know what these tasks did to all of us?

They brought all of us together. In a world that was shrouded in pain and misery, these tasks distracted everyone from that pain, though for a while, and filled everyone with gratitude for each other. In a world that had grown so individualistic in approach, these tasks moved everyone towards a common collective goal. In a world that had grown so disconnected, these tasks connected everyone for the larger good. In a world that was immersed in negativity, these tasks brought positivity within them. In a world that seemed so lost and in despair, these tasks filled billions of souls with hope.

Is giving someone hope a bad thing to do? Is validating an act so important? Or does it become important because it comes from the leader of the nation?

I ask, "Is the job of the leader always to do the practical thing?" Is sensibility a trait that has to weigh over empathy, and gratitude? Is being emotional and sensitive towards the situations and people - whose representative the leader is - wrong? Is it in any way an indication of being weak or foolish?

Isn't it the job of a leader to infuse solidarity in the nation? Isn't it his or her role to motivate the masses to stand for the larger good and fight the battle together? Isn't it important for a leader to prepare the nation for the war that has to be fought? Isn't it important for a leader to muster courage in its public?

Isn't calming people down under such circumstances the role of PM of a nation? Isn't giving the public a sense of direction a part of the job description of a PM?

And I think, maybe these tasks were an attempt to jolt people out of the shock. These tasks were an attempt to instill the sense of urgency and gravity of the situation. These tasks were an attempt to let everyone know that every single soul was important. These tasks were an attempt to instill solidarity in 1.38 billion people irrespective of any caste, color, and creed. These tasks were an attempt to bring everyone to the common ground. These tasks by the Big Boss were an attempt to let everyone know that *together we could face, fight and win any battle.*

This incident not only brewed in my head alone for a long but was talked about in other various parts of the world as well. While many inside our country mocked these tasks and found this an opportune moment to ridicule the PM, I remember many leaders abroad applauding and replicating this in their countries as well. I am not justifying the tasks or validating them as the right or a wrong thing to do - scientifically.

But the entire episode was an epiphany of one very important lesson not only for India but also for the rest of the world. The need for an effective leader.

The need for a leader who could bring the nation together. The need for a leader who could be the guiding light for the masses in the darkest hour. The need for a leader who could instill courage in the public. The need for a leader who the public listens to and responds to. The need for a leader who can stir the spirit in its public in the most stressful times. The need for a leader who can connect with the public. The need for a leader who can be empathetic and yet affirmative at the same time. The need for a leader who can think of the larger good. The need for a leader who could sail through the most turbulent times and gives others the confidence to do so as well. The need for a leader in whom the public can rest their confidence and trust.

The need for a leader who could help *Abhimanyu* walk out of the trap. Abhimanyu remained stuck and died inside the *chakravyuh.* Will humans be doomed to the same future as well? Or will there be a way out of the *chakravyuh called Corona?*

In the next few days and months, the news channels broadcast the videos of public banging utensils and clapping on their rooftops, a complete blackout lit by flashlights, and diyas and aerial views of India going black. The same videos buzzed facebook feeds, trended on Twitter, and replayed on Instagram stories and IGTV. #Thalibajao, #Diyajalao joined other famous hashtags of the times -

#DalgonaCoffee, #SafeHands, #Whoismore, #Untiltomorrow, and #quaranntinetravel.

The hope and solidarity trended for a while, stayed a little longer, saved as Lockdown 2020 highlights needing to be nurtured forever.

Chapter11:
Mothers without Instagram

Maa, "jhaadu to mara par gand nhi nikla."

Maa, "yeh poche se to mitti chipakti ja rahi hai."

Hello Maa, "yeh peeli daal bhi raat ko bhigoni hai kya?"

Maa, "parantha ghee mein banta hai ya refine mein?"

Maaaa, "yeh to ande ke shilke bhi tawe pe gir gaye, half fry kaise bnaate hain?"

Maa, "kuch meetha khaane ka mann hai, koi easy recipe btaao."

Maa, "maine aaj halwa bnaaya tha, bahut bekaar bana"

Nahi maa, "kapde press nahi krwa rahe aajkal, tracks aur night suit bina press ke hi pehan lete hain."

Maa, “yeh covid ke chalte sab kaunsa kaada pi rahe hain? Kaise bnaoon?”

Maa, “bhartan dhoye, sabun ka jhaag to badhta hi jata hai.”

Maaaaa, “I miss you.”

The 3 golden words our mothers yearned to listen to since their beloved kids left home to fuel their dreams and made their careers. Only if mothers knew that their kids would become so busy and engrossed in themselves, they would probably not have taken that tough decision to part ways with them in the first place. The pandemic made the unusual possible. Else, this was never going to be the conversation we would have had with our mothers.

Every time we run into trouble, mothers come to our rescue. Every time my heart aches or my stomach churns, Maa knows what will cheer me up. Every time I find myself entangled in a million thoughts, Maa knows the therapy. Every time I have empty eyes, sullen soul, and silent lips, Maa just knows what is bothering me. Every time, I have a word or two stuck in my throat, Maa knows those exact words before I even utter them. Every time I have done my best to make the *raita* of my life, Maa has helped to set my priorities right. Every time, my life has offered me too many lemons, Maa has ensured that I better make lemonade out of them, slurp, and enjoy. Maa, the wonder woman who shoos away all that bothers me. Every single time something befalls upon us, we rush towards our mothers - like the pac-man before it gets engulfed in the mouth of misery - cocooning ourselves into her lap before we are entrapped completely.

This time we could not do that even. The pandemic snatched away that too - the feeling of comfort and assurance from us. It distanced us from our mothers. But maybe, we all deserved it.

In the pre-pandemic world, when everything was normal, all of us were always busy with either work or catching up on a web series, hosting a house party or visiting a mall, a PVR show, or meeting a tinder date or socializing with folks. We had no time at all. All the time that we gave our mothers was limited to - those 2 minutes of her confirming our well being -

Maa: "Beta, khaana khaaya?"

Maa: "Beta, office kaisa chal raha hai?"

Maa: "Beta, raat ko neend theek se aayi?"

Maa: "Beta, ab ghar kab aaoge?"

Maa: "Beta, mausam badal raha hai, sehat ka khayal rakhna."

In our busy lives that we set up for ourselves away from home - mothers became our alarm clocks, our doctors, our counselors, a 24x7 all-in-one virtual assistant. They became everything a mother could be. They became the rivers of our life - they always were - which only had something to give to us but we never had anything to offer them back. Not even our love, completely.

And when the pandemic came banging our doors, the hell broke loose. The entire world was made standstill. Everybody got stuck wherever they were. Travelers were stuck at their vacation spots. People who had flown for work got stranded in the strange cities. People who were posted outside their hometowns remained stuck at their posting locations forever, not getting to see their families and relatives for long. Students in college remained there till things were a little better. People in metros or towns, cities or villages - every single person was stuck wherever they were in their unique conditions.

Even worse, everyone was expected to arrange for their living and manage their daily household chores. From arranging groceries to buying stuff for home, cleaning and sweeping homes, to cooking and washing utensils, ironing clothes to emptying the trash cans, washing the balconies or cleaning the washrooms, dusting the furniture to keeping the crockery dry, sorting the dishes to changing the bed sheets regularly - every single task had to be done by yourself. Mothers were not around to take care of these small little things - which were not so small after all - but we took for granted.

All of us millennials and GenZ - who were raised by our mothers as the pampered kids - found this not only challenging but extremely excruciating. We had only seen our mothers doing all of it. We had only lent a hand once or twice but not taken charge of everything on our own solely. The pandemic made it happen. Today when I think of the pandemic and those two years of my life, it seems as if the pandemic had arrived only to question the status quo. It seemed as if someone got damn bored by the current order of things. It seemed as if the pandemic came just to turn the tables around.

Well, days, weeks, and months passed and nothing seemed to change. Except for the social media handles. They became active yet again, with fresh and new content - presented directly from the kitchen and the lobbies of the homes all over the world. Bloggers, Youtubers, travelers, fashionistas, bakers, chefs, poets, writers, painters and artists, developers, software engineers, marketers, architects, - think of a profile - and all of their social handles looked all alike. The millennials and GenZ were all out there doing a cool display of them getting better at managing the household chores. Play, mix, repeat! As if the formula to get new followers, more likes, and subscribers had just been launched. The lockdown social showbiz had just begun - virtually though!

The couples posted fun videos of them brooming and mopping the house together over Facebook. With songs like '*Yeh Kahan aa Gaye hum*', '*love me like you do*' playing in the background. Love found new definitions, new goals. The ones who could act chose tik-tok to produce hilarious videos of housecleaning with dubbed dialogues. Instagram stories and feed buzzed with '*home-cooked food*', '*home-baked stuff*', '*my first cake*', '*imitating maa's recipes*', '*self-made rajma-chawal*', '*Illish-mach*', '*rogan-josh*', '*homemade ice-cream anyone?*', '*my first round-roti*', and the list went endless. Snapchat had new snap filters. Instagram had new hashtags such as #Stayhomestaystrong, #Gharperaho, #COVID19, #Homemade, etc. which could be used to find new related content.

Siblings who were together shared images from *Ramayana* and *Mahabharata* being broadcasted on DD National with captions like "Nostalgic after a long day of household chores", "*Back to school days*", "*Bhai can't cook*", "*She is just Mom*", "*good old days*". Missing Maa together became a thing. Connected by the womb, separated by careers, re-connected by household chores during the lockdown.

Youtubers curated vlogs about 'how to mop and clean your house', '10 Hacks to get your house clean faster', 'Top 10 easy dishes to cook at home during lockdown'. Many of us took to social media to share our experiences and learnings about how you move forward while brooming and move backward while mopping. It was like an Einstein moment for an entire generation. All of us who had only observed our mothers or helpers doing all these chores at home but now we had the first hand experience ourselves.

Women - wives, sisters, or girlfriends - took dig at men for spending hours washing utensils and still not able to clean them properly. Men left no chance to highlight that it took 8 *pedas* to get that first-round roti. There seemed to be healthy competition and collaboration.

There's one good thing though that came out of this social extravaganza of lockdown. It broke all the gender stereotypes. It made no difference if you were a male or a female. You are a male who could be good at cooking and you could be a female who is good at brooming. One could be washing utensils and the other chopping vegetables. The idea that household activities were to be shared amongst the family members equally irrespective of the genders was learnt well. I think with changing and evolving social diaspora, learnings like these were basics and we took too long to realize this. It took a pandemic to bring us to reality from the ignorant past. If changes like these are accepted at large at a societal level - it becomes a little easier to bring in that much-needed revolution - we have been fighting for years.

For now, you could check out what everyone was up to at their homes on your social feeds. Social media was so filled with everything household, that even if you wanted to know how to unblock your kitchen drain or fix a nail, there were already videos uploaded for that. And by any chance if you were not a part of the crazy social network or you could not find anything - you could call up Mom.

Millennials and GenZ who were not brought up to deal with the household chores were found upskilling during the pandemic and constantly boasting about the same on social media.

While the *household party* was on, my head constantly thought about being unfair to our mothers all those years. Each little task that we considered pity was not pity at all. The expectation that everything our mothers did had to be perfect was unfair. The expectation that we should always have our glass of milk on time, the lunch box to have newly cooked items every day, the room to be done-up well when we were back home after school or office, was not justified. Not standing with her every time she made sacrifices for us was selfish. Knowingly or unknowingly, being a reason for her not being able to accomplish her dreams was wrong. On all big and important matters, to shut Maa up by saying "*Aapko Kuch nahi pata*" was outrageous. But rushing to Maa on not being able to find a pair of socks was plain simple and fine. How?

I wonder if maa also had an Instagram account to showcase how much and how laboriously she worked for me and our family, had her value been more in the eyes of our society? I wonder if she would also have gone broadcasting, uploading statuses, stories about all little things she took care of, and dependencies we had on her, would we value her more?

The pandemic made me feel strongly about being unfair to our mothers largely. And you and I alone are not responsible for this, the whole society has been. There are undue expectations, exorbitant societal pressure, and so much justification to give if you are a mother. When the pandemic happened, all of us deep down in our hearts started valuing our mothers more. Our dependency on our mothers was not wrong to say but not letting her be own in that mesh of love was surely wrong. We got to live the lives of our mothers though for a while but it made us realize how grateful we should be to our mothers for all that they have done for us. Interestingly, we had social media to express our emotions and feelings, our mothers only had us express all their love and emotions.

However, one thing that kept pestering me all this while was the rampant use of social media. While the social feeds brought laughter to everyone in such stressful times of pandemic, social media otherwise had started taking up a vicious role in the pre-pandemic times.

I have been an active social media user. But my challenge is with how social media has been construed as a validation tool. Who's got a bigger house? Who's got a better car? Who has more beautiful pets? Who has more to flaunt at a wedding? Who is traveling where? Where's the party tonight? "And Oh! I just booked our next vacation *sigh." And yeah "Am I looking dazzling in this outfit?"

The buck doesn't stop here. "Reading this...", "Watching this....", "New Check-In..." "Feeling low", Feeling loved", "Feeling blissful", "Started a new job", "Left a job", "Traveling to", "Eating at", "Gymming at...". Had it all been just a matter of expression, it would have been fine. But it didn't remain that way. The endless cycle of posting and pushing each minuscule detail on social media caught like a rage. From giving wings to one's sense of freedom to express - it turned out to be becoming slaves of social validation. From what we wear to how we feel inside - from the outside appearance to the inside matter; everything was up for an exhibit.

We started watching out for more likes, comments, and shares of what we posted on our social handles. It became a way to judge our family, friends, and relatives' affinity and inclination towards us. If somebody likes and appreciates (though for the sake of it) is an ally, else opposition. The true feelings didn't matter. The real bonds didn't matter. The currency of exchange of love became likes on social media. You like my post, I like your post.

This was just the tip of the iceberg though. We eventually started becoming unreal. We wanted filters to make our images lit, photoshop our vacation pictures, edit the noise in the party pictures and sometimes filters to hide our dark circles, edit our pot-belly, lighten our face, and add blush to our cheeks. So much to conform to the "society standards of what is defined as Wow!"

It filled us with this intense desire to outdo others. We always had this urge to be looking better, being better, and doing better than anyone else who is a part of our network. It made us look at each post as a competition with folks who we called "our friends".

It made us reek of jealousy, dubiousness, and unwanted comparisons. Validation from others became so important for us to survive. In this entire social setup, we ended up creating a facade of ourselves.

We wore stuff we were not comfortable in. We watched stuff we didn't enjoy. We read books that bored us to death. We went to places we didn't like. We ate stuff that was unhealthy for us. We ended up buying stuff that we didn't need. We made friends with people we genuinely abhorred and we distanced ourselves from those who genuinely made us feel at home. Only to conform to what appeared better at the outset.

In this entire process of becoming someone else, we ended up losing ourselves. We became fake beings in a world full of fake people, fake profiles, and fake accounts. Our uniqueness was lost.

Thank God, our mothers were without Instagram. It saved them all the unwanted social pressure and comparisons. Or else we would have gone to compare a mother's love with that of another. Our (ab)use of social media had grown so shameless.

Out of a few good things, the pandemic brought to humans - one was the realization of social networks being a mere source of entertainment and fun and not a place to live and exhibit your life. It took us a while but we did realize that real conversations happened outside the messengers of the world, real friendships flourish over a cup of *chai*, real relationships survive the mettle of sharing physical presence forever, the genuine people stick with you at your best, and as well as worst and the real bonds are formed outside the virtual network.

During the pandemic, another good thing that social media did to us was:

aakhir kaar jo bhi ho;

Ghar bada ho ya chhota ho, safai sab ko karni padti hai,

Aadmi ho ya aurat, khaana sabko bnaana padta hai,

Working ho ya non-working, bhartan dhona aana zaroori hai

Jhaadu ho ya pocha, kaam baantna padta hai

Maa tumhari ho ya meri, pyaari hoti hai

Maa door ho ya paas, maa maa hi hoti hai

Mothers. One master key to all locks. One solution to all problems. One remedy for all wrongs. One blessing to fight all the curses. Someone rightly said, "Since God couldn't be everywhere, he made mothers." I cannot agree more.

The pandemic was a ploy to spare Mothers and Gods of their onerous duties for once, stop blaming them for everything and own up our shit.

Chapter12:
The Joy of Doing Nothing

When I was a kid, I always used to think when mom gets some free time. She was awake before I got up and she went to bed after I was asleep. When I used to reach school, I was constantly thinking that will she get to rest after dad goes to work? But when I was homesick, I found that Mom is not free even after dad leaves for work. Then weekends came. Dad was free. I was free. My sister was free. But Mom was still not free. She didn't have any weekends.

As I grew up, I found that our routines changed - Dad got retired, he had more free time. I started working and stepped into Dad's routine. Being in the private sector, even worse. The day had a start time but no punch-out time. My sister turned a teen - hitting the bed late and catching up with the sun a little later after it had risen. We inherited each other's routines. But none of us could inherit mom's routine. None of us could dare to inherit her routine. Her routine - she was busier than before. A free-er husband, a teenage daughter, and a young son - clearly she had more demands and tantrums to fulfill. She had more things to take care of than before. She still didn't have any weekends.

It's been 32 years. And 2 things haven't changed a bit. She remains busy. And my question remains, "When does Mom rest?"

Does she get to enjoy the comfort of doing nothing? Will she ever experience the joy of doing nothing? Is it important to experience that joy? It is.

Amidst the continuity of that thought, the pandemic happened. The pandemic forced each one of us to get into the routines of our mothers. We found ourselves getting up early, cleaning the house, mopping the floor, emptying the trash cans, dusting the furniture, and putting the clothes in the washing machine. Once this running around the house was over, we switched to the kitchen - chopping vegetables, washing rice for the afternoon meal, cooking the breakfast and lunch leaving the dinner to be cooked in the evening hours. All of this had to be done in three hours before we took a shower and got ready for the office to begin. The buck didn't stop here. And yes, before we sat down to kickstart our work-day, put the clothes out on the stand for drying.

All of us needed tea or something to munch in between. But now we shared responsibilities amongst each other. I thought, but we never shared responsibilities with our mothers. It was her who had to break her routine every time any one of us needed anything. Whether she was on a call, reading a magazine, watching a serial, or probably engaged in her own thing - knitting or yoga - it was always she who used to leave her "chain of activities" to cater to our demands and fulfill our needs.

When things came upon us, we took turns. Oh thou pandemic, you took too long to arrive! Come vice, come virtue!

The day would slowly move on with the work, unending repetitive calls, and insatiable desire to eat. As the evening would approach, we would take turns preparing evening snacks and *chai*. *Shaam ka naashta*, ready to binge!

One would go pick up clothes from the stand, the other would fold them and if need be, iron a few of them. Then everyone would get together to prepare the dinner. We were left with no time, literally. Now we knew what it meant to be busy in our lives. Managing ourselves was a demanding task. And *Maa* would manage each one of us. Imagine! My thoughts still hung to my head like the clothes on the rope for drying. Why does Maa not rest? Why do we all not pause once in a while? How comforting it would be if someone would help you break the monotony of your life?

The surprising part of our lives is that we - the GenZ and Millennials - were busy (read seemingly busy) even before the pandemic happened. We were always busy. You may ask, busy in what?

We thought going to the office was enough. It left us drenched out and tired for the rest of the day. So we chose - lying on the couch infinitely, scrolling up and down our phones, consuming IGTV videos, reels, and stories on Instagram and Facebook, catching up on WhatsApp statuses of family, friends, the office boy, cabbie, and every other person who was in our contact list - all of this to be busy. We chose to swipe people left and right to keep our weekends occupied. Yeah, I am talking about Tinder, Bumble, OkCupid, and all those apps that gave us options to choose our fuckbuddies and at times soulmates too.

If this was not enough, buying stuff online, ordering food online, or watching a web series that we left in the middle, the previous week, or catching up on new releases on so easily accessible OTT platforms. All of this kept us busy. But when the pandemic happened, our facade of being busy bit the dust - to find ourselves truly busy in things we needed to be busy with or at least be equipped to manage on our own.

Moving from one edge of the spectrum of being busy to the other side of being busy reinforced my thought of pausing for a while and the need to rest. We all needed to pause, rest, reset and refresh. This had to be a continuous process. But we could not fathom the importance of the same. The pandemic jolted us out of our state of oblivion and the forever busy zones.

It is quite strange that some of us find this uncanny satisfaction of being busy all the time. Unfortunately, it is not all that cool, how it seems to be. But all of us were caught with this cult of being busy all the time. I was glad that my mother was not alone. The only difference being - she was busy by force, we by our choice.

Today, when I think of it, being busy 24x7, is not that a great thing. It does more harm than good to us. Our pre-pandemic kind of business fused thoughts and desires into our heads - continuously. It kept our heads occupied with one thought after another. It created more tangles than we could handle. It made our lives complex like a mesh we could not find our way away from. It kept our heads cluttered. It made us more demanding. Our business during the pandemic times - mom kind of business - left us more tired both physically and emotionally.

Neither kind of business was(is) good for our health. And this makes it important - for all of us to find joy in doing nothing. How comforting it would be to break the chain of thoughts! We do not realize. We did not realize.

This is the challenge of keeping ourselves occupied all the time. It makes our brains passive. We go on to follow our routines blindly. It kills our sense of creativity. It makes us passive, leading to mindless consumption of everything - food, content, thoughts. Our actions are no more consciously - thought about - driven activities rather activities and tasks driven by an involuntary mind out of habit. It makes us resistant to any kind of newness. Eventually, we become human beings who have lost purpose in our lives. Maybe this sounds far-fetched a correlation but imagine the same activities and habits being carried on for 10, 20, and 30+ years of your life. It is bound to have some impact on the evolution of our brain and how it thinks, reacts, and responds to various situations, circumstances, and people around. I believe, we stop feeling anything for anyone around us or we start feeling too much for everything. And that is why it is so important to press the reset button and calibrate our thoughts. Rest is not a bad thing after all.

We can choose days or moments in each day when we play the pause button. We can choose our moments and times or specific days. I do it monthly (approximately 12 times a year) and a larger reset annually near my birthday month. But the pandemic reinforced the need for all of humanity to *Play the Pause button* more often. Nature has its ways of teaching lessons. This time it chose a pandemic to make us realize what being truly busy meant and how important it was to rest at the same time.

I couldn't agree more. There are so many ways we could choose to *do nothing.* We could lie down and relax like in *Shavasana*. Staring at the wall could be another way of doing nothing. We could also choose to breathe in and breathe out. Chanting *Om or a hymn* could be another spiritual way. Going out for a walk or a run could be a nicer option for hyperactive ones. I would love to go and sit by a pond, lake, or in a park and absorb the beauty of mystic nature. If you are near the sea, heading to the beach could be a joyous way of doing nothing. Just sit by the beach and let the waves play with your feet. If you happen to be in the mountains, you could hike a trail or probably find yourself a corner and let your thoughts and breath reverberate. There are umpteen ways to do nothing if you get to think about it.

This act of doing nothing fills you and me with a fulfilling experience of *nothingness*, where everything seems empty yet everything feels complete.

This *nothingness* is the joy of doing nothing I was talking about. This feeling is what all of us had forgotten to experience in our so busy mundane lives before the pandemic hit the world.

Foremost, It clears my head. It untangles each thought in the web of my brain and declutters my thoughts process. It removes all the toxic thoughts and fills me with positivity. It makes me complain less about life rather feel more gratitude toward it. It not only cleanses my brain but also my body. It makes me feel light, literally. The body I was dragging till yesterday suddenly feels ready to take a flight.

It makes me question my actions. It gives me the energy to think in retrospect and evaluate my decisions and acts. It allows me to introspect and course-correct my attitude and approach towards life. It helps me draw a line between the right and the wrong; the good or the bad. This nothingness tells me what my heart wants and what is my calling. This noise-free mind invigorates me to ask all the right questions which is sometimes even more important than finding all the answers.

It makes me more cognizant of what's happening around me. I stop consuming things mindlessly and start absorbing the beauty of everything around me - be it nature, friends, family or relatives, possessions - material or otherwise. I grow more mindful of each activity - even breathing. And I end up being more sure about who I am as an individual and where I am headed to. And this nothingness then dawns upon us like a silver lining in a sky full of clouds and fills our hearts with immense joy. Because all we want in life is clarity and this joy of doing nothing brings in exactly that.

No wonder, I thought that this joy of doing nothing needed to be experienced by one and all. Only a pandemic could cause such realizations at scale. The sad part would be if we choose to ignore this in the times to come and continue to remain busy all the time - just like before.

I must confess that I am not against being busy but I am against getting into a mindless rut and chain of mindless activities. I am against the monotony of routine and stickiness of thoughts that we ignore to break. I am against not giving ourselves enough time and space to breathe and think clearly. Being busy consciously is good. Sometimes that is the only option you have got. And also, only if you are busy enough and your mind has been occupied for a while, will you discover and experience the joy of doing nothing. The pandemic made us see both sides of the world. To be busy and be very tired and realize the importance of doing nothing at the same time. All I am saying is let us not wire our brains to be busy every time. The bodies need to rest. The brains need to reset. The thoughts need to recalibrate. The souls need to be refurbished. And we - the human race - needed to learn this sooner than later. The pandemic accelerated that learning curve.

However, we need to admit that in this hyperbole called life, we did pick up a few (I am being kind) bad habits. (Pretending to be) Being busy all the time was one of them. Somewhere along the journey, we forgot what was good for us and what we genuinely needed, and the basics went wrong. And that is what we were paying for?

Chapter13: Basics Gone Wrong

A few years ago, I was on my trip to Bhutan. I went there to witness the beauty of cherry blossoms that I had seen in pics - decorating the boulevards, alleys on both sides of the roads, along the mountain trails. They were a sight to pause all the time for. They were a sight to stop by, the beauty of which you could not absorb all at once. The transparent blue skies, the after-winter brown colored mountains, the free-flowing rivers and streams, all seemed to merge well with the wide metalled roads, the sun-lit rooftops of the houses, and trees that surrounded the space in all their flamboyance. We crossed from town to cities trespassing villages and forest areas - each nook and corner was spick and span. We visited the Memorial Stupa, Buddha Dordenma, the king's palace, Dzong and Lhakhang monasteries, and the much famous Tiger's nest. I was in total awe of this place.

The bright sun, the warm sunlight; the strong winds, and the air felt light; the steep mountains, the natural walls of protection; all complemented each other so well. Amidst the immense beauty bestowed upon the Land of Thunder Dragon, what stood out were the quiet and beaming-with-happiness people. One could not make it if it's people who were adding tranquility to the environment or is it the serene environment which had turned people likewise. There was no noise, no hue and cry, and no drama. There was no rush. Everything seemed to move in a very coherent way and unison with each other. Entire Bhutan resonated with peace and happiness. It seemed a world very different from the world we all belonged to. Our trip came to an end. We came back with a lot of wonderful memories and some beautiful pictures of the places.

It had been a few days after I came back that I read about an article on the Gross National Happiness index of Bhutan. It sounded familiar and intriguing. I recalled our tourist guide mentioning this once during our trip to Bhutan. So I started reading about it. I read it a little, a little more, and fell in complete love with the concept. Oh, man! The Pursuit of happiness is for real. Someone is genuinely concerned about the well-being and happiness of its population. There is a country that thinks that their true accomplishment lies in seeing their people mentally healthy, happy and providing them with a fulfilling livelihood. There are a set of folks existing on the earth who weigh happiness as a more important quotient than the otherwise defined metrics of success. Was it only a concept in theory or practice? Was it all for real, I pondered?

No wonder the world of Bhutan seemed so different from the rest of the world. Now I knew why the air felt so light and comforting because people were not breathing their worries out but only happiness.

(Gross National Happiness is a philosophy that guides the government of Bhutan. It includes an index that is used to measure the collective happiness and well-being of a population. Gross National Happiness Index is instituted as the goal of the government of Bhutan in the Constitution of Bhutan, enacted on 18 July 2008. It emphasizes harmony with nature and traditional values as expressed in the 9 domains of happiness and 4 pillars of GNH. The four pillars of GNH being: 1. Sustainable and equitable socio-economic development 2. Environmental conservation 3. Preservation and promotion of culture 4. Good governance. And the nine domains of GNH are psychological well-being, health, time use, education, cultural diversity and resilience, good governance, community vitality, ecological diversity and resilience, and living standards. Courtesy: Wikipedia)

The rest of the world had a long way to go and chase the right set of things. Their priorities were muddled. The pursuit was materialistic. The parameters under the Gross National Happiness index of Bhutan were (still are) secondary and most esoteric to the rest of the world. Our basics had gone wrong.

2020, the pandemic came for the entire world. It came like a hurricane. It was so scary that it felt as if someone threw us from our bed while we were deep asleep. How the pandemic arrived would remain a mystery for all of humanity until and unless the "powerful" of the world decide to disclose it. But how the pandemic affected each one of us and how the world reacted to the pandemic was out there on display for each one of us to see, consume and reflect upon.

The pandemic made us witness misery every single day around us. It made us ask uncomfortable questions. It questioned the status quo. The pandemic went on to question everything we did, everything we thought we did right. It put a big looming question mark over even how we lived.

The days and months of confinement demanded people be wilfully and mentally strong. The pandemic demanded people be intrinsically happy to sail through the otherwise so stressed and depressed times. The shutdown markets demanded us to be demanding and consuming less. The curtailed activities left us with lesser options to choose from. The inoperative modes of travel made us comfort our loved ones from miles apart and share the happiness and goodness with them virtually. With less to do, less to consume, less to participate - the pandemic left us lurking looking more inwards. The pandemic poked and incite us to find our sense of purpose and fulfillment while being at home. But we were not trained to do so. That mindset was not a part of the DNA we had construed in the last few decades.

After all, we were not the ones chasing happiness as an index or metric of accomplishment in our lives. Our basics had been skewed. Our measurement of fulfillment was different. Our sense of success and accomplishment was measured by who has got more - more money, more power, or more fame! Any of it or all of it! And we all were equally infected by it, even more, infected than by the coronavirus. Still, no one took notice!

This all-pervading sentiment trickled from homes to communities, to societies, to towns, cities, countries, and the entire world (minus Bhutan for obvious reasons) and vice versa. This persisted in the ways we lived at home, the ways we chose to entertain ourselves, the food we consumed, the lifestyles we maintained, from the time we were born till we met our graves. But our skewed ways of living had a huge price to pay which the world saw and realized when we were hit by the pandemic out of nowhere.

The pandemic arrived at each house as Air-Conditioners arrived at each home 10 years back. Nobody remained untouched. I remember a few years back, almost 24 years ago, there used to be erroneous power cuts. Sometimes for 8 hours a day stretching to 12 hours a day. There were no coolers in summers and no portable heaters in winters. The inverters were missing. AC was a prestige. You could tell how rich a household or a family was by looking at these few possessions. But then one fine day, we started seeing each family replacing their dessert cooler with the in-room portable coolers with more direct air but less effective cooling. But it became a trend for those who could not afford an AC. Then a few years passed by, and each household had an AC as well. 1 ton, 1.5 ton, 2 ton, and even larger ACs to match the size of the rooms. Each one of us picked the rage. The rage started with having an AC in one room and spread to have AC in all the rooms. Only if somebody could tell these lovers of AC that ACs produced more heat in the environment and the ecosystem than the cooling it brought to our houses. Eventually, each house had a cooler plus AC plus inverter. Times are not far when each household will have a genset as well to operate all these devices.

For all good and bad reasons, our family was not an early adopter of technology but laggards. The years passed by and my father prudently kept deciding which devices and equipment to install at our home. We were catching up with this pace when suddenly the markets were flooded by all things cool and jazzy. All things, new and fancy. All things, tech, and suave. All things, comfort and cost. All things, sweet and poisonous.

The Air Conditioners entered the cars. Cars replaced scooters and motorcycles. The two-wheelers replaced the foot. Any distance for that matter 300 meters or 3000kms - we had a conveyance for each kind of trip. Walking as a habit vanished. We could not stop tripping over our cars. Only when people realized that they were growing unfit sitting in homes and offices fitted with ACs and roaming around in the cars that had ACs too - gyms mushroomed.

We woke up from our AC room, drove in an AC car to a fully air-conditioned gym. We only worked out but didn't sweat. Wasn't sweating the key to all the walking, running, cycling, and working out? Looks like it was not.

The viciousness didn't stop here. Just outside the gyms, we had outlets selling subs, donuts, momos, and chowmein. Food served just at the right time. To the hungry and the confident us. Hungry because we had just worked out and confident because we had just worked out. We deserved this treat. Didn't we? It became hard to break the chain of tacit capitalism.

Now that we were going to the gyms, we needed sportswear along with the duffle bag and a sipper too. We went to malls to buy this and some other stuff as well which we didn't need. We needed 5 types of attires - the nightwear, the casual for hopping to the mall and PVRs and catching up with the friends, the formals for office and the bar lounges, the travel-gear and the sports-wear. And once in a year - the wedding types (traditional). The attire included not only clothes, but a matching pair of footwear, accessories, watches, slings, and wallets, and any kind of customization you and I could think of.

But was this enough? Obviously not. All the members of the family needed to buy all of the above. All the members had to go to the office, malls, and gyms too. So, all of them needed AC cars. Each house with 4 members had 4 cars as well. And everybody clamors about the rising petrol and diesel prices. If they knew the economics, higher the demand - higher the prices especially if the supply was limited. Petrol was (is) a limited resource only if these buyers of the cars knew.

We kept on gathering more and more stuff which then we needed to flaunt too. So we celebrated more and more occasions. From my pet's 1st birthday to an after-exams party. From 6th month engagement anniversary to the last of twenties (29th) birthday party. From celebrating 4 years of friendship, 36 months of engagement, 24 months of marriage to the breakup party. We found and discovered occasions to celebrate (read flaunt stuff we gathered). And once people came, we shared with them the upcoming vacation plans.

We found our cities noisy and cramped so we headed to other cities to find solace and make them cramped as well. We found our localities unhygienic and polluted, so we traveled so we could make other places equally dirty as well. Our insatiable hunger took us under the oceans and over the mountains. We wanted to visit the places that others had not or could not. The destinations became important. The state of mind, irrelevant.

When we got tired of all this hustle we created to please ourselves, we got back to our homes. But that could not make us happy either. So we ordered more stuff online. And we ordered more than we needed, thanks to our poor assessment of what and how much we needed in our lives.

Did all of this make us happy? Probably not! And I wondered if there should be a Gross Consumption Index to measure the happiness of people of the world minus Bhutan?

It is a strange world we have built for ourselves. Strangely, there are no more paper boats. Nobody dances in the rain but looks for water parks. Nobody welcomes the weather or prays for a healthy harvest. The Spring, Autumn, and Winters - they all come and go. And no one notices the change of weather in their AC-fitted homes. The kids do not play outside, nor do they cycle anymore. They have found the ease of clicking buttons and touchscreens to game and score. Detergents are available but clothes do not get dirty anymore. Somebody needs to tell them that *Daag Achche hote hain.* The innocence is gone too soon and demands increase sooner than before.

Friends or family - we only planned to get together but when we finally met, we were always glued to our phones. Nobody asked and cared about the whereabouts of their neighbors. Some of us didn't even know who our neighbors were. Why didn't they find each other interesting? I wonder why people do not talk and converse. They pool cars and food. Can't they pool their emotions too? It is strange only that *tapris* are considered unhygienic but the hotels serving food to strangers in the same crockery and cutlery are considered safe. Sitting on the floor and eating food is traditional and orthodox but *Chokhi Dhani* is too cool. We became strange beings. We measured the food we ate, hours we worked out, but felt shy to measure the screen time and our carbon footprint. We created a weird world with skewed priorities.

I wonder why no one gave any more hand-made cards. Why do grannies not knit sweaters and socks and gloves for their adorable lads and dolls? When did homemade pickles become exquisite and packaged food so common? Why does no one paint anymore? Why are there fewer people who write, and compose? Why does nobody love reading while reading also takes us to different places? Why is traveling the only thing considered?

Our home exercises became obsolete, gyms became a trend. Eating home food was boring and outside food fun. It became okay to take medicines but not so okay to eat a balanced diet. Playing DOTA, AOE, CS, and virtual games was too cool, playing outside in the streets was foolish. Each member of the family had their collectibles. To each its own, sharing was not a virtue we nurtured anymore. A single-family ended up having multiple homes - across villages, cities, and a town. We cascaded our wants and started presenting them as our needs - justifying our ways of living.

We created beautiful homes but the roads outside the homes remained dirty. We chased beautiful places but we ended up polluting them too. None of it mattered. What mattered was how much we could consume without even bothering how much waste we generated. The root cause of this vicious cycle was the way we measured success and fulfillment. Our sense of accomplishment was derived from who had got more - more money, and more possessions.

In this blind race of consumption, we ended up resulting in a generation that not only lost connection with nature and each other - we also lost connection with ourselves. Will it still be wrong to say that our basics had gone horribly wrong?

None. None of us stopped, paused, stood up, and asked - Where were we headed to? What was the unending race for? Why distort nature and the entire ecosystem? Why put so much pressure not only on ourselves but also on the earth as a whole? We all just went with the flow. Because one did, so did others. Because one did, let everyone suffer.

We made money the core of the circle of life. Our accomplishments and success mattered more than the collective well-being and harmony. We didn't bother how our lifestyles impacted everyone around us and how it escalated to a larger catastrophe. We corrupted the entire system so much so that we ended up commercializing everything. Even the roles of teachers, doctors, and public officials. The need for money became so stark and important that the sanctity of professions, roles, and jobs was diluted and the means to make more money were invented. We went too low as a race to meet our undue *consumerist wants.* And what remained behind was a void, a carcass of the earth created by us humans ripping off the earth of all that it had and building our kingdom of dreams. Clearly, Gross National happiness was not our cup of tea.

But then the pandemic happened and it pushed us to the four walls of our houses, rendering every material possession of ours meaningless. No more going out to the malls, gyms, parks and cinemas, dining, or gatherings. No more parties or celebrations, no ganging up at the bars and cafes. Work from Home orders was passed. Our cars were parked forever and we needed fewer types of attires. The gadgets lay on the tables, clothes hanging in the wardrobes, the watches kept staring back, shoes on the rack, wallets in the locker, the laptop bag, and the sipper were dumped in the chest of drawers, and all kinds of apps remained silent on the phones. Traveling - local, national or international - was banned as well. The safety measures stopped us from ordering food and even limited our rage of placing orders online. Nobody cared how much money you had, for all was parked in the bank and any spending was deemed futile, all that we thought was important for our life was marked USELESS.

What mattered was a roof to live under, the family to support, the company we kept, the food we ate, and nature that fused in some sense of hope. Rest was all for namesake.

The world knew it was time we corrected our course of activities and lifestyle. It was time we set our priorities right. It was time to keep a check on our materialistic aspirations. It was time that we lived a fulfilling life rather than a life filled with just possessions. It was time we took care of each other rather than being too individualistic. It was time we adapted sustainable ways of living. It was time we cared and upholstered nature at its best. It was time that all of us lived on this earth as one single unit - in coherence and harmony with each other. It was time to introspect and bring the much-needed change. It was time we corrected the basics that had gone wrong. It was time for the entire human race to be cautious - of its ways of living and of the pandemic that was looming over the head like a dragon spewing fire.

The Cautious Me

The world was

oh so trapped

grown so bizarre

and forever lost

in its own creations, and

we lay there with our

disheveled thoughts,

sad eyes,

tired bodies,

and souls so deprived

in our so called busy lives

when the untoward happened

when the pandemic arrived.

But just because
the earth didn't shiver
nor did the oceans
took us in their garb
the mountains didn't quiver
and we didn't flow in the mud tar
doesn't mean – that nothing happened.

Nothing happened,
if you would love to think so
is just an illusion,
perspired in our apathy
and our constant state of oblivion.

The world was shut down
mass lockdowns imposed
the seasons came and went by
while we remained indoors
we were alive, when we witnessed
what could be a world apocalypse
but stopped at being a pandemic
Maybe! we all hoped so.

Our moral compass dwindled
and the fight for survival began
chaotic and clueless
we were left with no place to ran

The times they were
stirring up the conscience for it approves
of what we do not and what we do!
It didn't stop there
it was just beginning of The End
and what we were stepping into
doing nothing seemed the best we could possibly do
for the times we sailed through
for the times that were yet to arrive
for the choices we had to make
for us and our generations to survive!
The Cautious Me!
The Cautious Me!
dwelled in all those doubts.

Chapter14:
The Lockdown Continues

It all started from Janta Curfew followed by a series of lockdown announcements. From Lockdown 1.0 to extended lockdowns to further lockdown, there seemed no end to it. People were going dizzy and the economy was growing frizzy. The entire world was split into two. The better half and the not-so-better half. The caged-captive and sheltered half. The roofless, free, and wandering half. The partying half. The starving half. The medically protected half. The uninsured-unprotected half. The ones with comfort-cushy jobs. The other half was without any job. The ones waiting to roam free again. The other half hoped to go back to their usual pain. While one half of the world was battling themselves locked inside their homes, the other half of the world was fighting tooth and nail to find themselves a home. The world dwindled, repercussions of which were felt across the hierarchies at the helm of affairs.

But lockdown was a must if corona woes were to be controlled. Even if that meant at the cost of a bucket full of other woes. We were already in June 2020. It had been more than 60 days of strict lockdown. Unlock 1.0 was already announced starting 8 June with a few relaxations and certain restrictions and limitations. But the journey till here had been no bed of roses. It had been an arduous one full of tumultuous times, horrendous hardships, difficult decisions, and mostly anticipations. Those decisions were a must to safeguard the lives of millions and billions pining hope at the Karta-dhartas to bring relief and normalcy to their lives.

India had 511 cases of corona-infected people as of 24 March, a day before the first lockdown began. There were 10 deaths already. And the cases were doubling in 3.4 days. To slow down this rate, all the connections with infected people (symptomatic or asymptomatic) had to be truncated. Any possible touch had to be avoided. The ones who tested positive had to be in complete isolation and quarantine from the rest of the family members and society. To make this possible, the government declared a complete shutdown of all possible activities - factories, services, any kind of travel or transport, private cars/cabs and public transport, shops and markets, IT parks and SEZs, public offices and retail outlets, banks and post offices, malls and cinemas, gymnasiums and fitness centers, salons and spas, street-food outlets or fine-dine, restaurants and hotels, street selling and even vendors selling door-to-door were not allowed. In short, any possibility of where people could come in close contact with each other or gather in masses or huge numbers was eliminated. The entire world came to a complete state of halt.

Only the essential services were allowed which included - grocery, healthcare (hospitals, pharmaceuticals, and chemists shops), and defense. At the same time, the government worked with eCommerce majors to ensure a continuous supply of goods to the public and drive digital commerce till the physical markets could be allowed to reopen to meet the daily needs of the public.

The people were in awe. There was deafening silence everywhere. The roads lay empty. The markets were stranded. The huge concrete structures echoed emptiness. Everything we had built to serve our convenience and pleasure was abandoned overnight. The lockdown sent shivers across the population of the country. It opened Pandora's box, especially for the urban poor.

Suddenly, millions were jobless. There were thefts of not only money and goods but of food as well. Everyone was rushing to the grocery shops to buy essentials. People started queuing up in front of shops starting at 6 am. Shopkeepers were bullied and brutally assaulted on exhausting the stock. There was panic buying everywhere. The workforce started waiting infinitely at the bus stands and railway stations to rush back to their home towns and villages. There were herds of people who along with their families started their journey home on foot. With no money, no to less food, no means of transport - these people, majorly the migrant workers, continued their onward journey to their homes under the scorching sun and stormy nights. Then there were a few who looked for a spot to conclude the last rites of family members they lost during the journey. In the pursuit of home, they ended up being in heavenly abodes. All you could sense and feel in the bulletin hour was a grim situation, restless people going through extreme pain. One could only feel helpless and sad about the overall scenario.

The government announced a 1.7 lac crore stimulus package to cater to the needs of the poor. It included medical facilities, free cereals, and the provision of cooking gas for the poor households for the next 3 months. But to no good. The package was not enough. It needed to reach into the bank accounts of the beneficiaries fast. The challenge was to ensure a direct bank transfer to the rightful beneficiary. Our systems were not equipped to implement this at scale.

By now, I had talked to my helpers - whom we had sent on a paid leave, security guard - who stayed downstairs in the building. I checked with them if they needed any help. We tried to help the delivery boys who delivered our essentials at the doorstep by giving them some extra money. It was nothing in lieu of them putting their lives at risk just to ensure my essentials were delivered on time so that my family could survive. We only tried to do our bit.

But they were not alone fighting this battle. There were so many of them. Momo wale bhaiya from Darjeeling went shopless. The beautician didi who used to come home for my wife and sister went back to her home in Assam. Dhobi Bhaiya never picked up my phone afterward. Golgappe wala, where my wife and I used to go during the evenings, went back to his village in Bihar. I am not sure what happened to the naariyal paani wala, and the bhutte wali aunty. One of our helpers and her family went back to their village somewhere between the state border of Karnataka and Andhra Pradesh, never to return. By the time the first phase of lockdown came to an end on 14 April, India had 10, 541 confirmed cases. The economic activity dipped and unemployment was on the rise. The overall cost of this economic inactivity during those 21 days was estimated at Rs 32,000 crore/day (US$4.5 billion). The only good thing out of this ruckus was that corona cases were now doubling in eight days instead of three. A dim ray of hope.

There were 37, 978 relief camps and 26, 225 food camps set up across the country to take care of the migrant workers and laborers who were suddenly without a job or home and were forced to shun cities waiting to reach their home villages soon. With no buses or trains, the migrant workers, laborers, and daily wagers remained stranded for long. It included contractors, masons, plumbers, electricians, cab drivers, rickshaw walas, delivery guys, factory labor who had moved to the cities to find better income for whatever skillset they had. Their dreams lay crushed there. Didn't they know that they will have to rush back like this in a hurried-scurried manner leaving and exhausting all that they had built over years of hard work and toil?

The problem was further triggered because of companies like Ola Cabs, Uber, Urban Company (former Urban Clap), and other cab or service aggregators losing business to the restrictions imposed because of the pandemic. To avoid chaos and confusion, the government had to start special train services called Shramik Special that carried migrant workers and laborers to their hometowns. The Indian Railways passenger operations which were otherwise suspended as a part of the initial lockdown had to start again. This was the first-ever complete shutdown of the rail network in 167 years.

This exodus of the labor force turned out to be a huge impediment to the revival of the economy in the days and months that followed. Even when relaxations started getting announced, the factories had no workers, the infra projects had no labor. Karein to karein kya? The unorganized sector was severely impacted as well. From retail stores and outlets selling crockery, utensils, clothes, stationery, electrical equipment, plumbing supplies, or construction material - all the small-scale businesses and MSMEs took a big blow in their business. With no takers in the market, the overall circulation of the money slowed down. This curtailed the to and fro of money in the shadow banks, small finance businesses and even exhausted the savings at home. The liquid money started drying up fast.

There were those as well who were indirectly impacted by the severity of the situation and lack of money in the ecosystem. Suddenly there were no municipal workers to pick the garbage from homes. They were hesitant to come because no one offered any extra money like before. Maali Bhaiya reduced his frequency of visits too. Then one fine day he completely stopped coming. We were informed he went back to his hometown in Chhattisgarh. Rag pickers vanished from the streets as they got no buck for any collection they made. Newspaper wale bhaiya also complained about the reduced business and many households disrupted the newspaper subscription. The fear of the virus was for real. What if there were strains of the virus over the newspaper, people thought. Doodh wale bhaiya was lucky amongst all small-scale businesses as it was covered under essentials without any doubt or subjectivity. Cable waale bhaiya was even luckier than the milkman. The supply kept coming and he came only once a month to collect money. There was no or minimal loss of business for the cable operators.

Lockdown was a costly affair. But will it ever be completely over? Well with lockdown 2.0, starting 15 April, the government did announce a few relaxations. It allowed agricultural businesses to open including dairy, plantation, and aquaculture along with the shops selling farming supplies. Cargo vehicles could run. Small retail shops were allowed to open with half the staff. Public works and programs could be reinitiated. The government allowed inter-state transport to allow stranded people to reach their destination. This movement was subject to testing the arriving people, 14-day isolation at the special quarantine centers established followed by periodic medical checkups. All this was not a full-proof solution or a long-term remedy to fight the corona battle and lockdown woes but it surely helped in reducing the stress with each passing day and made our life a little easier.

All these relaxations were subject to the condition of reimposing the lockdown if the corona cases were seen to increase in any area. The entire state and districts were divided into red zones (where the spread was still severe), orange zones (indicating lesser infection and spread), and green zones (with no new infections in the last 21 days). It turned out to be like a level-up in your game! Higher the precautions, lower the cases - brighter the chances of opening up more facilities in your area! This motivated people to follow instructions of social distancing, and wearing a mask in public places. A collective win-win!

One lockdown paved the way for another relaxed lockdown allowing for the economy to open up a little more. As the second phase of lockdown approached its end, the major cities of India including Delhi, Mumbai, Chennai, Bengaluru, and Ahmedabad were all red zones under strict lockdown. India was struggling with 39,980 confirmed cases and mourning the loss of 1323 lives. The economic activity index had fallen from 82.9 (pre-lockdown) to 44.7 (during the lockdown phase). The government, finance ministry, RBI and the think tanks like TIFAC in the country were all working on the recovery plan for the economy which was spiraling to its death and negative growth rate.

As the third phase of lockdown started on 4 May, there were 130 districts marked as red zones, 284 districts as orange zones and 320 districts were green zones. India was doing considerably fair in comparison to the rest of the countries of the world. The green zones allowed the movement of public transport at 50% of their capacity while only private and hired cabs were allowed in the orange zones. The status of each zone was reviewed once a week. There could be no lacunae in ensuring the safety of the lives of citizens of the country. It was a constant battle between life and livelihood.

The states of Maharashtra, Gujarat, Delhi, Madhya Pradesh, Rajasthan, Tamil Nadu, and Uttar Pradesh were the worst-hit states of India at that time. Despite China being the epicenter of the pandemic, India, at 85,940 cases, surpassed China in terms of the total number of cases reported. The finance minister announced a second and third stimulus package giving relief to the small business players, taxpayers, power distribution companies, real estate, organized sector, and agriculture and allied activities - fisheries, animal husbandry, dairy, and food processing - respectively. India also initiated Vande Bharat Mission flights to bring back the stranded Indians from countries like the UK, the UAE, the US, Maldives, Singapore, and Bahrain.

With 96,169 cases and the loss of 3069 lives, India entered its fourth and final phase of lockdown beginning 18 May. Red zones were further divided into containment and buffer zones. The local bodies and states were given more authority to react to the prevailing situation in their vicinity. To ensure more transparent availability of information, every citizen was asked to update their health status on the Aarogya Setu app, specially designed and built to fast track the status of individual citizens. This became a de facto checkpoint for anyone who wanted to travel outside the city.

Lockdown raised questions at multiple levels. It highlighted many inadequacies prevailing in the system and lapses that could have been avoided. With 1,90,609 total cases reported and 5400 deaths so far, India became the 7th most infected nation in the world. India's GDP dropped by 23.9% during the lockdown. 80 million migrant workers were impacted because of the pandemic and consequent lockdown. There were a total of 350 deaths reported because of starvation, suicides, exhaustion, road and rail accidents, police brutality, and denial of timely medical care. 140 million people lost their jobs. 53% of the businesses in the country were thought to be severely impacted. 45% of the households saw a drop in income in comparison to the same period, the previous year. India was headed to depression, according to CRISIL, the worst ever since independence.

Amidst this depression, both economic and emotional, I wondered about the guy who used to draw sketches sitting at one corner just outside the mall. And what about the guy who used to sell cheap Chinese tech gadgets and those long pens at the signals? Also about the girls who used to sell me roses while I was in the cab and told me to give those to my girlfriend. And those who sold dusters and cleaning clothes after cleaning the front mirror of our cars. And the one who sold tickets in black. The dose-wala anna, to chai tapri wale bhaiya, vade stall wala, to phool wali amma - my heart ached and wondered for them. Would they have survived the pandemic and the lockdown that continued for months or did they succumb to the wrath of the lockdown? Would the gubbarewala be able to sell happiness packed in balloons and bring smiles to the faces of children crying non-stop? Would there be anyone who would have brought smiles to all these gubbarewalas and everyone, during the lockdown, who was severely and badly impacted by the pandemic and even more by the lockdown that was imposed to protect the very life?

In the constant battle between life and livelihood, we have been always choosing livelihood. The times we were going through, we had to choose life. There was no option left.

Chapter15: Ambush

Exhausted. Depressed. Exasperated and claustrophobic, I decided to wake up early and take a stroll outside the building. Will it be safe? I got up at 5 am (to avoid any human touch), wore a mask, and went outside. The road was empty and covered with a thick sheet of fallen leaves. Over that sheet lay a beautiful thin layer of fresh cherry blossoms that left their branches on the trees to hug the earth so tight to finally merge with it. It looked like a pink carpet spread for the warm welcome - especially for me. I watched my steps to avoid trampling the fallen flowers. The edges of the boundary walls of the houses which met the roads had fresh green herbs and small plantations grown from the crevices. A few of them spotted white and yellow flowers such as Yarrows. The empty plot which used to be a garbage dump for all the nearby houses had turned green with huge plants grown on their own. It had become a shelter house for stray dogs. As I looked up, the trees covered the entire view of the sky. The sky shone blue and white from the sneak peek I could get from in between the leaves. I would have walked for a little more than half an hour - to and fro on the same road from one end to another. Everything on the earth - the trees, the cherry blossoms, the yarrows, the plantations, and the dogs - basked in the glory of the sun. As the sun started shining a little more, everything started turning into a little more gold. I looked here and there and took off my mask for a while, breathed deeply a few times, and wore back the mask.

The air was light but as if it controlled everything there. It brushed me a few times as if to make me feel its presence. The trees stood tall, a little bent towards the earth as if patrolling the roads. The sun - the guiding light; the sky - the omnipresent; the plants - the dancing barons; the dogs - the owners; they all were a team. I - the no one - was the odd one out. I could hear laughter - loud and clear - coming from all nooks and corners. I could feel someone walking beside me. I could feel the presence of someone other than humans on that road at that instance - seizing the moment. Amidst all the misery and sadness, if there was someone who was having a great time it was nature. With the onset of the pandemic, nature took the reins of all that belonged to it back in its hands. All that we had snatched away from it. Call it *tandav*, call it *nritya*, the scene on the road outside my house was mesmerizing and captivating. The same scene was prevalent all over the world.

The skies became clearer. The rivers gushed transparent downstream. The air was cleaner than ever before. The wildlife - the rare, the endangered, and thought to be extinct - they all came out. They all showed themselves up at the lockdown party where everyone but humans was present. The humans - caged behind the four walls of the houses like animals in the zoo - were up for display where animals came to watch them out. The pandemic was here. It had turned the tables around. The animals now roamed out freely in the open without any fear of being killed while humans stayed indoors for the fear of being killed by the invisible virus. The environment had never been so green and clean before. What could not be done by pumping billions of dollars for years was achieved in a few months of complete human inactivity. Everybody could guess who the real trouble was.

As lockdown and shelter-in-place orders kept being passed around the world, there were unusual sightings everywhere. From clear sky-views in Jakarta in Indonesia, Manila in the Philippines, where particulate matter dropped by 180% since quarantine measures to empty highways in Los Angeles with one of the busiest road networks;

people witnessed the unthinkable. The downtown views and skylines were visible which were otherwise always shrouded in dust and smog. From better air quality in Spain to a visible Eiffel Tower from suburbs in Paris, the air pollution levels plummeted at unprecedented rates. Folks in Kathmandu could see the snowclad Langtang mountain range at the backdrop of Swayambhunath Stupa.

With 2.6 million corona cases, 1.83lakh deaths all over the world, and stay-at-home orders the environment was no more the same as what we had grown up to witness. People in Kashmir valley cheered up at the sight of the clearer Pir Panjal range and folks in Jalandhar, Punjab were awestruck at the sight of the Dhauladhar mountain range. Nobody from the current generation had ever witnessed the sight in the last 30 years. Nobody knew that the mountains and peaks they visited during the summer, 210km straight, were visible from their rooftop as well. On the other hand, people in the town of Saharanpur, UP could spot the snow peaks of Gangotri. I was appalled that it took humans to be locked inside for nature to show at its best. Nature's message was clear enough - Touch me Not! Unfortunately and sadly so we had done a lot of devastation and brought more harm than good to nature. It was nature's turn to take revenge and show us the right way forward. Were we listening? Only time would tell.

The complete lockdown, shutting down of factories, absence of vehicular traffic, work from home orders restricting humans to their own houses dropped the pollution considerably. Nitrogen Dioxide level in Delhi dropped to 90 umol/m2 in comparison to 158 umol/m2 the same period the previous year and 162 umol/m2 just before the lockdown began. Mumbai saw a drop in the NO2 levels from 117umol/m2 pre-pandemic to 77umol/m2 during the lockdown. The same pattern was observed across all the major cities and townships of India. Besides nitrogen dioxide, which is the most harmful of the pollutants, the air also had less suspended particulate matter. To the surprise of everyone, all 4 metros met more than 30% of their NCAP target set for 2024. The average PM2.5 value for Mumbai was 20, Delhi - 49, Kolkata - 22, Bangalore - 23. What alibi did we have to suggest humans were not responsible for polluted earth? None.

While the skies were shining blue and bright, and the air was clean and light; the water sources were flowing freely with less toxicity and turbidity levels. Zero emissions from the factories, no industrial effluents being dumped into streams and tributaries that joined the river along the journey made the rivers look clean. There was less of what humans created as waste flowing into the rivers. Maybe the apparent results were temporary but they were an eye-opener for the entire human race. All these positive changes in disguise came to the environment as a breather. Nature lived to the fullest yet again. What remains to be seen is will these patterns sustain when the pandemic is over and the world is back to its usual? Or will humans continue to rampage nature like before in pre-pandemic times?

For now, one could spot South Asian River Dolphins (popularly known as Gangetic Dolphins) at the *ghats of the Ganga* river in Kolkata after 30 years. A sight that was not unusual decades back was lost owing to ever-increasing industrial waste and chemicals being released into the rivers. On average 6500-7000 million liters of industrial waste was released into Ganga every day along the UP stretch alone before the pandemic hit the world and the lockdown was imposed. Out of which 10% was considered highly toxic. With lockdown bringing all the industrial activities to a complete halt, the quality of the river water was found to be fit for bathing and propagation of fisheries and wildlife at 27 of the 36 real-time monitoring points along the river stretch. Ganga water at the higher reaches of Haridwar and Rishikesh was deemed fit for drinking because of a 500% decrease in sewage and industrial effluents. It was found that Ganga water became fit for *achman, ritual sipping* after decades. So much purity for the world that was doomed.

With each passing day, it became evident that the river systems worked well on their own. The snow melts, rainfalls, ingress, and outflow of river water could keep the river system and biodiversity in check. All it needed from us was regulated water withdrawal from the river ecology for industrial, irrigation, and domestic purposes and in return dumping less to no waste and industrial effluents back into the rivers. However, we aimed to clean the river while polluting them at the same time. No project however ambitious it may be like *Namami Gange* could ever clean the river ecosystem. It only became a vicious circle. What we needed to look at was how to reduce and then eventually eliminate the outflow of the wastes into the river systems not only in Ganga, Yamuna but other river systems in the Indian subcontinent and the world.

From water canals in Venice that turned clear and transparent to *Erode Kalingarayan Canal* in Chennai that turned as clean as it was two decades ago, nature regained its lost glory. Aquatic species reclaimed their legitimate place all over. The surprising and the most dreadful part of the story was it just took an invisible virus a few weeks to push "the great mankind" to nadir and bring nature back to its best. It would be foolish to believe that we could play around with the natural cycle at our own will and forever.

150,000 flamingoes descended over Mumbai turning the wetlands pink and a sight that went viral all over social media. The same thing occurred in the Camargue region of Southern France as well. Thousands of birds flocked to Aqua Dulce beach in Peru which was missing millions of beachgoers in action. Abandoned by humans, claimed by an army of seabirds. The bar-headed geese - which breed in China and Mongolia - and migrate to India in winters were spotted in huge numbers at the mouth of the Vembar river in Thoothukudi and Tirunelveli in Tamil Nadu. Waders, Gulls, and various species of terns were spotted as well.

From Deers being spotted in Raby Castle, Britain to visiting pelicans at a public park in London - the wildlife was enjoying nature and parks to themselves devoid of any humans around. Cougars were reportedly spotted prowling the streets in Santiago, Chile and wild Kashmiri goats meandered through the town of Llandudno, Wales. The dolphins danced wild and free in Bosphorous, Turkey (one of the busiest marine routes of the world which was now inactive).

The silence by human inactivity caused wildlife to roam freely in the otherwise busy city streets looking for food and made them stay longer in deeper pockets of the towns. Sea lions were there on display in the streets of Galapago islands in Ecuador. Deers gatecrashed homes in the bustling city of Mumbai.

One could see fox hunting squirrels on the streets of Toronto in Canada. A pack of jackals, which is a rare sight, was seen in Hayarkon Park in Tel Aviv, Israel. The badger was seen roaming on the streets of Prayagraj, India. From peacocks in Lodhi Gardens, Delhi to swans in Nymphenburg in Munich; from goats strolling in Trinity Square, North Wales to greylag goose in Hungary - the world witnessed the most unusual as well the most spectacular sights. Nature walked with aplomb all over the world.

My favorite among all the spectacular sightings was Olive Ridley Turtles turning up in lakhs on the beaches of Odisha, India. 3.7 lakh of them laid eggs at Rushikulya Rookery, while 4.2 lakh Olive Ridleys turned up at Gahirmatha Beach for laying eggs. I don't know why but none other news of unusual sightings made me feel so bad about the entire situation, about us being locked inside and the wildlife beginning to enjoy its newfound space. I felt this like a punch in the gut of my stomach. So, it was not us who believed to be in complete control of what conspired on the earth. That thought was delusional. It was nature that eluded us of all the beauty that lay hidden in its garb. Nature considered us unworthy of witnessing all this beauty. That is why it waited or conspired for us to be locked indoors so that it could show a glimpse of what it held close to its chest and without us being able to hurt its prized possessions.

They say "The Jungle is always alive. Always watching." It depends on us when we can cut the clutter and listen, observe and see beyond what is usual. It seemed as if Coronavirus was nature's vaccine and we were the virus. The all-pervading, all intrusive and seemingly all-powerful - the humans - stood humbled by an invisible virus.

The pandemic made us realize that we were just a pawn in the chess called *life.* It was nature that made all the moves and decided who won and who lost. The bigger challenge looming over the human race was that if we were ready to coexist with nature via sustainable ways yet or were we waiting for the pandemic to get over soon to get back to our older wilder callous ways?

Our continuous home to office and travel back; the vehicular traffic - via road, rails, and air; marine sailing and trading; our incessant travel desires to mountains and higher reaches or towards the sea and beaches; our consumption of plastic in terms of packaged food, water bottles, cola, and other beverage bottles, and dumping of the same into our usual home-waste and other sources of water; poultry waste or barber-shop waste; and all kind of domestic waste; industrial waste of being it tanneries, or manufacturing sector, clothing or chemical sector, agricultural refuse or any other kind of waste; emissions from ACs, heaters and cars; construction debris, defunct equipment or huge towers; rampant deforestation for the so-called development projects - all of this together devastated nature little by little and more. Our exploitation of nature needs to be stopped with immediate effect and it needs to happen collectively across the globe. Remember - *I fail, we all fail.* The complete lockdown put a full stop to all these human activities thereby relaxing the levels of air, water, land, and noise pollution, temporarily though and thereby increasing the lease of life.

We all know and realize that putting a complete halt to human activities beyond pandemic times might not be a practical solution which then puts the bigger onus on finding alternatives so that nature and humans can coexist. Because as a matter of fact, we need nature more than nature needs us. If we are deemed unfit for the survival of the ecosystem, we will soon be eliminated from the equation called life. If we can not heal nature, nature will find its ways to reclaim what truly belongs to it and forever. It is a matter of time that nature finds it even uncomfortable to share what is hers - the natural resources, what she has been sharing benevolently with humans for millions of years now. But we have not been able to be thankful enough for what we have been bestowed with rather we took all that nature provided us with for granted. Let's not forget that nature can take care of herself, we need to take care of ourselves and be more cognizant of our activities.

If we continue to behave irresponsibly, like in pre-pandemic times, the temporary ambush by nature would be replaced by a permanent one which would be worse than the pandemic and much more catastrophic. The pandemic was a wake up call for all mankind to step back and contemplate our ways of living. The thought and the urgency need to be globalised. The future is ours, the choice is ours too. It is now or never.

Chapter16: The Irresponsible Ones

It was a huge temple on the top of a mountain. The mountain stood tall surrounded by shorter mountains and peaks. All of us - our entire family - climbed our way up to that temple following the trail left by other visitors. Countless *diyas* decorated the temple like infinite stars lighting up the sky. The sky was colored in yellow-orange sunset hues. It was time for *evening aarti.* The priest held the *panchbhooti* strongly in his right hand and rang the pooja bell with the left hand in a tune synchronous to the aarti. *Lord Shiva* sat along with divine Shakti - *Maa Parvati* at the sanctum sanctorum of the temple enclosed by a boundary erected by a strong iron fence. Nobody was allowed inside that area other than the priest. All I could hear was loud *Om* chants echoing from peaks surrounding the temple. All I could see was people absorbed in the prayers and submitted to the power of the divine - their bodies swinging left and right.

Between the mountains, in the narrow gorges, a river - dark green in color - flowed smoothly like a silk sheet following the curbs and bends of the mountains. But with chants getting louder, the river water kept rising and becoming turbulent. With each chant, the river water became unstoppable and uncontrollable. Slowly it reached the pavement of the temple. The sky turned dark. The mountain started quivering, the water created whirlpools, the winds became strong, the mountain opposite collapsed and merged into the river and vanished in a few seconds. People started trembling in the fear of death with chants becoming even louder, asking their supreme to save them for one last time.

I was completely drenched in sweat when my alarm clock rang and woke me up from sleep. "Thank God, it was a dream," I told myself. I was scared. Did the dream mean anything? "Maybe, maybe not." I got up, took a shower and performed my daily *pooja* ritual, and sat in complete silence. As I regained consciousness, I realized the Gods had already shut their door upon us. The pandemic had stopped us from visiting a temple, mosque or a church, gurudwara, synagogue, or any other place of worship. We were supposed to find God within, inside our homes, till we were allowed to visit our places of worship again.

Any public gathering for that matter - religious or social, formal or casual was not permitted under any circumstances and was against the guidelines of protection to prevent the spread of Coronavirus. "*Par Rab ke bande rab ke ishare kahan samajhte hain? Yeh to bas rab se arziyaan karte hian*" (But do these creatures of God understand the omens of the very God they pray day and night? They only know to ask for their wishes to be fulfilled.)

The hospitals were full. There were not adequate medical facilities available to cater to each person falling ill because of the pandemic. The health and medical staff seemed less and insufficient. People were dying. There was not enough information available to diagnose and cure the illness caused by the virus. Some people had no symptoms but still carried the virus (the asymptomatic victims) leading to a bigger fear of spreading the virus fast and wide. No one was able to make complete sense of what was happening around. To avoid complete disaster and save maximum human lives, the best we could do was avoid any human touch, lock ourselves inside our houses and follow the safety precautions as guided and directed by WHO (World Health Organization) and IMA (Indian Medical Association).

And the only way to achieve that was to avoid any mass gatherings, public outings, and get-togethers.

But oh people! They won't listen! Not only in India but also outside of India, not once and twice but multiple times, people gathered in large numbers to rally, protest, celebrate and rejoice. There were umpteen reasons that got them together out in the streets but one reason to stay inside - to save each other's life - did not seem enough. But if we truly believed in God, then we must believe in its creations as well. And we must do all it takes to protect and safeguard its creations. But did we? No. How could we behave so irresponsibly?

9000 people gathered at Markaz Mosque in Delhi, the headquart2ers of Tablighi Jamaat, from various states of India including 960 attendees from foreign countries. This led to more than 4500 confirmed cases of corona and more than 40,000 close contacts of attendees at the conference being quarantined and medically examined. The incident resulted in the loss of 27 lives. Any loss of human life was painful and when the loss was due to our ignorance and negligence, it became shameful and sad for the entire humanity.

We didn't realize that incidents like such caused undue pressure on the medical fraternity and the government to track, quarantine, and look after people who otherwise would have been perfectly fine and alright. This caused travel authorities, local bodies, police, and hospitals to be on high alert at least for the next 14 days till everyone reached back home and was declared fit. Religion didn't matter, humanity did. But looks like we had become good at failing at it time and again.

While people here were gathering for religious congregations, there were protests in many parts of the world questioning the citizens' right to freedom and liberty. Why should one wear a mask, and not gather in public? How can a government impose restrictions on our fundamental rights? How can they stop us from living freely? Albeit, one needs to be alive to enjoy all sorts of freedom. Was it too tough to understand? The strange part was while these pseudo activists protested for their rights, they supposedly didn't attend their sessions on fundamental duties. They forgot that It was every citizen's duty to enable the government to run the country peacefully and successfully. But as always rights weighed more than the duties. People protested and demonstrated their anguish. The ones who had locked themselves inside their homes looked at these people in skirmish-scornful ways.

If this wasn't enough to question the sensibilities, we also had folks who gathered for pool parties, enjoying their summer and festivals without any protective measures in place. They probably believed in the phrase, "Live life like there is no tomorrow." And surely so, if they continued to live like this, there would be no tomorrow.

2.7 million tourists gathered in Wuhan in Hubei province where corona had first emerged for a massive pool party against any health advisories. Hundreds and thousands of people gathered at Ozark Lake and Daytona Beach in Florida for Memorial Day celebrations. Owing to summer and Liverpool Football club's first league title in 30 years - there were multiple instances of public gatherings in the UK. People thronged beaches, and there were street parties everywhere. Folks across the world gave up their cooped-up coronavirus existence for one reason or another.

In India, we were busy shopping. We waited for an opportune moment to escape to the market. The major reason being - wedding and festival season ahead. Everyone was doubtful about the guest list but no one was unsure about how much to shop and where to shop. As soon as the markets and shops would open, people gathered out there to buy the stuff. And eventually, when there was not much one could do about the guest list, we ended up inviting everyone. We celebrated, drank, danced, and dined as if there was no corona. If Gods were watching from the above, they must be, they must have wondered about where did humans leave their common sense? Did they believe this coronavirus was a myth? Were they not ready to believe that COVID-19 was a deadly virus indeed?

A similar and even bigger mass congregation happened at Maha Kumbh. 9.1 million *sharadhalus* thronged Haridwar for the Maha Kumbh over three months. Out of which 3.5 million gathered for the holy bath on 12 April 2021, 3.2 million on 11 March on the occasion of MahaShivratri, and 1.3 million arrived on the occasion of Baisakhi. This happened just before the second deadly wave of Corona took India by storm. One could only wonder if my *bhakti and devotion* were subservient to one visiting the holy site? Were my intentions and my karma not enough? These were not normal circumstances, these were not normal times! But we didn't pay any heed.

The sharpest blow came from the never-ending Farmers Agitation in India and Bengal election rallies. These were brutal, to say the least. Somewhere around 300,000 (3 lakh) farmers converged at various border points of Delhi. In another instance, 40,000 farmers gathered to protest against the Farm Laws. Tens of thousands of farmers held a parade with a large convoy of tractors and drove towards Delhi. While farmers *gheraoed* Delhi, the political parties surrounded Bengal amidst election rallies. Lakhs of people turned out to attend the rallies where the Prime Minister of India and Chief Minister of West Bengal were to speak. In one of the rallies, there were reportedly 1 million attendees. Were these people not afraid of the virus anymore? Was their love for these leaders so much more than their own life? Were they ready to risk their own life for these leaders? But then why were these leaders not equally worried about their voters' lives? Why didn't they stop these rallies from taking place? Interestingly, the number of COVID cases out of these 2 events was never reported.

The real challenge begins here when the real protectors of the public go on to behave irresponsibly setting the wrong precedence for the public. When the processes, system, and safety procedures are tweaked to suit one's interests and ambitions overlooking the larger good of the society, the credibility of leaders and leadership is put into question. Amidst coronavirus spread, the government must have taken it upon themselves to handle these situations wisely and differently. But the harm was already done.

Shops were full. People were partying. There were long queues outside liquor shops across the world. Pool Parties happened. Religious gatherings happened. Rallies happened. Protests happened. Agitation and demonstration took place. And when I would switch to my social handles, people didn't leave a chance to foray out to their favorite destinations. All this while the entire world was shadowed by a deadly pandemic - the cure for which was not yet found.

There were elderly at home. Some battled chronic ailments and suffered from other diseases. There were newborns. If not for relatives, neighbors, or community and society, we could have chosen to be cautious at least for ourselves and our family. Rather we indulged in what was a perfect recipe for disaster. We could not have been any more foolish. We could not have behaved so irresponsibly.

Incidents like these make loud noises in my head and scream, "Why is our relationship with our God so lopsided?" Why is it that every time we are in conversation with our God, it is him/her who we expect to listen to us and all we want is to bear fruit out of that conversation! Why do we not expect ourselves to listen to God as well? God who manifests itself in nature has been screaming loud and clear to find the balance, respect nature, and behave responsibly. To stay indoors!

How much worse could it be that all places of worship were closed and shut too? If God stopped us from stepping into the corridors that we considered God's abode, then what made us think that stepping outside and gathering in hoards was a perfectly fine thing to do? Or did we consider our whims and fancies more important than God? Or were we under the impression that come what may, our God will save us from the claws of the virus? Lest we forget that God helps those who help themselves. Didn't we think once that our God - that we get ready to kill for - was angry with us? Didn't we consider that God was trying to signal us something? *Tham Ja re bande.*

I thought, did my dream mean anything? Was the river symbolic of the pandemic? Were the chants equivalent to human cry? Was the fence symbolic of God not allowing humans near them? Was the crowd symbolic of people congregating when they were supposed to be indoors? But my dream was left incomplete in between. Would God have saved the humans or let them flow with the river like the mountain that was squashed and merged into it?

Did my dream mean that *The End* was near?

Chapter17:
Did we think we are indomitable?

What made us behave as we did? What made us think that we could risk our own lives and others as well? Or what made us think that we were not putting anyone's life at risk? What gave us the confidence to roam around freely and gather in huge congregations against multiple health advisories? What made us so careless yet so full of conceit? Did we think that we were indomitable?

The human race was basking in its full glory when the pandemic hit the world in 2020. Humans have always been curious creatures and that curiosity has led to the greatest inventions and discoveries of their lifetime. Our urge to know more about each and everything around us has been unstoppable. Not only earth but the humans went on to conquer the extraterrestrial spaces as well. The world shrank in the last few decades. One could fly from Bangalore to Jammu or San Francisco to New York in 3 hours over a nonstop flight. I could talk to my friends and family in Cambridge or Amsterdam, Singapore, or Dubai in seconds over a video call. We could find our lost school friends or college mates in a few searches and clicks. Our connectivity was instant. We could explore everything in this universe at a tap of a few clicks and hits. Distance didn't matter anymore. Time zones were no barrier. The language was no obstacle. From human anatomy to spatial intelligence - humans had conquered it all.

The exponential advancement in technology made humans undefeatable. But then the pandemic happened and the entire human race stood humbled by an invisible virus. All the intelligence was put to question. All the knowledge was rendered useless. All the experience was doomed. All the confidence was shattered. What went wrong where? How did the virus push the entire race that had worked so hard to reach where it was - behind the four walls of their houses? Why could no one anticipate the pandemic? If anyone could anticipate it, why could no one prevent the harm it brought along? Were we so engrossed in what we had built for ourselves? Did we think nothing could harm us anymore? Did our achievements make us think that we were indomitable?

114 years ago no one knew that earth was a billion years old. That number is nothing in the timeline of human existence, which is only 6 million old species on this very old earth. Humans as we know today - *Homo Sapiens* - are just 200,000 years old. And the civilization which we believe to be existing forever is only 6000 years old. The consumerist us are a result of Industrialization which began recently in the 1800s. But today all of this information is so redundant that no one bothers to remember it or factor it into our history of evolution. Does it matter to you? No, right? And we continue to live so unapologetically as if this has been our usual since times immemorial.

And why not? After all, in the last 100 years and more so in the last 30 years - humans made enormous revelations in terms of our understanding of how the universe behaves, how galaxies are held together, human ancestry, genome editing, and beyond. From launching the Hubble Space Telescope to setting up the International Space Station, from exploring the planets of our solar system to discovering solar systems and planets outside our solar system; there has been a lot of effort put into knowing the mysterious outer space. Today we have discovered 4768 exoplanets. Humans have unearthed much more than what was even known to exist at the beginning of the century. Our desire to know and explore more of what lies beyond us is unquenching. But we have been relentless in our quest.

I am sure you would have heard of the Higgs Boson particle. We discovered it as a part of the Large Hadron Collider experiment by CERN. The particle gives matter its mass. It remains the fundamental particle responsible for our existence - for that matter, any matter that exists. It was one of the biggest discoveries of the human lifetime. It inched us closer to understanding our existence. This opened avenues to study *Axions* in detail which are considered responsible for dark matter that holds galaxies together. In 2015, approximately 100 years after Albert Einstein proposed *the Theory of relativity*, which he doubted was proved to be true and relevant even today. The human race turned everything impossible into possible.

But we did not arrive here so easily. We made gradual progress that accelerated as we rushed into the 21st century. We expanded our exploratory excursions eventually with more resources available at hand. We made successful landings in space. We set our foot on the Moon as well as on Mars. We launched spaceships, reusable rockets into space. We made *Cassini* orbit around Saturn for 13 years, *Juno* around Jupiter, and *Curiosity* landed on Mars. And now we have Jeff Bezos, founder of the eCommerce giant Amazon, headed to space. It is strange that 100kms straight on the earth needs no special preparations but 100kms upwards to the sky needs a whole lot of specific intelligence, resources, and acumen. But humans had got it all covered. Why would then one not believe that humans had become unconquerable in the last few decades of the history of earth?

We tried our best to discover the life and existence of water - the basic source of life - on other solar planets and outside the solar system as well. We studied and observed the movements of interstellar interlopers such as Oumuamua and others. We launched NEAR (Near Earth Asteroid Rendezvous) to study asteroids and decipher the history of the universe more than we already knew.

One must then wonder - what accelerated our discovery of all things universe much beyond earth in the last three decades so much? The answer is simple - *the technology revolution.* Our computation speeds became 100X, our communication became instant - all supported with the advent of the biggest invention of a human lifetime - the internet. It brought the world closer to each other much more than we could anticipate. This was the beginning of all things great that followed.

The Internet was born in 1973. Since then there has been no looking back. We started using websites with their names instead of IP addresses in 1983. The ubiquitous world wide web (www.) was made available to the public only recently in 1991. This made the human race use the internet and the web at scale without any pre-required technical knowledge. It was simplified for use by everyone. This revolutionized the way people collaborated and communicated with each other across the oceans for work or casually. It not only made connecting to fellow beings present in other parts of the world easy, but it also seemingly made travel look and feel more comforting. It made crowdsourcing much easier with like-minded people and organizations coming together to collaborate on bigger unfathomable projects. The Internet could mobilize the entire human race in a fraction of seconds.

Don't be in awe! The White House and United Nations went online in 1993 as well. Yahoo came and became obsolete in just a few years since its inception in 1994. Do you find jeevansaathi.com and Tinder weird and interesting? Only if you knew the first online dating website came into existence in 1995. Google - the know-it-all, without which humans cannot survive anymore, did not exist before 1998. Then came Facebook in 2004, Twitter in 2006, Instagram in 2010, a year after Whatsapp was launched. So much in so little time. One invention gave way to another.

Today Whatsapp boasts its 2 billion active users with 390 million coming from India alone. Facebook and Twitter played a crucial role in the *Arab Spring*, one of the firsts civil protests orchestrated and executed almost completely via social media. Such has been the extent of social media.

One cannot easily fathom the power of social media. From connecting with friends and family to finding jobs and soulmates, fueling passion and dreams, and running home-owned businesses, social media revolutionized the way humans interacted with one another. Not only the citizens of cities but also the ones in far-flung physically distant places could see their dreams seeing the light of the day. Social media gave freedom to each individual to maintain their unique identity. It would be funny if we told kids born in the late 2010s that social media didn't exist a few years ago. They would rather pass it as a joke. No wonder, we called them digital natives!

Social media truly globalized the world's manners. If we look at the chronology, we humans started our explorations by finding our fit in the larger picture of life called the *universe*. Once we started setting our foot on outer space and realized more could be achieved with systems that were fast and cheap to produce, we switched our attention to faster computers and computation systems. It brought along mobile phones and Internet technology - evolving from 0G, 1G, 2G to 3G and now 4G and 5G, as we use today.

The faster and slick desktops and mobiles became the infrastructure. The internet became the fuel. Social media were applications to be installed on this infrastructure. All of these together could be deployed and used to decipher any big or small discovery and invention. From human-human connection to human-space interaction, the human race made it all possible in just a few years. There should be no surprise, there was none either, that humans utilized the gifted intelligence to the best they could.

It is fascinating to see that while we were expanding the stretches of the space we knew, we were bringing the world closer to each other on this earth. The attempts were on to understand the infinitesimally small elements that made us and infinitely big things that we were a minuscule part of. Why would then we not consider ourselves indomitable? We were trying to connect one end of the universe to another - fully assimilating our past so that we could better our present and predict the future.

We came a long way from using mobile phones that were 40kgs in weight to using 1.1kg heavy mobile phones in 1973 to smartphones of today. Motorola became the first company to launch a handheld mobile device for the public. Then came Nokia, Blackberry, Samsung, Apple, so on and so forth.

One can only imagine how fast the revolution came and changed our habits forever. From SMS to using instant messengers - the way we converse with the world changed drastically. And all of this happened in just the last 30 years.

The most fascinating thing about these rapid transformational changes in the last thirty years of evolution has been the pace of one invention outdoing another. Technology gave very little time to humans to pause, think and gauge its usage and repercussions. Instead, we all were forced to adapt to the changing ways lest we were left behind in the race.

We made a similar advancement in the field of medicine and pharma. From finding cures to common ailments to inventing vaccines for the deadly Ebola, which ravaged West Africa in 2014-16. It prevented a world pandemic. We also found a cure for HIV in the form of antiretroviral drugs. A universal flu shot would soon become a possibility. We could use organoids, that are generated from human stem cells, to replace any degenerative brain cells and soon will be equipped to replace the cellular architecture. Humans ensured that fellow humans could enjoy the most in a given lifetime. The life expectancy of humans at birth increased from 65.2 in 1989 to 76.5 in 2018.

One may ask, who was responsible for all these accomplishments and the pinnacle in the history of our lifetime? The Humans.

Our race to become the most powerful species on the earth didn't stop here. From DNA sequencing to genome editing, there was already enough progress made to understand how our genetic past shaped modern humans. From finding a hybrid human fossil dated 90000 years back to editing the genome sequence to prevent diseases or incapabilities transcend the human race - science made magnificent progress. This not only helped in identifying our past but also discovered our vulnerabilities to various microbes or viruses to prevent any pandemic-like situation. But look, where were we? Amidst a pandemic despite all this progress and advancement.

The pandemic happened and all we could do was to see it taking us by storm and feel helpless about what was happening around us.

The pandemic questioned all human intelligence. It questioned all the knowledge we had accumulated in the preceding years. The pandemic hit us hard. It caught us by surprise and left us speechless. When there was so much we had evolved from, there was so much that we were working on - it was almost unbelievable to realize that a virus could pull all the strings. There must be something wrong that we did all these years. There must be something that we, the humans, gave a miss while trying to solve the equation called life.

The pandemic raised multiple questions for all-pervading human beings. It reminded us of us not being indomitable for sure. We might be the most intelligent species on the earth but surely not the wisest. The pandemic left us with more questions than the answers we had found in the previous decades. It shrouded our surety about everything in the dust of confusion, chaos, and helplessness. There was so much that humans had accomplished in so little time but the pandemic made it all seem so meaningless. It pushed us back by years. It applied brakes to our much-accelerated journey on this earth.

The only positive thought that I could carry with me was our ability to be an indomitable spirit and not give up anytime soon. We surely were not indomitable. The pandemic had shown us our reality in a few days. But we surely could be indomitable spirits, that is where our beauty lies. That is the best we could try to become in the days to come.

Chapter18:
The Anticipation of The End

There were 2240 souls aboard *The Unsinkable Titanic* on its maiden voyage. People cheered, flocked in huge numbers when the ship set its sails. The first class enjoyed their private promenade decks and the third class enjoyed the fact that they were traveling on the largest man-made object on the earth at that time. They all rejoiced that they could. The star-studded sky above and the blue clear waters beneath - with a township sailing through. Each moment spent on the ship - indoors or out on the deck - must be breathtaking. It must have been an exhilarating experience for each soul present there on the ship. *Champagnes popped. Orchestras played. Sky shots fired. Umpteen tea served. Cigars smoked. Who's Who among paupers.* The party was on!

But none of them would have thought on the day of departure - 11 April 1912 - that they would meet their fate on this eventful journey. In the wee hours of 15 April, amidst the transatlantic crossing, Titanic met its fateful end. It took 3 hours, after the ship hit the iceberg, for the unsinkable to sink and hit the ocean bed. Only 706 people survived. Rest is History.

None of the passengers would have anticipated their end when they started the journey. Nor the 706 remaining would have thought that they would survive when the ship started to sink. The unsinkable sank. The unthinkable happened. The reality turned out to be way different than what was anticipated.

No one anticipates death at the beginning of the journey. No one anticipates death at any point in time of their life. This is hilarious though. Right? In our entire lifetime, we are always dealing with all kinds of uncertainties. Even our birth is a huge uncertainty. Till the time we are born, no one knows that we are going to be born. But the moment we are born, the only certain thing about our life is our death. That we will die one day is a surety. All of the rest has to be experienced and lived as and when it reveals to us. But during our life, we choose to spend our lives as if we will live forever. This *forever* emotion is a delusion we create for ourselves, we have always created for ourselves.

Not many would know that after Titanic sank, among many conspiracy theories and hypotheses on how Titanic sank, there was an unpopular opinion as well. Many viewed the incident as the remains of human hubris. The fact that creators and builders of Titanic believed that it was unsinkable and could not be defeated by laws of nature was considered the primary reason for its doomsday. You just don't challenge nature! That's an unsaid rule.

When I think about it, the pandemic arrived at the cusp of a similar kind of smugness that suffused humans. Maybe, once again! After years and decades of immense success and glory, humans had started to believe that they were all-encompassing. Humans thought of themselves to be the lords of all things big and small. From microorganisms to humans, from earth to outer space, humans believed they had conquered it all. But they hadn't. Humans were supreme, that was not true!

Time and again, humans have been left in a state of shock. History keeps repeating itself to give humans a reality check. It takes us to the pinnacle only to bite the dust later. The only option then humans are left with is to feel helpless and wonder - *Why did it happen?*

A few years ago, a similar incident sent shockwaves across India. Uttarakhand Floods of 2013. The incessant rains and sudden cloudbursts caused devastating floods and landslides in and around the regions of the Kedarnath shrine. The nonstop heavy rainfall caused the melting of the *Chorabari* glacier sweeping away the entire towns, settlements, and market areas. Everything that came its way was wiped off, such was the wrath of the floods. The massive landslides caused heavy damage and loss of lives. Somewhere around 300,000 pilgrims were stranded or trapped and 5700 people died. Entire families went missing. In a group of 14 or 17, only 1 or 2 survived, the rest of them got washed away in the floods with their dead bodies never to be found again. Who would have thought that the people who had traveled all the way there as pilgrims to pay obeisance to their God would meet their end? None of the pilgrims would have anticipated such a gory and terrible conclusion to their pilgrimage. Against the anticipated, it did happen. When the visuals of the havoc started appearing on television, they were so horrifying, to say the least, that all we could do was close our eyes and pray for no one to face such an end.

But as a matter of fact, who anticipates its end. No one. No one wants to die. In our day-to-day life, no one even thinks about death. Once in a while when incidents like *Titanic* or *Kedarnath floods* happen, we are appalled. We are in a state of shock for a few days maybe. And maybe a little more surprised and depressed if we have lost someone known in such incidents. Otherwise, nothing matters much and moves us to think more. All these incidents become a mere thought that gets faded in months or days or hours. Remember, *State of Apathy*! Until and unless something hits us directly, we are not moved by it.

However, one might start thinking that *the end* is mostly catastrophic, devastating, and extremely painful. And if you happen to watch movies such as *The Wave* or *2012*, that belief is only strengthened. Our anticipation of the end indeed becomes associated with wreaking havoc upon us. But as I said, as you start anticipating something, expect the unanticipated.

That is what happened with humans, with the onset of the pandemic. At the party called life, there arrived a villain called COVID-19. It came silently. It came without wrecking any mountains or roaring tsunamis or rivers gushing and sweeping our homes. The earth didn't shatter and engulf us. The earth didn't move faster on its axis nor did it stop revolving around the sun. *The end* came silently drawing upon us.

Contrary to how we anticipated the end of the earth, the pandemic was calm in its occurrence. There was nothing magnanimous about it. It was not overwhelming like the sinking of the Titanic nor was it appalling like that of the Uttarakhand floods. It came in the size of a virus - invisible. It didn't bulldoze but still could suffocate you. It didn't make any thundering noise but still brought the world to a state of hue and cry. It didn't leave you stranded in the valleys or the middle of an ocean but still trapped you inside your homes. It didn't have any favorites - the rich or the poor, the strong or the weak. It just impacted all of us differently. It didn't kill us instantly but killed us each instant. It didn't numb us but still didn't allow us to think about anything else other than the virus itself. It didn't wipe all of us at once, rather took us slowly one after the other. It didn't give all of the pain together for us to forget in a few days. It made us feel the loss of every person - neighbors, family, or friends - for us to realize its presence even after it's gone. The memory of which would not be gone in hours, days, or months and not even years. It was not catastrophic in a literal-physical sense yet impacted more than any other catastrophe in the last 100 years or so or even more. Was it *The End?* Who knows!

If you think of it, there was nothing extraordinary about this virus yet there was nothing ordinary as well. To say, it was just a flu but it cost us our lives. It didn't touch anything other than humans and kept everything humans created untouched but only rendered them useless. It also remained a mystery like other catastrophes on earth. It also left a looming question over our heads - *Why did this happen?*

The only thing this virus wasn't was it didn't match our anticipation of the end. The only thing this virus didn't harm was nature.

The End came silently, drawing upon us with more force with each passing day. It didn't attack us in complete surprise. It gave each one of us enough time to see, observe and understand what was happening and what could be done to protect ourselves. If we still didn't pick up hints, that was our problem.

The whole world survived on hope. The hope for things to get back to normal.

Chapter19:
Unlock - Business as usual

Will we ever get back to normal? 7.6 billion people on the earth had the same question. No one knew the answer. After months and months of being under strict lockdown and confined to our homes, we all waited for the lockdown to get over and humans to be allowed to roam and wander freely. Just like before in the pre-pandemic times.

The lockdown had caused a huge blow to the economy of countries of the world. Millions went jobless and homeless. Many had to face salary cuts and many were given pink slips. Industries were shut, companies went bankrupt. In the unorganized sector, local shopkeepers and local vendors suffered huge losses to their business. The worst came for the street hawkers, costermongers, and door-to-door sellers. People suffered a loss of income and their life savings. Many on the streets and homeless starved to death. There was the loss of lives and livelihood, everywhere. The world had been cursed with the pandemic. The lockdown just made matters worse.

We all wanted, wished, and waited to rush back to our "usual" as soon as we could. I remember every morning when I would get up, the first thing I would do was to go to the kitchen balcony and touch the tree in the common compound. And then look outside on the road to see if anyone was out there. I used to pick that as my signal if things were back to normal yet or not. We needed proof to feel that we were alive.

Lives were absolutely important but with each passing day, livelihoods seemed even more important, if humans had to survive. It was during this period I realized that livelihoods were quintessential. They gave humans the hope to live. They kept humans going. There was an important lesson for all of us: Chalti ka naam zindagi. But the pandemic didn't allow us that freedom. It was not an option we could exercise. It was taking that zindagi away from us. Maybe because we took that zindagi for granted.

But being under lockdown was also no longer an option. Staying indoors was not a long-term solution or sustainable way of fighting the virus. We all wanted to breathe again freely. We all wanted to live again. Everybody waited for the cases to go down and things to get better. The governments were closely monitoring the situation so that they could give the orders to re-open and start operating as soon as possible. The propellers of the economy had to get started for countries to thrive and survive.

After three months of strict lockdown and complete human inactivity, the cases finally started seeing a dip. Still, by then a total of 6.6 million people all over the world had been infected by the coronavirus and 0.4 million people had lost their lives. In India, we had a total of 2lakh confirmed cases and lost 5,626 people in the battle with coronavirus. Unlike the US and Europe, which had suffered badly at the hands of the coronavirus, India was not severely impacted during the first wave of the pandemic. We had a narrow escape.

Considering the situation, the government issued orders for the phase-wise reopening of the villages, towns, cities, and metros. The demarcation of red, orange, and green zones from the lockdown months continued into the unlock phase. Depending upon the spread of the virus and infection hotspots, red zones were further split into containment and buffer zones, where the unlock proceedings were slower as compared to other districts and zones. Social distancing, wearing a mask, sanitizing the hands - all the corona times protocols - continued to remain in our arsenal for protection against the virus. Humaare suraksha kavach.

As they said during those times, "Unlock ki prakriya ab shuru ho gayi thi." The cars were back on the roads. The shops started opening again. Some shops were open with shutters half-open and half-closed. Liquor shops were full of queues that extended kilometers. The malls were fully prepared with sanitizing tunnels to spray sanitizer on incoming visitors. Public transport started operating at fifty percent capacity. People booked cars on the car rental portals for long drives to places like Nandi hills, Raasta cafe, etc. We booked a car as well and did a city trip. The city seemed silent and quiet where you could still hear the rustle of the leaves in Bangalore that had grown green-er during the lockdown. The city seemed to be recovering from a storm that had just passed by. There was no hour-long waiting at the signal like before. Traffic was back but not at full throttle yet. We enjoyed the unusualness of Bangalore traffic.

Street hawkers - not all of them - were back selling their products - mostly old stock - in hushed tones. As if the coronavirus might sense their presence if they shouted loud. The leaves outside my building hustled and lined sideways making way for the cars. I could hear the exhaust fans roaring in the office behind our building. The construction work in the adjacent plot picked up pace as well. Residents started moving in and out of the building. Some went to markets to shop and some were off to their offices.

Not all the offices opened at once. There were a handful of them who had started calling people back to offices. They had roosters built for different teams. They also arranged for cab services to minimize the risk of traveling in an unknown car or vehicle. Salespeople were asked to go out in the field and start selling. Luckily for the three of us, our companies continued to work from home.

However, we took a trip to nearby cafes once in one of those evenings. Cafes had turned smarter between pre-pandemic and post-lockdown periods. They now had a high-speed Wi-Fi connection installed in most of their facilities. They established DND (Do Not Disturb) zones for folks who wanted to come and work from there. Work from the cafe, it seemed! It meant good returns for the lost revenue during the lockdown phase. A meaningful business proposition, I thought! The cafes aka the new workstations followed all the standard safety protocols. Social distancing was followed in their seating arrangement. The staff regularly sanitized the used spaces and seatings. There were air sprayers that purified the air. Everybody who walked in was asked to wear a mask. That was mandatory. "This is going to be our new normal?" I asked myself in dejection.

For now, only cafes and dine-outs were allowed to open for limited timings. Most of the cafes preferred allowing take-aways rather than a dine-in experience. Each cafe owner couldn't have an elaborate setup adhering to the safety standards. PVRs were allowed to open that too at fifty percent capacity but during the later phases of unlocking procedures. Night curfews continued throughout. Starting from 9 PM to 5 AM to eventually being relaxed to 10 PM to 5 AM, the practice continued for a long time. With all the uncertainties and circumstantial changes of guidelines, the businesses found it tough to adhere to the safety protocols, make amendments and keep running a business successfully.

Will the business ever be back to usual? It was tough to say.

Public gatherings were never allowed. They were not a part of the plan quite late in the Unlock series. There were no outdoor events - commercial or personal. Any form of public gathering or congregating in large numbers was strictly prohibited and a punishable offense. As the unlock progressed, religious, entertainment, political, sports, academic functions, and gatherings of up to 100 people were allowed. Weddings with a gathering of 50 people and funeral/last rites with 20 people were allowed. We were surely living through strange times. We could neither celebrate nor could mourn. The allowance only started to relax towards the end of

2020. The onset of the pandemic had canceled our bachelors and the aggravation of it delayed the wedding. We were just happy at the idea of the wedding taking place that year and the fact that more relaxation came our way as the unlocking progressed.

Eventually intrastate and interstate travel was allowed. This caused mayhem in the beginning with more and more people traveling back to their hometowns or places of establishment with people gathering at the bus stands or railway stations. But it brought much-needed relief as well, as people headed back to their safe-havens. Sigh! Slowly-slowly recreational activities were allowed as well, which included swimming pools, gymnasiums, theatres, entertainment parks, bars, auditoriums, and assembly halls. Limited international travel was permitted with stringent protocols for travelers both at the departing and the arriving destination. Unlocking came with many T&Cs.

I think the student community made the most of it as educational institutions remained shut for most of the time. The schools were advised to only conduct classes online. Students ate, slept, yawned, gossiped, pranked, and did everything during those online classes except studying. Some of them just went online - keeping themselves on mute - only to fall asleep for the entire session. Students were the only cohort of people who were truly back to their "business as usual". The rest of us - were just dragging through.

To say, with unlock, everything was then back to business as usual! Was it?

Was everything back to normal? Not yet! It was not normal-normal like before. There was a sense of fear in each movement I witnessed around me. People moved slowly, so did the cars. People talked slowly, so did the horns. Everyone indulged in very precise and brief outings. Cautious. Alert. Afraid. Alarmed. People even breathed as if gripped in a constant state of frenzy. We were not carefree as before. Maybe we were never supposed to be as carefree as we were. The entire movement seemed like a clandestine motion. As if playing hide and seek with someone. That someone being the invisible virus. When I looked at people, it seemed like someone wanting to move yet afraid of being caught in a trap. Like someone caged wanting to fly free. The fear of the virus was for real. And it persisted.

I am not sure if we were really back or not but Kalavati didi was back and for real. That was a moment of glory and extreme happiness. To see another fellow human was a treat to the soul. Our eyes gleamed with joy. After months, we had those sumptuous aloo paranthas. We had a happy stomach because of the paranthas and happy eyes because we saw and met another human being after a long time.

It breathed freshness into our lives for that moment and a few remaining days we were going to be there. She was equally happy to be back. She narrated her struggles and hardships during the lockdown to us. All of us had a heartfelt conversation with each other just as if close friends had met after a long time. She curtailed her work to only three homes in the same building thus creating a bio bubble for herself. She would go to and fro from her home to our building alone. We also restricted our movement outside to the most we could. Especially now that we had decided to travel back to our hometown. We continued to order grocery and other stuff online. We only moved downstairs to the porch or upstairs to the terrace for those evening walks.

Counting days and hours to be united with our families soon!

Chapter20: Ghar Waapsi

It had been six months since we had gone home. This was the longest we had been away from home in the last few years. The last time it happened was fourteen years ago because of my college exams followed by an internship stint. But I didn't feel that bad and was not caged at all. Nostalgic, maybe but then the thought that I would reunite with my family as soon as the internship gets over made me feel relaxed. This time, it was different. We were caged for months. We were not here by choice but because we were forced. We didn't even have any clue when we would be able to fly. There was no timeline to foresee. It all seemed blurry. "*The sense of freedom is bigger than the freedom itself*", *I thought.*

While the unlocking was in progress, we were waiting for the restrictions on the incoming travelers to stay in the established quarantine facilities to relax in our hometown - Jammu.

We read daily about the poor infrastructure, makeshift complexes, shared toilets, unhygienic conditions prevailing at these government-established quarantine centers. The resources were to be shared by all those quarantined. We read about the casualties happening at these quarantine centers. The RT PCR test reports came in two days and at times even later after the day of the arrival. Till the reports came there was complete uncertainty about the number of travelers who were positive and who we were going to share the quarantine facilities with. And irrespective, travelers were supposed to be in those quarantine centers for seven days or two weeks, depending upon directives by the government officials of the respective States and UTs.

Although, there were hotels and paid facilities as well for those incoming travelers to stay during the quarantine period. The bigger the hole in your pocket, the better the facilities you got in return. But we read about the mismanagement, mixing of the reports, and safety protocols not being adequately followed. All of this only pushed our decision to book our flight tickets because none of us wanted to be caught in that trap.

Traveling was not easy either. Each traveler was supposed to carry a negative RT PCR test report not older than 72 hours. In certain states, that restriction was even more stringent being 48 hours. This demanded so much coordination on behalf of a traveler. We needed to synchronize our timing of the covid tests, departure time of the flight, arrival schedule of both the flight and the test reports. It was a must to have a test report in hand when you landed at the airport of the arrival destination. That too, negative.

We finally got to planning our itinerary. We booked our flight tickets three weeks in advance. Before booking the flight tickets, we called the hospital to check and confirm the availability of the covid tests possibility and the time it would take to get the reports.

Reaching the hospital was another task on its own. We booked the cab. The cabs were no longer the same. There were plastic sheets used to isolate all the four passengers in the cab. There was a box of face masks and a bottle of hand sanitizer placed in the cab. All of us wore hand gloves, face masks, and face shields and took the cab to the hospital. We got ourselves registered and queued up for the test. Finally, our turn came. The swab was painful. It went too inside the nostril and shoved too much down the throat. The doctor snapped the swab into the test tube of a special red-colored solution. And put the test tube into something that looked like an icebox. We coughed a little and our eyes welled with tears. But thankfully, it didn't take us more than two-three hours to reach the hospital, get our tests done and reach back.

In a few minutes, we had received the message of us being registered for the COVID RT PCR test. Well, something worked well during all the crises. Sometimes, a timely message is enough to assure you that all is well. We got the test done four days before our date of flying. We had therefore passed the first step in our journey of reaching home.

The reports came, a day before we were flying. Hurray! We all were negative. It seemed a bit obvious though considering we had not stepped outside for the last three months. The only time we had stepped out was to get ourselves tested for COVID. But we were glad that the reports were just in time - valid to be accepted at the arriving destination.

We had never been so excited to travel back home.

Our preparations began the very day we booked our flight tickets. All three of us had made up our minds to travel back home, come what may. Except that neither of us should be tested positive in which case we would reconsider our decision. Luckily we didn't have to go through that litmus test.

Instead, we indulged ourselves completely in packing the stuff. The commotion in our heads was unexplainable. How long are we going to be at home? What kind of clothes should we carry home? A few, some or all which would mean too much luggage? But what do you mean by 'kind of clothes' when you have been living in Bangalore for the last five years. There is only one kind of clothes that can be worn throughout the year. But Jammu needed five different kinds of attire for all five different seasons. What if our companies called us back? Should we empty our house or keep the possession till we had more clarity? All these questions were not easy to answer at once. They created more confusion in the already stirred up times. So we decided to take it further step by step.

We made up our mind to keep possession of the house, contrary to what many of our friends, and cousins decided. We started cleaning the entire house and covering the unused utensils, equipment, and furniture one after the other in a phased manner as we approached our day of departure. At the same time, we started packing our clothes as well. We picked the ones first which could be worn throughout different seasons for the next two to three months. Loungewear, jogger pants, t-shirts, full-sleeved shirts, sweatshirts, socks, inner-wear. Irrespective of the season and weather, all of this could be put to some use. Then we picked up a bunch of warmer clothes we had like a blazer, a few jackets, and warm sweatshirts, and those counted one or two sweaters. Now that we have been in Bangalore for the last five years, we didn't have much winter clothing. Didn't we know then that we would be in our homes much more than we could ever anticipate? Our stay in homes would be compensation for all the time we had lost being away from our homes all those years.

Well, we packed clothes for the current weather, imminent season, and winters if we were to be there for so long. The winters in Jammu could be harsh especially if one was not accustomed to them.

It was not until we started packing a few souvenirs that we felt something. After all the packing was done, we packed a few things that were close to our hearts. My sister picked up her favorite pictures hanging on the wall, a hanging that said *Om Mani Padme Hum*, her dream catcher with snowhite and sky-colored tassels. My wife picked her favorite soft toy called David Jones, her only pair of artificial earrings, her favorite wallet which she seldom used but often adored. And I picked up my favorite wooden calendar, an idol of Lord Ganesha, and two notebooks full of poetry. I handed over the bamboo that I nurtured with so much care and attention to our neighbor. All of us suddenly felt a void inside us. The house looked a little too empty, and our voices echoed a little too much. Were we leaving

Bangalore forever? Was it the end of the chapter called Bangalore in the book of our lives?

It was a bag of mixed feelings. While we were happy that we would be home soon, there was as if something - a potpourri of bitter-sweet memories - we were leaving behind. We would miss our *Mani's Dum Biryani*, cafe outings; breakfast buffet to pub crawls; unlimited PVR sessions to binge-watching at home; mid-week outings to late night cravings, our house parties to lazy Sundays, *Shubh's pani puri* to *Pappu Chaiwala ki chai. The Forum Mall* and the Bangalore rains. Our routine and our hardships. Our struggles of managing home and work at the same time. We were going to miss all of it. But God had been so kind to all three of us that he gave us a chance to live together, once in a lifetime opportunity. Bangalore was going to be a fond memory etched in our hearts forever.

But for now, it was time to depart. It was time for *Ghar Waapsi.* The day to fly arrived.

We had pre-booked our cabs. They came with all the safety measures. The luggage was too much so we had to book two cabs for three people. We wore face masks, face shields, and hand gloves. We also carried with ourselves the body cover - like a raincoat. We had planned to wear it throughout our journey from Bangalore-Delhi-Jammu and removed it before we walked out of the Jammu airport. There was a constant fear to not be the carrier and end up infecting our parents.

We reached the Bangalore airport and it never ceased to amaze me. There were zero human touches at the airport. From the security check at the main entrance to frisking, checking the body temperature and identification cards, from putting the luggage on the conveyor belts to the security check at the gates, it was all contactless. The entire process was so well-timed that we didn't have to stay much at the airport. Though we hurried our way in between to grab our favorite dosa and idli at the *Tiffin Centre* it was shut because of the pandemic. All we could get was button idlis that too in a walk-away order. We didn't want it. I loved that serving of the food in those heavy steel plates and tea that was served in copper-plated cups but none of it was available. "*The world was never going to be the same*", I told myself.

We reached the departing gates. The crew handed over the PPE kits to the passenger seated in the middle of the row. It was me. I wore it on. We showed our boarding passes. As we walked through the gate, all of us looked back for one last time bidding adieu to *Namma Bengaluru.*

After three tiring weeks, we finally got to rest. Both of them slept as the flight took off. I thought about the 10 million migrant workforces that returned to their homes during the pandemic times and lockdown. Were we counted as a part of those 10 million migrant workforces that decided to go back to their homes? Did we also sum up to the 80 million migrant workforces in India?

The daily wagers, laborers, construction workers, plumbers or masons or electricians, contractual or permanent employees, software engineers, or corporate honchos, IT teams or marketers, poets or authors, actors and dancers, and all kinds of artists - each one of them found their way back home. They all went back to their roots where they started their journey from. They all onboarded for *Ghar Waapsi.*

Was their *Ghar Waapsi* equally strenuous? Much more - strenuous, exhausting, painful, full of misery, and in some cases costing a life. Going back home was never a part of the plan. Getting back to homes, which we had left in pursuit of a brighter future, was never going to be easy.

It is often said, "Home is where the heart is". In modern times, this was twisted too, "Home is where the wifi connects." All of this is in good spirits. But for me,

"Home is where the comfort is. Home is where we feel safe and secure. Home is where worldly worries vanish. Home is where we feel stronger. Home is where we have lesser things to bother us. Home is where we sort our lives. Home is where sorrows are halved and joys are doubled. Home is where the feeling of pain is reduced. Home is where the

approaching end doesn't deter you. Home is where the possibility of The End seems weak. Home is where the courage to fight all the battles is more. Home is us. Home is family."

".....Welcome to Jammu Airport. It is a defense airport and so clicking pictures is strictly prohibited....." These lines woke me up from my partial slumber. 10 hours of the journey - that included changing planes at Delhi airport - finally came to an end. *Ghar Waapsi* was surely a mission. A mission that we had well accomplished. A mission that millions of others struggled to achieve.

We got off the airplane and queued up for the rapid test. With one report in our hands, luggage waiting on the belt and the queue that just got bigger and bigger with time, and no one to guide the way to the incoming passengers, it was a complete ruckus. No safety protocols being followed, no social distancing, the masks were down on the chin, the face shields flew off, PPE Kits coming out of the bins - a perfect recipe for disaster during pandemic times. Just noise, no system.

"Welcome to Jammu ", I said out loud and everyone around laughed it off because that was the Jammu they all loved so much. That was the Jammu, they had all come back to.

We had asked one of our uncles to arrange for a cab (yes there were no cab apps functional in Jammu) so that our parents didn't have to come to the airport for pick up. The cab was waiting for us outside the airport near the petrol pump.

We were waiting eagerly to reunite with our family and so were they.

Chapter21: Of Families

Only the airport was crowded. The *Jammu city* looked abandoned. The roads were empty. The vendor carts lay stranded on the side of the roads. Jammu's *Chaupati* was unattended. My favorite *ganne ke ras wala*, who I used to see on my way home, was missing from the scene. A few cars that were on the roads didn't abide by the traffic signal. The city looked greener than usual. The yellow-orange-red barricades stood there strong in the middle of the junctions.

We all loved crowded cities and empty airports. Isn't it? But the pandemic came and reversed everything.

Traversing through the city, we finally entered our lane. Our tired bodies had hearts full of energy and joy waiting for the car to park in front of the gate. There, we were! The car stopped. We all sighed a breath of relief inside our masks. We got down from the cab and stretched our limbs after a 10 hour long journey and three weeks of strenuous preparations for homecoming!

Mom and Dad were already standing at the gate waiting for us. They had a wide grin on seeing us and their eyes beamed with happiness behind the masks. All of us caged in our travel zombie bodies looked at them with all the longing and smiled wider with our eyes shining bright. No hugging, no touching of feet - all we had were smiles to exchange. We got our tons of luggage down from the cab and got inside our home. Home is where you could breathe freely.

We took shower. The lunch was ready. Rajma-Chawal with *Shashha* (mango chutney), *paneer ki sabzi*, and *boondi raita*. The food was yum. Maa had also prepared *phirni. Maa ke haathon mein jaadu hai.* There is magic in mom's hands. She cooks delicious food. Food, whose remnant taste we had savored for months. Food, our heart was yearning for. Food which we missed the most, we always miss the most. Food meant nostalgia when we were away from home. But then we were back. So food meant celebration. This reminds me of one of the famous quotes, "A *family that eats together, stays together.*"

We didn't have a heart full of conversation with our parents yet. They would keep all our food, and consumables, and things of need on the table kept outside the room. We avoided any physical proximity with our parents. We isolated ourselves for two days. We closely observed ourselves for any symptoms. But all three of us seemed fit and fine.

Maybe we should have isolated ourselves for more days but we didn't. We had just tested negative a few days earlier and our rapid tests at the Jammu airport on arrival were negative as well. Plus it was *Raksha Bandhan* in two days. We could not miss that fun. This was one festival which we mostly missed. The one we mostly celebrated away from home. Mostly because a longer holiday awaited Diwali, always. But this time we were home so we didn't want to miss the festival.

Face masks, pocket sanitizers, sanitizer in the car, a box of face masks in the car, face shields, This was the new world, thanks to the pandemic. We took all safety measures, and protection for everyone's safety and our safety as well. It was time to catch up with cousins and extended family.

There is this immense comfort in vibing with our tribe. It never felt to have lost connection with them irrespective of the number of years after we met. And why would one feel so! We shared cultures, values, ethos, food, pranks, countless memories from childhood and the gone times. There was a time when none of us imagined a world without each other. But then we grew up, taking our ways to discover and experience life.

Today we were back with all those learnings and experiences celebrating *Raksha Bandhan* together after ages. There was no end to the conversation. Everyone discussed and talked about their professional lives, their nature of jobs, friend circle before diving into more private and intimate topics. And even before that, everybody had so much to share about the lockdown diaries and how they survived those days. Interestingly, survival seemed to be a concern for each one of us present there.

"*The pandemic was here to teach everyone a lesson*", I told myself.

The festival was over but the celebration of reuniting was not. The families took turns to host all others. There were snacks, tea - served to taste, meals followed by desserts. In Jammu, there are no parties, there are jamborees. There were laughter riots. Jokes from the past dugout. In between, we played *Antakshari* and sang in the coarse-st of voices. But everything seemed melodious. The elders always wanted all the children to be in front of them.

Was it insecurity? Was it *bebasaai* that children are not gone too soon even before the parents realize they were here. After getting back home I realized one thing, that our parents missed us more than they expressed. They missed us more than we missed them.

Coming home was a strange feeling this time. In the last few years, 14 years to be precise, every time we were home, it was for a holiday. This time we had to live our routines while being at home. The office continued. The meetings continued. The office banter continued. There was work and more of it than usual times. Video calls or just calls, there was a plethora of activities for us to do. Amidst all this, there was a home, and we were back to being a family. Home is where discipline and fun can coexist.

Did you also believe that you will relive the home, the family, and the city of the past? Did you also think that when you will be back home, everything would just be the same as you had left years ago? I did. I was wrong.

There was nothing the same. Things change, people change, cities change. Everything changes with time. I changed, my perspective changed, and so did everything else in all those years as well.

The city was the same, the streets had changed. The names of the stops and *chowks* remained the same, but the vendors putting up the stalls had been replaced. The shops remained the same, the shop owners changed. The restaurants remained there, the chefs had gone. The hangout spots remained but there was no action there. The *addas* were there but no chai stall was to be found. A few streets I could not recognize anymore. A few areas I had never been to before. There were routes, where *No Entry* board was put up and routes that were now one-way alone. More houses had mushroomed in localities but people didn't know each other. Neighbors didn't visit each other anymore. Some areas and grounds were bulldozed and societies had sprung up. There were famous eateries that today's kids didn't know. There were new attraction points that we - kids of yesterday - were not acquainted with. The city was not the same anymore. It swang between the vagaries of the past and fancies of the future in an attempt to be a modern metro-like city. So, was Jammu the same? Was this the Jammu we had come back to? Was it the same with other towns as well?

Didn't we love our towns because of the slow pace they maintained, more space to breathe, less time to commute, more people to talk to, more people we knew? Didn't we enjoy the camaraderie with shops and shopkeepers that we treated like our own, staff in hospitals and restaurants we knew personally? Wasn't it this sense of belonging, the sense of knowing that made our towns our hometowns?

All these years our parents had not remained the same anymore. I felt a similar lack of - a sense of belonging, a sense of knowing when it came to our parents as well. My hometown and my parents were no different. They had changed too. Living with parents was not the same as it was when we were young and when they were young too. Our parents had grown old - visibly. Physically even more so. I realized that their bodies had wretched beyond repair. Life had never been too kind to them. They belonged to the times where there were too many responsibilities that were thrust upon them when they were our age. They didn't do that to us. They let us make our own decisions and live our lives the way we wanted to. They bore all the burden that they could and they were still doing so.

Living with parents after all these years made me discover my parents yet once again. The version of my parents which I would have never witnessed if not for the pandemic. I saw their erratic sleeping patterns. They popped medicines as children popped candies. There was a schedule that they religiously followed to pop those pills. "When did all this medication start?", I wondered. I discovered their new hobbies which I never knew existed in their universe. They twitched and played with mobiles and tried to make the best out of those smart devices. Over the years, out of love for their children and the desire to stay connected with them, our parents became tech-savvy. *Google, Facebook, Youtube,* and *Whatsapp* were their newfound friends. Loneliness engulfed them all the time no matter how busy they became or pretended to be. I listened to their words and sensed their worries. I gauged those thoughts that they never expressed or said but which brewed inside them continuously. Home is where sweet lies and bitter truths make lives better and comfortable.

By this time I had started doubting if the pandemic happened for good or bad?

That lawn at home was a major missing for all those years I was away from home. So, I got up early to water the lawn and the plants. It had taken a lot of patience, persistence, and discipline to nurture those 200+ species of plants. Maa had taken care of them as she took care of us, always. We shared our time from bed tea to all the meals. We talked about almost everything under the sun. They say each family has a vibe. What is yours? Ours was philosophical. All of us tried to find meanings behind each act - be it the act of god or any fellow human. This always helped us to stay unbiased towards others and stay unperturbed by the acts of others. This one thing didn't change about any one of us all those years we were away from each other. It was a daily ritual to don that spiritual-philosophical hat once in a while and cleanse the system. We synchronized our timings so that all of us could be available for all the meals together. Remember, A *family that eats together stays together*. We lived that quote all the while we were with the family in

Jammu. We took breaks in between work. We had tea or fruits during the breaks spruced with tons of gossip we missed having all those years. At times, all of us walked or just sat outside in the verandah post our evening tea. Doing nothing, plainly ogling at the sky cutting through the roofs of the neighborhood. Or scroll through the mobile and sharing that joke with everyone that made us laugh. We watched *Ramayana* and *Sri Krishna* on DD National once our work was over later in the evening with everyone. We discussed and opined about incidents from these great scriptures and tried to learn the best we could. We talked about things that could be implemented in today's world and how. The pandemic brought back memories of the past. Walks. Ramayana. Politics. Gossip. And Philosophy. And all kinds of banter. We were back to our homes and families.

These small little acts of togetherness - watching television, listening to music, sharing ideas and thoughts and opinions, eating food, watching each other's discomfort, observing likes and dislikes, sharing each other's happiness, living each other's routines - all these brought us closer as a family, once again.

We were still in the phase of unlocking. The world had not completely opened up yet. But being with family, we didn't realize if things were not normal outside. With family, the days didn't seem long and never-ending. We didn't feel caged at all. With family, we were not sullen anymore; rather we looked forward to each day and lived it to the fullest. Home is where you could feel normal in the most abnormal of situations. Families gave us the courage to feel that way.

Meanwhile, the parties were not over yet. The seriality continued. We kept hosting house lunches and dinners. There were new dishes, new desserts. At times, we played housie indulging everyone. At times we played cards. There were board games too. There were more jokes, more laughter. It took a while for everyone to gel well, again with each other. But we were getting there. Eventually, we were opening up about our relationships, flings, and hookups, and all that conspired in all those years. Not all could be talked about with elders around so there were stayovers at one place or another where only youngsters were invited. The booze was not easy, the smoke was not an option. Simple soda somber nights with more fun than ever. Home is where booze is not needed to feel high. Families made us feel that way.

The days just passed by with families around. We all got busy with the wedding preparations. The wedding was scheduled for August and finally happened in November. The wedding of the brother whose bachelor got canceled because of the pandemic. Back in my hometown with families, there was never a dearth of action. One thing or the other keeps you occupied always. Home is where you could keep busy all the time and still not feel tired. Families made us feel that way.

The pandemic revealed altogether a new world to all of us. The pandemic showed us those shades of our hometown and parents that we would have never experienced otherwise. The pandemic pushed us out of our comfort zones. The pandemic showed us that there was a life that existed beyond the taps of the cells and screens. The life that was much more real and worth living. The pandemic brought families together which otherwise would have remained lost somewhere in the business of day-to-day lives. The pandemic gave all of us a chance to express our love towards our families again which otherwise would have remained hidden in the subdued voices over the phone or hushed-hushed distracted calls that we made out of our so-called "busy lives". The pandemic made us open our hearts towards each other which otherwise would have remained sealed forever. Home is where you could find goodness even in the worst that happens to us. Like we found the silver lining in the pandemic. Families teach us that.

"But all these years when we were away from our families, it was only friends who made us feel that way and filled in for our families." I thought.

Chapter22:
Yaar Anmulle

You cannot have a serious moment with your friends. Can you? There is always this underlying joke that cracks up everyone in the room every time there is a serious discussion going on. But this reminds me, *'Life is not to be taken too seriously*, always'. These friends, we needed them more than ever during those cruel times.

The pandemic took a toll on everyone. It eventually started getting on everyone's nerves. Some who were away from home grew nostalgic and depressed. They had nothing to look forward to. Wake up, do daily chores, work from home, daily chores, binge watch, sleep or no sleep and repeat. Some who were with families felt claustrophobic. Some missed their freedom. Some grew tired of their liberties. Some grew sick and badly. Some were hospitalized. Some felt traumatized. Some had no shelter to keep, some went hungry to sleep. Some had more than usual work and some had no work at all. Those who were out working prayed for their lives, those who were stuck indoors wished to go out and get a life. The pandemic affected each one of us in its unique ways. It broke us - financially, physically, and mentally. Nobody was spared.

During those times, I missed my friends. I am sure we all did. With friends, you could share random stuff, how you felt, how you made others feel, what went wrong, what possibly could have gone wrong, your fears, your anticipations, all things sane and insane, all those random thoughts that kept you awake in the middle of the night and all those dreams big or small that you always wanted to chase. All this sharing was lost in the garb of the pandemic.

While the pandemic brought families together, it drifted friends apart. Years back when we moved out of our homes to chase our small little dreams, we found companions for life. Or we thought so. We made friends - *Bengali, Bihari, Odia, Punjabi, Marathi, Tamilian, Telugu, Kannadiga, Konkani, Malyali* - from all over India and the rest of the world too. Some of us continued to work in the same cities and some of us hustled in between various cities all these years. But we continued catching up. At pubs, bars, and cafes. At a common friend's place or for a stayover at each other's place once a while or whenever we visited our friends' cities. The connection stayed. As years passed by the network shrunk but the news kept coming in. That large group of friends was now a sub-sub group of that group. A few were friends with some and others were friends with the other half of the group. And that is how we survived friendships all those years. And then the pandemic happened.

All of us rushed back to our hometowns only to find that there were no friends and friendships left anymore there. The school friends had made their network and sub-sub group by now and we had our own. The hometown echoed a weird emptiness, only friends could fill in for. The parties were missing. Those untimely and unwise jokes were missing. That banter and sarcasm were missing. Those guitar and keyboard *ustaads* were missing. That loud singing of the songs was missing. That profanity after each sentence was missing. Those sudden long *gedis* were missing. That *chai-sutta gupshup* was missing. Those late-night pick-ups and drops were missing. Those unplanned trips were missing. That loudness and simplicity of life were missing. I wonder how friends made life look easier. With them, we somehow saw the brighter side of life, always.

In the last few years, however, things didn't remain the same. Some of us got married. Some of us even had kids. And the rest of us got too busy to pursue our careers. There was nothing wrong with moving ahead in life. But in doing so, in the race called life, we kept getting drifted away from our friends. The regular catching up reduced to phone calls which further got reduced to only pings. Well, I have always hated *Whatsapp* for the same reason. It creates an illusion that we are connected when in reality we are not. We just become numbers. The numbers that we slowly forgot to dial. It happened to me. It must have happened to you. It happened to all of us.

Today, when I think of those times spent with friends, it all seems like a long-forgotten story. It is tough to believe if that happened for real. Friends and friendships meant life to us. We could go miles for a friend.

From the playground to sharing lunch boxes, from copying homework to completing practical files together, from murmuring viva answers from behind to helping with answers during the exams - the school friendships were the most innocent and selfless. From bunking classes together to help us meet our crushes, from giving proxy for a friend to help them handle their first drink, from living the crazy hostel life to all-nighters, from standing shoulder to shoulder over a fight to abusing for the fucktard things we did - the college friends made teenage seem less complex. From those hours long counseling sessions to help us overcome our breakups to advising tips and tricks for the corporate world, from discussing dreams and passions to making us our favorite cocktail, from discussing the next big move to joining in for the next silly action - friends helped overcome the denial of adulting.

In each phase of our life, friends were inextricably connected to our lives. Our life and their life was intertwined in uncountable and unimaginable ways. But then we finally grew up! The race of life became aggressive. The competition crept in. Envy, ego, comparison - they became part of our perspectives. Opinions became points of view. *Bakchodi* became socially awkward. Loudness was no more appropriate. Jokes turned into personal remarks. And eventually, friends turned into socially amicable fellow humans. The importance of friends and friendships changed in our lives. We had friends but only those that suited our interests. *"But jo itni naaptol ke ki jaaye wo dosti hi kya!"*

With the pandemic, we missed our friends even more. We needed someone to crack those jokes. We needed someone to cheer us up. We needed someone to lift our spirits and make us feel better about everything that was happening around us. We needed someone to make those times bearable for us. In that way, the pandemic came as a blessing rather than a curse. It made us realize the value of each person, thing, or relationship we took for granted. Friendships were to be cherished forever. And now that we were miles apart from our friends, we missed them even more.

"Could we have all of them together locked inside one room during the pandemic?" I wished. That would have been one heck of a lockdown to remember. But that was only a wish, far from reality.

The reality was painful. The cases were increasing every day and more casualties were being reported. The medical facilities fell short of catering to the crises we had at hand. Everyone avoided traveling as much as they could. Amidst the entire chaos and confusion, I had friends in hindsight and was concerned if all was good at their end. It had been months since I talked to some of them. I had no clue how they were, where they were, and if everything was fine at their home and with their families. Weren't friends supposed to know the whereabouts of their friends? When our families were missing from the scene and we were away from our homes, it was friends who got our back and stood with us through all thick and thin. But today we suffered a long pause in that connection. That pause had to end.

I picked up my phone and called my friends one after the other. They were safe and healthy and so were their families. I was relieved. To that point, I decided to be in touch and stay connected with my friends - pandemic or no pandemic - because, *Yaar Anmulle.*

Chapter23: Tested Positive

It didn't matter if we took all precautions or not. It didn't matter if we wore face masks and face shields. It didn't matter if we sanitized our hands every time we picked up a parcel or came back home from outside. It didn't even matter if we took steam once or twice a day. It didn't matter if we regularly chewed Vitamin C and did Betadine gargles. It didn't matter if we adopted all the *desi totke* and consumed that homemade *kaada* or not. As time went by and the pandemic kept getting its grip harsher on the human race, we realized none of the above mattered. What mattered was how strictly we could control our urge and desire to go outside and roam around wild and free. How honestly we could resist the temptation to travel and turn our vacation mode on. How zealously we could find ways to entertain ourselves and our families while staying indoors.

Because the moment we stepped outside our homes we made ourselves vulnerable to COVID19. It all came down to social distancing and avoiding public gatherings.

Wedding or Death. Mundan or Birthday. Bangle ceremony or Haldi. Muh Dikhai or god Bharaayi. Bachelors or Baby shower. We needed to put a stop to attending all those ceremonies irrespective of how close the relation or family was to us. But we couldn't resist. We gave in to all the temptations. I believe more than the temptation, we gave in to our incessant desire of stepping outside our homes.

We were going through strange times. It was a strange turn of events. When we were living in a free world, we detested all those family gatherings and outings. We thought it to be too boring hanging out with the same set of folks, talking about the same old familial issues, and ranting the same stuff. But now when we were supposed to be locked inside our homes, we found new reasons to hang out with the same "boring" bunch of folks bringing us many breathers and an escape from the cage that we all were dwelling in.

Every time such a contradiction happened, my belief in the pandemic's arrival to question our choices became stronger. And the pandemic was full of such contradictions.

Everyone waited for the relaxation norms to be announced every Sunday of each phase during unlocking. What everyone wanted to know was the number of guests allowed per gathering. To be honest, that announcement was just a relief from the moral and civic guilt. Irrespective of the permissible number, neither the hosts nor the hoteliers cared about the number. They booked back-to-back halls as two unique bookings belonging to the members of the same family. This way the hosts or the organizers could invite almost as many people as they wanted to and hotels could walk away freely without really flouting any rule. And everybody thought it was a win-win situation. Unfortunately not!

It was inviting devils home!

By the time September ended, we had already lost a few folks, who we knew up and close, to COVID. The loss was irreparable. We could hear the cries and feel the pain but could do nothing about it. All we could feel was the covid wave slowly inching closer to us with each passing day and ready to barge into our homes as well. We could not afford to lower our guards then.

Amongst the people we lost, we also lost the uncle who had arranged for our cab for the final leg of our journey to Ghar Waapsi. We could not believe that he was gone too soon. Did he mean to live to play a role in us reaching our homes safely? There are losses that we cannot fathom ever. This was one of them. This tragedy jolted all of us. He had fallen sick miserably in the past but ventured out of all that misery and pain every single time to everyone's surprise. But this time, he just succumbed to fever and loss of appetite. And lo! We lost him forever. In a state of shock, we prayed for his soul and asked for strength for his family. Some of the family members did attend the last rites standing far behind at the boundary walls of the Shamshaan ghat as per the law of the land.

And like that, we lost so many loved ones to the pandemic. The pandemic took so much and so many loved ones away from us. It was strange and extremely painful to be losing loved ones to the invisible virus. No ailment, no mishap, no suffering - just you were caught in the trap of the virus and you were gone. Either you got better and tested negative in fourteen days of time or everyone watched in anticipation (rather anxiety) of you getting better without developing any complications. Everyone dreaded getting admitted to the hospital. That was considered as the sign of Yumdoot's arrival to take us with him. If you walked out fit and healthy, it was an omen that you were here to survive and see more of what pandemic had in store for the human race.

Wasn't it better than just dying? After all, we all wanted to defeat the virus. We all wanted to know what lay ahead of The End. But that was not easy. It was not in our hands. The pandemic came with a dose of pain prescribed for everyone. In what proportions, only time could tell.

They say no pain is severe unless it is infested upon us directly. With each day bringing one bad news or the other - we could just brace ourselves for the worse. The world got up each morning with a fear of what the day would bring to them and a hope that everything will be normal soon. We did too.

But it was too soon to expect things to be normal. We got news of my uncle and his family falling sick and having a high fever. In another two days, we saw them running from hospital to hospital in search of oxygen and a bed. He and his daughter had oxygen levels going below 70. We could do nothing but feel helpless. There were no beds in the hospital. One needed to be tested positive to be admitted into the COVID ward. Unfortunately, my cousin didn't test positive but her oxygen level kept dropping. So she remained in the government hospital without a bed but with oxygen arranged. She spent three days on the iron bench in the hospital. My uncle, though tested positive, was shifted to a private hospital with better facilities and amenities. Their oxygen level was horrifying. My aunt and her other daughter, who tested positive too, were isolated in their home. The pandemic prevented anyone from being with the family during the toughest of times. Everyone had to deal with their misery, pain, and trauma on their own. No help, howsoever desperately one wanted to offer, could be delivered.

It took both of them, my uncle and his daughter, approximately two weeks to get better and get back home from the hospitals. They were tested negative but they did not completely feel alright yet. This incident sent shivers down our spines. In those fourteen days we tried to remain optimistic but all negative thoughts deluged our brains. We had lost all hope of their recovery. But loss is not something we were ready for. No one ever is. And after such a long stay at the hospital, with limited to almost no connection with them, we just prayed and prayed for them to recover fast and soon. We had not seen anyone in the first family falling sick so badly because of the virus. No one at that oxygen level survived. We waited for the miracle to happen. Thankfully, it did.

But miracles didn't happen for everyone. People suffered at the hands of the virus. We were not alone to survive that pain and helplessness. So many families lost their loved ones. So many families would remember covid times as a dark phase in their life that took their loved ones without any reason. They were there the previous night - smiling, breathing, and eating with their families - and just gone like that the next day. It didn't give people a chance to talk to their loved ones for one last time. It didn't allow people to look at the deceased before the last rites were conducted. The pandemic didn't allow people to bid adieu to their families, friends, and relatives. In that sense, the pandemic was too cruel for mankind. And having seen that, we just got lucky. We were lucky that my uncle and his daughter were back home safe and healthy. We knew that they were here to witness what the pandemic brought for the human race in the days and months to come! But my heart never stopped questioning, "What were we - the human race - being punished for?"

For now, we all rejoiced. But these incidents made everyone more cautious about stepping out and flouting any of the safety protocols. Only when someone would have seen somebody so close suffering so badly because of the virus, would they know how traumatic things could be! Every person, no matter how normal they pretended to be, was scared of getting trapped in the chakravyuh of coronavirus. Nobody wanted to be Abhimanyu. Once trapped, gone forever. But that didn't seem an option. Looking around, it seemed everyone was going to be infected once, while the virus was here. A time came, when every non-infected dreaded the day it would be their turn.

And the day came. My entire family was tested positive.

I had a high fever and shivering for a night. Dad and sister had a fever that was gone and slightly sore throats for almost two days. But we took these as signs of changing weather. The weather had suddenly turned cold. Dolo was not effective for more than four hours and my fever kept coming back that night. I was asleep when Mom came to the room telling me that Dad and sister had tested positive. She tried to remain calm and poised behind all the anxiety. They had gone to the nearby dispensary to test themselves when I was asleep. I jumped out of my bed listening to the news. I immediately took Mom and wife to the dispensary to get rapid tests done. We thought it was important to ensure that the non-infected could be isolated from the infected ones. We never thought that all of us would be tested positive. For surety, we got RT PCR tests done as well the very same day. The reports came and we were all positive. It was confirmed.

Mom and wife were asymptomatic mostly. Mom had severe shivers one evening but nothing more than that. The first two days of falling sick were fine. We constantly monitored oxygen levels and there was nothing to worry about. The real battle began when we started our medication after consulting the doctor. We knew the medicines were effective but the repercussions were strong. We felt nauseated and had convulsions in our stomachs. The bodies became weak and wretched. Mom and Dad had severe body pains. The three of us didn't have any major post-covid symptoms but our bodies were really weak. Throughout the time, the brains felt fuzzy, there was this constant desire to lie down and rest. Our bodies became like immovable objects that didn't wish to move even at the strongest urge. This weakness was terrifying. Any single time our oxygen levels dipped below usual, we would start taking deep breaths. It caused extreme anxiety at the same time. The more we slept, the better we felt. But even after just five minutes of movement, we felt terribly weak. Just so that the doctors could predict the severity of the infection and any further remedy, the doctor advised us for CT Scan. The reports were normal and we went home happy.

It was a different emotion hearing about somebody falling sick because of covid yet extremely different thing to live and experience that emotion. Our bodies felt wretched beyond repair. The bones were sore. The muscles pained continuously. There was a loss of sense of taste and smell. The virus impacted our bodies as if it had come to alter the human system. All those days, I kept telling my family that it seems to me as if the virus has been designed to harm the human race in the long term. The consequences of which would be seen in generations born to the covid infected generation. My family thought I was being too harsh on the virus and was weaving a conspiracy theory in my head. But I genuinely believed that to be true. I furthered my argument by telling them that when there was no cure for a disease, how could they prescribe humans any medicine? It was a sham of the highest order. The medicine was an attempt to further make our bodies weak in our natural functioning. I saw the coronavirus as an attempt to wreak havoc on the most intelligent species available on the earth - the homo sapiens. My family thought the virus had a side effect on my thinking and cognitive capabilities. And we all laughed out at my conspiracy theories and more on how passionately I went on to present them to everyone.

But as a matter of fact, the virus had both physical and emotional impacts on humans. It made our bodies weak, and minds fearful.

Our connection with the outside world snapped. The family that was full of social butterflies was stranded and secluded inside the four walls of the house. We remained isolated for almost three weeks. I was right in believing, the sense of freedom is bigger than the freedom itself. We kept a chair near the gate so that our relatives could leave the food there outside on the chair. What could be more painful than our loved ones not being able to communicate to us directly? What could be more heart-wrenching than our inability to cater to our daily needs? We had never felt so helpless. The only silver lining was we all were tested positive so we all could sit and eat food together. That came as a blessing in disguise at that time.

We were thankful to God and glad that we didn't have to suffer as much as others but we all prayed that nobody tests positive anymore. But that prayer was not to be heard anytime soon.

We lost relatives, family members, and friends. We lost people in the neighborhood that we used to see during the morning walks. We lost an adorable uncle who would always cheer for life. We heard stories about children being orphaned. We heard of multiple deaths in a single-family. We heard about young people succumbing to the wrath of covid. We heard of couples leaving for heavenly abodes within a few days' gaps. We heard of people giving away their breaths in hospitals with their bodies not being handed over to families for last rites. COVID didn't see any age, bar, sex. It didn't discriminate. It didn't spare anyone. "But for how long?", the question that the world could not stop asking.

"What were we up to? How long will this pandemic last? What was our role in the larger schema of life? Why the most intelligent species could not decipher the virus and find a cure? What stopped us from winning over the virus? What role did we have to play? Were we supposed to decode a message that was being delivered to us via the virus? Did we miss anything? Were we missing anything that needed our attention? What possibly could be done to prevent the virus from spreading? What could we do to put a stop to the virus? Were we not competent enough? Was it a penance for something wrong we did?" All these questions occupied my mind all the while we were tested positive and forced to remain in bed for most of our days and nights.

Testing positive was a curse we all had to fight together. We all had to find a solution.

Chapter24:
To Seeking our self

All those days when I was sick, I spent most of my time in my room. I used to step out of the room for meals, at times for tea or a stroll inside the house just to see each other and ensure everyone was doing fine. The fear and uncertainty gripped me. None of us had much energy left to talk and be seated on couches for long. I would eat, sit for a while for a change of ambiance and come back to lie down on my bed. I had a discomforting feeling about all that conspired in the last few days and weeks. A weird kind of sadness surrounded me.

After returning to my room, I kept ogling outside the window. A huge eucalyptus tree stood there tall and sturdy. I could see the movement of its branches every time a bird or flock of birds made that branch its host for the evening. The branch delicately managed all of them together swinging up and down. The tree hosted many kinds of birds and kites. Every time the tree hosted new guests, I had a private repartee with all of them. They became my newfound friends while in isolation. Each day was like a lifetime spent. The slow sullen days filled me with remorse, of what, I didn't know. I kept staring at the tree, observing its movement and the guests it kept hosting. When the winds grew stronger, the tree turned those strong winds into a comforting breeze. The tree was not shaken. It didn't shatter. *"The roots held the tree strong"*, I thought. It kept the tree firm yet the tree resonated with the wind as well. It didn't resist. During calm days, the leaves rustled silently now and then. I could not hear the sound of the rustle but I could sense with that slight visible movement of the leaves and the branches. I enjoyed the play of hide and seek between the sun and the tree. I woke up to the tree bathing in the golden hazel sunlight and slept to the silver silhouettes of the leaves adorning the night sky. I lived a little with the tree every day for all those days.

All the while I engaged with the tree, my head was swamped with so many thoughts and questions. *"Why has the pandemic arrived? Why us? Why is it killing people? There are so many species on the earth, why only target the human race? What is the way out of the pandemic? Are we stuck forever? Is this going to be the new normal for times to come? Seriously, stepping out of home will remain such an arduous task for always? Are we just not going back to our usual normal? Will we never be able to go to a party as we did? Will vacation and travel be out of the question for a few more years? Was it the beginning of the end? Was it supposed to happen this way?"* Every day I would think of new questions and then I juggled and hustled in my head to find answers to them.

It is said that when the pain and suffering become too much, too heavy to carry for a soul and our being, it stirs the deep inside of us, withering us with each passing day. It makes us question everything around us, even our existence. The pandemic had a similar effect on all of us. To say, it was just a virus. But it came, it toppled the world order, and it conquered over humans. We could only pretend as if nothing drastic had happened but that would have been a foolish pretense. Neither the virus was ordinary nor its repercussions.

I had disturbing questions hovering in my mind. *"What if I die because of coronavirus? What is the purpose I would have served here on the earth? What for I was born? What would happen to my unfulfilled dreams? Was I born just to die during the pandemic? Why was I working so hard If everything had to finish just like that one day? And why should anyone accumulate all the wealth and material possessions they do during their lifetime? Is all the hustle then worth it? Are we born with a specific purpose to serve on this earth? What would people remember me for? Was it even important for anyone to love and remember me once I was gone?* " Questions like these disturbed me beyond what I could think or imagine. A weird kind of loneliness permeated inside. Was I trying to find meaning out of what was happening around or was it a sheer madness that captivated me during those idle times?

There were days when I tried hard to find positivity in all that had happened. Or at least, I tried to convince myself. I had always wanted to be back in my hometown for longer than usual. The usual was a week or ten days at the most. That was all the time I could get off while working. I always wished to live with my parents again having moved out of home for more than a decade then. I just didn't know that it would take a pandemic to fulfill my wishes. I would smile and cheer up for a while only to find myself in the same rut of thoughts.

The pandemic made our life drudgery. It pushed us behind the four walls of our homes. It slowed down our pace of life. It restricted our movement. It challenged our intelligence. It shattered our belief in ourselves. It made us question every damn thing the humans had built over the last few years. It shook us at both individual and collective levels. It made us feel physically weak and mentally disturbed. The social setup quivered and the economies crumbled. It showed us that all that we had accumulated was useless. It made us question our ways of living, ideals, values, and morals. It left us more doubtful than ever in our lifetime. "*What the heck were we doing all those years?*" I asked myself in exasperation. I wish I could ask everyone in the world.

We were belittled to no more than the prisoners. *The Prisoners of The Pandemic.* We got up, freshened up, ate, worked, ate, watched something over television and our smart devices, and slept. Repeat. That is what all of us were reduced to. But that could not be our motto of living. Right?

It was times like these I wanted to be like that tree outside the window of my room. Nothing could deter and question its existence. It stood there tall and sturdy, much in confidence facing each day as it dawned.

But to be like that tree, it took a lot of courage to withstand all the storms, strength in the roots to hold the tree firm, and realizing of its mighty existence yet staying humble. The tree had it all, it takes to be there. I didn't. We didn't.

When you cannot find answers outside, you start looking inside more vigorously. Therefore we were left with no option other than to find answers to all those mysterious questions by provoking our inner self. And that meant seeking our self to be more sure about our existence and being.

After all the self-doubting and deliberation, I felt that maybe then the pandemic was pushing us all to pause and reflect on our lives. The pandemic wanted us to slow down and be wise about the choices we made for ourselves in the ecosystem. (There is no denying the fact that the pandemic was here to show that humans were a part of the ecosystem and not the ecosystem in its entirety.) The pandemic was here so that we could pause, reflect, look inwards and think deeper about our being, and be able to find our truest selves. Was it that tough?

I think it was. To break the shackles of our facade about ourselves must have been tough.

The pandemic deemed seeking of our self important if we meant survival. If we wished to stay sane during those insane times, we needed to know who we were. If we wished to find our connection with the rest of the ecosystem, we needed to find our purpose in life. If we wanted to survive and exist on this earth, our intelligence needed to benefit the ecosystem as a whole rather than the human race alone. If we wished to win the war against the coronavirus, it was excruciatingly important to be fully aware of ourselves.

The epicenter of all of which lay in *Seeking of ourselves*.

Maybe that was the reason, the pandemic granted us solitude and confinement along with all the ailment and suffering it bestowed upon us. So that we could think deeply and seek ourselves once again. So that we could find the meaning out of our lives that were lost.

The pandemic was the notice period given to us by nature. And the period of confinement was our buyout time to redeem ourselves, only if we realized.

So, I was relieved that all the ramblings of my heart and the weird thoughts and questions that occupied my mind for most of the time of my confinement period were not just aberrations. They were a step in the right direction because all the seeking begins with self-doubt. At times, it is not important to have answers to all the questions at once but it is important to ask the right questions at the right time. And I was just doing that.

In the days to come, I found that I was not alone. There were others too who had similar doubts and uncertainties. There were others as well who were disturbed by similar kinds of thoughts. More people like me were trying to seek themselves. They went on to question the existence and the role of humans in the larger schema of life very much like I did. They questioned the life they lived and what they derived out of it. "*The pandemic had pushed not one but many people into this mode of thinking*", I wondered.

Some businessmen thought that there was a life beyond profits and making money. And no money could be enough to satiate human greed. Some families thought that there were wrongs that they did to their parents which brought a similar fate when their kids grew up and they grew old. Some students spent more time thinking about what they would want to do with their life ahead once the pandemic was over. There were people from the corporate world who thought of work-life balance for real and for good. They thought that there surely existed a world beyond their so-called busy lives. So, each one of us was having a revelation during the pandemic and inched closer to making wiser decisions for ourselves. Maybe these were superficial revelations but the journey of seeking had to start somewhere. And it had begun. The silver lining in the cloud was that something had conspired in the minds of people during the pandemic that led them to thinking and asking all these questions. But there was still a long way to go.

Amidst all the chaos, confusion, and crises, all of us were trying hard to find ourselves in our best possible ways to the best possible extent. The pandemic had triggered that avalanche reaction and cascaded that thought process. The pandemic had dragged us - the humans - to such an extent where there was no way out other than to be more sure about ourselves and that surety was a direct consequence of seeking ourselves.

The pandemic made us break free from our monotony, pushed us out of our comfort zones and out of a life of oblivion that we had become so used to so that we could consciously watch our thoughts, and actions. As a race, we could not afford to fumble anymore and just be a part of the bandwagon. The times demanded us to be more grounded and firm in figuring out our ways of living. We needed to usher insanity in the insane world we were a part of. There was a need for us to have clarity of thoughts which eventually perspired into our actions. Humility and compassion were a must-have if we had to survive the times to come. And all of this could be possible only if we knew ourselves inside-out.

It was pivotal for mankind to know who we truly were. What comprised us and what did we comprise? What was our role in the ecosystem that nurtured us? How were we connected to other beings and the universe? What brought us here on the earth and what legacy would we leave behind? This was not going to be an easy win but there was no other way out to escape the harsh clutches of the pandemic.

The pandemic was here so that we could seek ourselves and seeking of ourselves was important so that we could escape the pandemic. But for that, we needed that seeking to happen at a collective level across the world.

All those days when I was sick and stared at the tree, I wondered how the tree made itself an unquestionable part of the larger existence despite its mighty presence. We humans could not learn to merge with the larger universe in all those years and centuries. We thought of ourselves to be unique and considered ourselves superior to the rest. In that ignorance, the pandemic happened. However, the fact was, *Aham Brahmasmi. I am the finite, I am the infinite.* That was the ultimate truth!

The seeking of self hence was important to attain that level of understanding of our existence. That was our way to leading a happy and peaceful life. It will always be. Because only when one identifies its true self could he or she understand its role in the larger play of things. Only then will we be able to nurture ourselves and think of the larger good. Only then do we begin to merge with the larger ecosystem and the larger ecosystem merges within us.

All those days of being tested positive and having spent in the room, that tree turned out to be my only ray of hope. It inched me closer to seeking myself. It became my companion who helped me sail through my days of confinement and solitude.

Chapter25:

Come 2021, Come Hope!

335 days had passed since the first case of coronavirus was identified in the world on 31 Dec 2019. A total of 65 Mn people had been infected since then till date across the world out of which 9.5 Mn cases were in India alone. Out of all infected, we had lost 1.5 Mn people all over the world to covid and post covid complications. The only positive thing that kept us going was a strong recovery rate. 49.6 Mn people had recovered in the world with a recovery rate of 96% and 98% approximately for the world and India.

India was cheering the 9Mn recovered against 9.5Mn reported cases of coronavirus infected. This was commendable considering other large and advanced nations had found it tough to contain the spread of the virus resulting in utter pandemonium. In India, on the other hand, people were recovering at a much faster and better rate. The medical infrastructure was less stressed. The health condition of the patients was stable. There was a relief to the health and medical staff after a long hiatus of keeping up with the ever-increasing influx of covid infected patients since covid had hit the world. The times ahead seemed promising.

This relief translated into hope. And this hope translated into normalcy-like conditions for everyone around. The ill were recovering and the recovered were feeling better. The homes could be heard of laughter and filled with positivity yet once again. There were more people out there on the top of their terraces or out on the balconies. The morning 5 AM clubs were back in action. The evening walkers were too. There were more people out there on the streets and in the malls, in the shopping arcades and the parks. You could spot *yoga* practitioners with their mats placed at one corner of the parks. The children were out too on their bicycles and in front of ice-cream cycle stalls. The street vendors were back on the streets and their stalls put up again at their designated corner of the roads. The hawkers and door-to-door vendors could be heard. The roadside eating stalls had people queued up again to savor their favorite dishes. The traffic jams were back after months of pause. One could hear the honking of the horns. Except for the public gatherings, schools, and religious institutions, everything was allowed. The world once again felt like ours, accepting us after having rejected the human race for all those months.

Life suddenly was back to normal or at least it seemed to be.

Everybody was getting prepared ahead of the holiday season in India. *Navaratri*, *Karwachauth Diwali*, *Bhai Dooj*, soon to be followed by Christmas and New Year. This period coincided with the wedding season as well. The markets were allowed to open for longer than during the lockdown times and initial phases of unlocking. The shutters went up with the hope of more shoppers thronging the shops. From gift shops to jewelers, from apparel boutiques to retailers, from confectioners to hypermarkets, from local sweet shops to wedding card designers and planners, from hotels to restaurants - everyone - from wholesalers and distributors in big cities to retailers in small cities and townships - saw a surge in the business ahead of the impending festival season. The money started circulating once again in the market. This circulation spruced up the things for one sector after the other. India, which thrives majorly upon the unorganized sector - lit up once again with the recovery of the covid patients. The businesses hoped to see this surge continue in the weeks and months ahead leading to the new year.

There were a few good things that came out as a result of the suffering and the aftermath. Public transport was not overcrowded. The sensible ones wore masks and maintained social distancing when out in public. All that arrived at home - family members, parcels, or grocery - was duly sanitized and cleaned. People took steam religiously. Everybody washed their hands regularly. People switched to healthy eating habits including increased consumption of fruit, homemade food, and reduced consumption of outside food. All these positive changes gave everyone hopes for better times ahead.

Everybody rejoiced. In Shakespeare's words, the sudden turn of events was like hope against the hope to be hopen. Especially after what we had witnessed in the last few months.

After months of pain and suffering, nobody could imagine a world for themselves that would be any closer to normal. After months of being under strict lockdown and restrictive movements, people had forgotten how the world outside looked like. After mourning the loss of their loved ones, people wondered if they would smile again. After being confined to their homes for so long, though people desperately wanted to get out and feel free - they were hardly sure about when those times would come. A sense of fear gripped all of us. All those who had suffered severely at the hand of coronavirus thought twice before stepping out. Everyone who escaped the wrath of the covid and witnessed death so up and close was grateful for the second life they were bestowed with. After those months of hue and cry, how could anyone imagine days full of laughter and celebrations? That seemed like a far-fetched reality to all of us.

During all those days full of misery and confinement, there was only one thing that kept everybody going. And it was *hope.*

It was then I realized that hope is a powerful emotion. It musters the courage inside us every time we feel weak. It picks up the fragmented pieces of ourselves and puts them back together, every time we feel shattered. It guides us through the darkness. When everything is going topsy turvy, hope holds each bit of us through a strand and yet keeps us intact. It fills us with positivity every single time fear strikes us. It helps us deal with tough times with its tender approach. The hope that gathers me also binds all of us together. Hope is powerful. It was hope that gave all of us the courage to fight those tough times, all those months. It was hope that made our survival possible when there was nothing that we looked forward to. It was hope that gave us the belief that better days would be ahead. It was hope that empowered us to push the miseries aside and welcome the good times that were knocking at our door. It was hope that killed my insecurities and doubts and made me confident to march ahead as things started to get better.

With that hope in our hearts, I also stepped outside of our home after having recovered from COVID finally. We took a long drive to the outskirts of the city to break away from the city clutter and noise and feel the fresh air. I played my favorite playlist and drove some twenty kilometers away from the city. We halted there for an hour or so. We opened the windows and after some time stepped out of the car and walked around for a while. It was overwhelming to experience that freedom after months. Freedom that was lost ever since covid had hit the world. Freedom that was truncated when we were tested positive. Thankfully, we had recovered and so had others around us.

There was an unsaid alacrity in the environment now that the winters had arrived and festivals had too. Christmas and New Year were just around the corner. 2020 was coming to an end. I wondered if we could baptize 2020 as *The Year of Great Realisations* taught by COVID. 2021 was about to make an entry. We all hoped and prayed for 2021 to bring freedom from the trap of this virus. For now, everybody enjoyed this newfound freedom. And the environment buzzed with all kinds of human activities, interactions, tell-a-tales, and cacophonies - all of which sounded soothing to the ears.

We also met our friends, visited a few relatives. We also took our childhood ritual trip to the Church, located at the heart of the city, just before Christmas. The church was illuminated in those wonderful golden ball lights from top to bottom. The sandstone-colored building glazed in the golden light. Mother Mary and Jesus held atop the Church blessing the city with the good times ahead and a dash of hope. The entire city bathed in the shimmering lights put up to celebrate the *New Year* and *Welcome 2021.* We watched from inside our car that people gathered in huge numbers at the eateries nearby waiting for their turn to come, each car with a kid called the balloon seller to give them a balloon shining bright with LED lights inside it, people ate the food ordered inside their cars totally immersed in their food and kids. It was a sight we had not witnessed the whole of 2020.

We could not believe that the whole of 2020 was spent being locked down inside our homes. Humans are under siege by a coronavirus. On 31 Dec 2019, none of us had thought that 2020 would be a complete bummer. It would bring in the worst of nightmares for mankind. None of us had ever imagined that we would be locked inside the four walls of our homes with all human activity put to a halt. Partying, traveling, clubbing, going out for dinners, hanging out with friends and family till late in the night, trips to the malls, and our incessant desire to be in movement and almost be omnipresent was clipped. None of us could ever imagine that there would come a time in our lifetime when humans would be subjugated to the horrors of an invisible virus. There used to be a proverbial phrase '*unites bees ka farak*' to depict dissimilarities of the faintest order. But with 2020 being starkly different from how 2019 was, people would never use that phrase again ever.

On 31 Dec 2019, we all ventured out to party hard and celebrate. We all decked up, looked our best, and booked ourselves a table at the best of pubs and lounges. We all were pumped up to welcome 2020 with all glitz and glamour. We looked forward to 2020 being full of splendor. We looked forward to the new year with our new resolutions. We hoped to take on 2020 by storm and fulfill our dreams - ever-pending dreams. We walked in with a commitment to make the better out of personal and professional lives. We thought of ruling the roost as soon as we stepped into 2020. None of that happened. 2020 was anything closer to what we had anticipated it to be.

On 31 Dec 2020, things were not the same. We all maintained lowkey. We didn't want to jinx yet another year. We didn't even have similar kinds of energy that manifested in us a year back. All we had was hope. All, our hearts carried, was a lot of hope for things to be better soon. All we prayed for 2021 to be was to be kind and considerate to all of us. All we wished for 2021 was - that it better be not like 2020.

On 31 Dec 2020, I stayed inside our home along with my family. We ordered some good food from our favorite restaurant in Jammu. We played the movie *Zindagi Na Milegi Dobara*. We looked at the picturesque locations and hoped that we would travel again soon. We felt the handicappedness of the characters and their desire to set them free. We cherished the camaraderie between the actors and hoped to nurture friendships likewise in our lives as well. We looked at the free sky, ogled at the vast crystal clear oceans, and experienced the road trips with the characters, and hoped to be free soon to experience all of it in reality. With each scene, we lived and experienced the life we had been denied in the year that went by. The lines from a poem in the movie "*dilon mein betaabiyaan lekar chal rahe ho, to zinda ho tum*" resonated with our then state of mind and touched our hearts deeply.

As the clock struck twelve, we raised a toast to the year ushering in, "*Come 2021, Come Hope! Zinda hain hum! Zinda hain hum!*"

Considering the improved situations in the country and a strong recovery rate, all of us started to behave as if we were back to normal - the pre-pandemic times. But that normal was an illusion. All of us started to take the liberty of relaxation in the safety norms. But that liberty was short-lived. All of us started being carefree and casual in how we operated. But that carelessness came at a heavy price. We thought we were back but we weren't.

Chapter26: The Anticlimax

Human beings have evolved into quite an impatient species. Though it's not entirely their fault. The last few years of technology explosion shaped us like that. We love our fast food. We enjoy prime deliveries. We love instant replies. If we have to wait for more than a minute to hear back, that annoys us. We love instant shopping at the tap of single clicks and hits. We love instant modes of payment. We love instant cab-booking facilities. If the cab is a minute late than the time it shows on the app, it pisses us off beyond imagination. We also love instant hook-ups and instant relationships. And if anything goes off or contrary to our expectations, we don't mind instant break-ups as well. We have grown up needing instant gratification. And we enjoy all of it. So, we love all things fast and instant. Unfortunately, that impatience made us pay a heavy price in the times to come during the pandemic.

We could not wait for the dust to settle down. The hangover of the New Year was not over yet. We were not yet completely over the miseries that the pandemic brought along with it. We were not yet done with the grief of the loss of loved ones. We had just begun to feel happy about the fact that things were getting back to normal. We had just begun our hither-thither movement in and out of the home to feel active and mentally relaxed. We had started to feel lively yet again after a long year of disorientation. We had just begun to start living our normal lives like in pre-pandemic times.

And probably that is where we got it all wrong.

It was unfortunate that while we all waited for things to get better and back to normal as soon as we could, things got worse and spiraled out of control. The daily cases in India had dropped to as low as twelve thousand in contrast to one lakh per day during the first wave of the pandemic. All of us saw it as a hugely positive sign and an indicator of things getting better from thereon. It looked like our hope - of 2021 being unlike 2020 - was going to be fulfilled. But our acts didn't support the cause. We became our biggest enemies.

We started getting out of homes too frequently. Our masks skid down to our chins from the nose. We hung masks over our ears to avoid paying *challan* to the traffic police. We started crowding in the markets and shops without maintaining any social distancing. We started getting into our mode of oblivion and in that mode, we skipped sanitizing our hands every time we came back home from outside. We started organizing and attending events and public gatherings. We were back to celebrating family functions with full fervor and zero attention to the safety guidelines. In our desire to be free and making ourselves believe that we were back to normal - we dropped our safety guard. We let go of our *Suraksha kavach.* We fiddled with our three *auzaars* in our security arsenal - *wearing a mask, social distancing*, and *sanitizing our hands.* We forgot that *aankh hati, durghatna ghati.* And *ghatt gayi durghatna.* The mishap! There were more Abhimanyus all over India stuck in the trap of the coronavirus struggling and battling for their lives in the hospitals.

The second wave of pandemic hit India out of nowhere. Or probably out of a consequence of our actions. Nobody anticipated that. The graph started picking up numbers from somewhere around mid-February reaching its peak in and around the first week of May. The daily cases reported during the peak of the second wave of the pandemic in India were approximately four lakh. Even more for a few days.

The entire nation panicked. The country rumbled under the attack of the coronavirus.

The news headlines in India and abroad shrieked about the miserable state of India. "*India ravaged.*", "*The coronavirus sabotages India's premature opening up.*", "*India's deadly second wave peaks.*", "*The virus' savage attack on India.*", "*How India failed to prevent a deadly second wave*", "*Has India's deadly second wave peaked?*", "*Lack of foresight caused COVID crises*", "*The tragedy of India's second wave*", "*Complete massacre of data*", "*Modi leads India into viral apocalypse*". The headlines like these dominated India's and international media coverage.

The opposition, International interest groups, other healthcare, and supervising bodies and committees were quick to find fault with the lackadaisical attitude of the government, poor governance, premature opening up of the economy, inadequate healthcare infrastructure, lack of preparedness for the second deadlier wave of the coronavirus. But rarely anybody pointed at the public stupidity that by and large was at the core of this bloody massacre. The government could not afford to put it all on the public. The government, in its lack of preparedness, was surely responsible for the disaster the pandemic had become.

The headlines were not important. What went into the headlines was supercritical though. India had recorded a peak of 414, 433 cases per day with a peak of 4,927 deaths per day during the second wave of the pandemic. There was no home, no street, no city or town that had remained untouched by the curse of the pandemic. And still, there were survey agencies and bodies that believed that the cases in India were under-reported.

To say that India was in a state of shock would be an understatement. India was under a severe medical crisis. There was a shortage of oxygen cylinders across the parts of the country. If oxygen was available, cryogenic tankers were absent. There were places without any oxygen plants. To ensure that COVID patients could breathe was the biggest nightmare and the topmost priority for every healthcare official and the government. India was not alone, countries like the US and Europe had faced severe consequences and suffered at the hands of the coronavirus during the first wave of the pandemic and second wave as well which had hit the countries much before it hit India. The disappointing part was India did not take its lessons from the miseries of the other countries.

By the time we knew, it was too late.

The public howled and cried and suffered miserably at the hands of the coronavirus. The second wave turned out to be monstrous and destructive. The patients were fitted with oxygen cylinders in their cars, or auto-rickshaws and ambulances because of the lack of beds in the hospitals. The condition was so bad that people breathed their last in the corridors of the hospitals while searching for a bed for themselves. A few could not even reach there. The healthcare system was strained. But they did the best they could to save the citizens of the country. The virus and the nature of the virus - its impact on human bodies and our reactions to the virus - were so uncertain that maybe a sure treatment was not even possible then. It was rather not available.

But the healthcare workers tried their best they could to save humanity if not humans. From making patients connect to their families over video calls from the hospital wards, from ensuring patients had their meals on time, to spending time with them to avoid depression-like conditions - the healthcare staff tried their best so that each life could be saved. They even performed the last rites for the people who lost their lives in the hospitals and whose bodies could not be handed over to the families because of the safety protocols. The medical staff set the bar for humanity high for the times to come.

Would it be wrong to say that our happiness was too short-lived? And the sorrow seemed to be forever!

All of us might not agree but the real reason for these disastrous consequences was us. It was strange that the very people who objected and questioned *Maha Kumbh*, Bengal election rallies, and cricket matches could not contain their excitement to step out of their homes. There was no denying the fact that allowing these public congregations of such a massive scale should not have been allowed in the first place. But there is no doubt that we should not have been so careless and carefree in our attitude as well. The pandemic was not over yet. The COVID virus was still there amidst us - only getting stronger and deadlier by interacting with more gene sequences. But it was tough to make each understand the dire consequences of the virus and even if they understood, it was practically impossible to stop everyone from stepping out of their homes. The frustration of the last year of house arrest was cascading.

The harm was already done. It was a perfect anticlimax we could have for our otherwise perfect 2021, that had started on a happy note.

Where did all of this leave us? There was only one thing certain and that was uncertainty. The uncertainty of the virus, its variants, their strength to impact us and affect us, the treatment, the efficacy of the vaccines. Uncertainty about the next day, two days after, the tomorrow we so wanted to look forward to, the future - our future - the future that belonged to each one of us. Or didn't it even belong to us anymore? The entire mankind was pushed to nadir.

We were left clueless about what we could do, other than to stay indoors, to get rid of the coronavirus. Will we ever be back to our normal - the pre-pandemic times? Or is this - the masks-clad humans - the sanitizer frenzy humans - the forever socially distant humans - our new normal? If this was the new normal, we did not like this normal. This new normal suffocated us, each one of us. It rendered all our accomplishments of the past decades useless. It clamped our wings of freedom. It even had started killing the hope that resided within us and filled us with despair with no tomorrow to look forward to.

577 days have passed since living in this new world and nothing felt good about it. All of us - every single human - were either living in the hope that one day things will get back to normal or were trying to pretend as if everything was already normal. The consequence of the latter approach is what we had already witnessed. That was not an option we could afford to live with. It was a perfect recipe for a world disaster.

With all these questions and fear looming over our heads, the world was just hanging in there by a thread. The world dwelled in uncertainties, which it desperately wanted to get out of. But no one knew the way out. Immense darkness surrounded us. We all felt frustrated at the thought of how and why we arrived where we were. It was established that we were not in a good condition. The world was not in a good condition. All of our frustration was eventually turning into a rage that demanded answers to all the questions and uncertainties. Will we ever find them?

But maybe we were not looking in the right direction to overcome this challenge that was thrown upon us. Maybe the virus was just a means to save us from a bigger disaster. Maybe the virus was just a clue in solving the larger jigsaw puzzle. Maybe the virus was just in time to save us from impending wrath. Maybe we were looking at the wrong side of the equation. Maybe we needed to solve a problem other than the virus. Maybe the virus was not important, but the lessons out of the pandemic were.

We were sitting on a time bomb. Nobody knew how long it would be before the bomb exploded. Would we ever be able to solve the puzzle? Would humans be able to solve the maze called life? Would humans be able to save their fellow beings? Would humans be intelligent enough to ensure their survival? Would humans survive the catastrophe and let the world know that *The End* was not here yet. Would humans be able to live again?

Only time could tell! If you ask me, I was only sceptical about our collective will to find a permanent solution to the problem.

The Sceptic Me

The world lived in between

the lockdowns and the unlocking

that continued for quite some time

but we didn't give up yet

'coz all was not over

Yes! we sulked and shrank

inside the four walls of our homes

and the nature walked all over

- in aplomb

ambushing all that we had created so far.

It scared me more to think

of all those who thought

it was just a passè

and nothing more than that

as if the pandemic was here
to not settle scores
and we were indomitable
here forever, maybe we thought

that is not how we had
anticipated,
The End to arrive,
afterall!

between the constant
toggle, that our life
had become,
we also packed our bags
for Ghar Wapsi, to return
to our safe holes, to our
families, friends and ourselves
who we didn't recognise anymore
yet amidst all the uncertainty
we waited hopelessly
for the hope
to arrive and
punch down all our woes

Lest we forget
that nature shimmered at its best all the while
with snow clad peaks, cleaner air
streams, rivers, oh so clear!
and the clearer skies
Lest we forget
that the nature breathed freely
and so did the wildlife
while the humans remained
caged inside, all this while

but I am scared for
tomorrow when
all of this is over
and past long gone
will we be back to
creating a life
what we had
before the pandemic arrived
what brought us here
and put us at strife
with our own selves.

Tomorrow, when this
becomes a thing of the past
Will it be a tell-a-tale,
of our bravery
or of Oops and Alas?
Tomorrow, when we rejoice
our survival through these times
maybe we do not forget
what all we went through
and lessons that pandemic taught

My heart shudders
with all these thoughts
squelching me harder
as the time passes by
The Sceptic Me
The Sceptic Me
harder it cries

Chapter27: The Seeking of the Truth

Once there was a kingdom. It was huge in its existence. The kingdom spread across mountains and oceans. In the millennia of its existence came a time when the subjects were at their most evolved and intelligent best. They could decipher the biggest of the mysteries. They made the most astonishing discoveries. The lords and the kingdom flourished with all this development and new inventions which the subjects made year after the other. This led to the common people also enjoying the fruits of their success. The public started frequenting from one island to another. There was increased mobility in terms of people, goods, and services. The far-flung areas were connected with advanced means of transport both via air and sea. The communication became fast and instant. The exchange of crops, art, and craft, indigenous cultures, ideas, and innovations catapulted as a result of the increased mobility and connectivity. No one fell ill and even if they did, there were cures for all kinds of ailments. There was prosperity everywhere. The lords, the chiefs, and other superiors along with the subjects took notice of their accomplishments achieved in such a short period in their long history of existence. They started becoming complacent and started considering themselves as the supreme beings in the kingdom. The more powerful ones damned the less powerful and started exploiting them. Since the lords and supremes found this an easy way to get more work done and make more wealth - this exploitation continued. As a result, the powerful started becoming more powerful and the weaker sections started becoming weaker. The complacency reached a new height when they started disregarding nature as well which was primordial to their existence. They stopped caring about the other species that existed along with them. They demeaned and defied the existence of any other being that existed beside them. They were supreme as they loved to believe. The systems of the kingdom became so corrupt that the entire kingdom was infected with malice of the lords and the subjects. They ended up in feuds and wars with each other. The one large kingdom, that it was once upon a time, was split into many small kingdoms and territories. All of them were hands-in-glove with each other in deteriorating their existence. No one or nothing could deter their arrogance till one fine day they woke up as equals suffering from an ailment no one could cure them from. Not even themselves - who they considered being supreme and the most intelligent. And they were told that this existence - what they called new - was their true form of being from thereon.

What would happen when one day you wake up only to find that the life you were living was a lie. All the glorious stories you were told about your victories and accomplishments were a sham. All the years you lived through believing that you were unconquerable and supreme were a delusion. All you had built, gathered, and celebrated was a mere illusion. What would happen when you would be made to live a life that was in complete contrast to what you were used to knowing life as. You would be in severe pain. It would ache you to see all that you had accomplished being rendered useless. The truth suddenly will become very important to you. The seeking of the truth will become your only goal of life till you breathe your last.

We all were going through the same pain and suffering. We all were living the mystery that was bestowed upon us. The human race was trapped in the pandemic and succumbed to the fatalities of the coronavirus. It had been more than a year. There was no cure for the virus. Though vaccination drives have started all over the world, there were still cases of COVID recurring in vaccinated people and vaccinated people succumbing to the virus. The scientific community believed that the virus was here to stay for more years or maybe decades. The pandemic was more likely to graduate into an endemic meaning the surge in corona cases could still be expected across geographies or in pockets though sporadically. There seemed no good riddance from the virus anytime soon.

The entire 2020 went like that. In a few months, 2021 was about to end. The virus took away 2 years of our life - a life that was beautiful and full of freedom. It took away our loved ones. It left us stuck inside our homes forever. It clamped our freedom. It instilled a strange fear inside us. We could hardly behave normally anymore. We were left in this frenzy of finding a mask, or a sanitizer every single time we thought of stepping outside our home. Travel became a far-fetched dream. We were no longer the same we used to be in the pre-pandemic times. We were no more the same we had become after centuries of evolution. The virus questioned our existence. We were getting more depressed and frustrated as days went by. Our world went upside down. And no one knew for how long we would have to bear the consequences of the virus.

Under such circumstances and situations of despair, the anguish that culminated in the hearts of the public seemed fair. Their exasperation was genuine. The entire world wanted to know how coronavirus came into existence. How did the virus spread among humans? Who was responsible for this pandemic? Was it a natural or man-made virus? Who could be accused and found guilty of pushing mankind to such horrendous reality?

But the truth is never easy to find!

There lay so many layers to peel off before truth unfolds itself. As soon as the first cases of coronavirus started getting reported, there was a widespread roar of a wet market known as Wuhan in Hubei province in China being the epicenter of the virus. It was believed that bats and pangolins were the hosts that transmitted the virus to humans. But later on, these findings were refuted owing to the non-availability of these two animals in the wet market. Instead, raccoons and badgers which are also likely to be the carriers of the "Wuhan virus", as coronavirus is popularly called, were sold openly in the market. It was found that there were more than 30 species of wild animals being sold illegally in the wet market that could have caused the harm. But with time, these theories found no solid ground and seem more like a camouflage to digress from reality.

As the days and weeks passed by, there were more conspiracy theories constructed to identify where the virus originated and how it was transmitted to humans. Another popular theory was the Wuhan lab leak theory, according to which, the coronavirus leaked out of the lab accidentally or deliberately. There were no claims and no sufficient evidence collected to support this theory as well.

Amidst all the chaos and anxiety, some groups accused Bill and Melinda Gates foundation of being a major conspirator behind the spread of the coronavirus. This was based on an early speech made by Bill Gates in 2015 in a TED talk where he talked about the pandemic-like situations shortly with no remedy and the need for the world to be prepared for the same. It was strange though that our desire to know the truth and the one responsible for the pandemic in the world grew so strong that we could go any length to connect the dots and find the accused.

On one hand, the world was suffering miserably and on the other hand the attempts to uncover the truth continued. While the mainstream media did not highlight these conspiracy theories without enough evidence in hand, the modern and non-conventional media fueled the fire now and then. The social media forums, the all-pervading internet, and our holy messenger apps left no stone unturned to invigorate the curiosity in us to know the truth. And in an attempt to do so, there were new rumors every day being circulated on all these channels.

There was another story where the United States of America and the People's Republic of China were projected as partners-in-crime. They both were suspected to be working together in creating a virus that could create havoc on the world. It was believed that the USA funded the project and China offered its intelligence and human resources along with the breeding ground for the virus - the Wuhan Institute of Virology's laboratory. This project was on for quite many years leading up to a world-war-like event in the form of a biomedical war. Surprisingly, when China got a breakthrough in the formula, it denied its existence to supremos in the US. This ruffled their ties and collaboration in the project. In the rift to steal the formula, the virus leak happened in the Wuhan wet market. So this story partially connected to the earlier story implying the epicenter of the virus was Wuhan wet market indeed but the source of the virus was not the market itself.

All of these were just brushed aside as mere conspiracy theories. However, the world started to believe that the Wuhan wet market, the Wuhan Institute of Virology (WIV laboratory), and China had a major role to play in the spreading of the virus resulting in the world pandemic.

But they say there is no spark without fire. A few months had passed into battling the pandemic when so-called amateur sleuths tried connecting the dots and spun the wheel and the world's attention back to Wuhan Institute of Virology in China. A group of curious souls inquisitive enough to find the real culprits. In an attempt to save humanity, they collaborated over Twitter and shared the information, correlations, reports, research, and their findings openly with each other and for the world to see. They found that China and the WIV laboratory, in particular, were actively engaged with viruses closely related to SARS-CoV-2, coronavirus causing the pandemic, since 2012 and Chinese authorities concealed these activities from the world. They also highlighted the fact that virus samples were being collected from the mines over the years and a few of the researchers contracted a mysterious disease back in 2012. Their findings also included active cases of coronavirus a few weeks before the outbreak happened in the Huanan market which was initially considered to be ground zero.

And then a classified report in the US established that three researchers at Wuhan laboratory were treated in November 2019 just before the virus started infecting humans. Interestingly none of these theories or reports established the fact of coronavirus being a genetically altered virus, the preparation of which happened at Wuhan laboratory. It was not deduced if the virus was transmitted to humans via contact with the animals or via an intermediate host. However, the constant denial from China in a transparent collaboration to work towards finding the truth raised more eyebrows than silencing the accusers. The investigation is still ongoing.

The truth remains untold, to date!

"In a world that was heavily moved by money and power, seeking the truth at the obvious epicenters was rather a stupid thing to do", I thought. *"If the truth must uncover and present itself, the world should rather follow the money trails. The world should seek the ones who benefited hugely from the pandemic and gained more power rather than seeking the truth. All this time while the world suffered at the hands of the coronavirus. The interesting thing to note here is when the pandemic happened most of the powerful countries of the world were being managed by the right-wing political parties. With time, their clout was only going to get stronger and the world order would have tilted in their favor. Maybe there is no correlation and the timing of the lab-leak was a mere coincidence or maybe the entire truth lies in the fact that who would establish the world order in the times to come."*

Mark Twain said, "*Truth is stranger than fiction*". And I believe that tomorrow or whenever the biggest mystery of the 21st century is unraveled, the world would be aghast.

I think that you do not seek the truth. Truth seeks you and presents itself to you at the right time in its due course of time. When it's ripe to be shown.

When we are prepared to assimilate it. One could only wait and watch. But having suffered at the hands of the pandemic, it was tough rather impossible to just sit, wait and watch and let the truth reveal itself to us at its own sweet time.

But was knowing the truth so important after all? The pandemic was ongoing, the harm was already done. Why bother about the origin of the coronavirus? Why bother about who brought the pandemic to the world? Did it matter now? WIll knowing that truth alter anything? No.

The only truth, for now, was that the entire human race was struggling for its survival and existence. The other big truth was our reactions to the pandemic, all those lessons we learned during the pandemic times, and nature's reaction to the pandemic. All those things that happened in front of us once the coronavirus infested into our lives, were the only truths we could rely on. Having seen how nature ambushed the world during the pandemic, I at times thought that maybe the pandemic was nature's conspiracy and China was unnecessarily being blemished. All that remained were just hypotheses to be proved.

The pandemic (and the suffering it brought along) and the ongoing conspiracies around it only stirred up more unrest and lack of trust of the public in its government and the so-called representatives of the world.

When did we forget that trust is key to our existence? There is no learning if students don't trust their teachers. There is no teaching without trust. There is no marriage or relationship without trust. There is no parenting possible if there is no trust. There are going to be no corporate success stories if the conglomerates didn't trust their employees. There are no cures and no treatments if patients don't trust doctors. There is no justice if the public doesn't trust the judicial system. There is no law and order if the public mistrusts the system. There's no policy if the public doesn't trust its policymakers. There is no God without trust. There is no use if we do not trust the laws of nature. So, yes trust is important. And it is the truth that manifests itself in the form of trust between various stakeholders of the ecosystem.

If we wanted to survive and continue our existence, we had to know the truth. The seeking of the truth was not a mere option or a choice, it was our only chance at our redemption from the pandemic.

But only time would tell if we would be doomed to ignorance forever or if the truth behind the pandemic would see the light of the day.

Chapter28: In a state of Oblivion

Amidst all the clamoring for survival and the truth, the remnant effects of the pandemic remained. The metro cities remained empty, less crowded than usual. The half-empty roads were devoid of any traffic jams. The cafes, pubs, and bars lay there abandoned, absent of all human banter and laughter. The business parks remained neglected without humans thronging in their various shifts, arriving and departing in autos, share rides, or cabs. It appeared as if someone gobbled up all the hyper motion of the metros. On the other hand, Tier II and Tier III cities swelled with people - all of those - who returned from their pursuits of success and excursions of fulfilling their dreams. Some completed, some half-baked, some had only begun to fly. All the dreams came back to where they originated, to have their *chai-nashta* and flourish in the very towns and cities. The towns reeked of fresh conversations and newness of ideas. Both sides of the world exchanged their bounties and curses.

Travel remained interrupted in some and suspended for other cities. The markets juggled between opening up and shutting down. People hesitated to take public transport. The masks kept skipping between chins and noses. Everything seemed half-open, half shut. The cities were wrapped in a strange gloominess. As if someone had woken up half-active wanting to start the day and yet half-asleep wanting to hit the bed again. The queues outside the dispensaries and vaccination centers kept getting longer. The vaccination drives were in full swing till vaccination was out of stock now and then. The hustles of the day to day life continued. We still would sanitize all the stuff we bought from the market or ordered online. The new habits we wanted to get rid of, continued. Work from home continued as well. More calls, and late shifts to complete the work still pestered us. We only got used to this new world of ours. Families gathered and rejoiced in their moments of togetherness. The world took comfort in its ephemeral joys. However, the fear of getting infected was deeply ingrained. The chaos and confusion seemed normal though. The families discussed and talked about how the virus had changed their lives and become a part of it. The virus and we had started to coexist.

Life had turned amorphous. During these amorphous days when the world and I remained frazzled by the virus, I tried to steal a few moments of a recluse when the work was over sooner than usual. I would climb up the stairs to our rooftop, sat there staring at the sky non-stop. The blue-colored blank canvas was painted by regular-irregular-shaped clouds. The so-vast sky, and so-minuscule us. I kept wondering. As the sun kept drawing the sunset hues in the sky, so many birds returned home. Together. Like a bunch swirling in the sky, sucking air from space, showing their might and existence before they head back. Those birds were everything we humans wanted to be. Free. Those birds became objects of my envy.

A part of me wanted to fight the virus and get rid of the pandemic. A part of me wanted to be like those birds. And not me alone, there were so many like me out there. Back in 2019, we all would wait for moments like these on our rooftops where we could get enough time to stare at the sky and wished for the time to pause forever. But today, we wanted this time to be fast-forwarded so that we could fly beyond our rooftop.

This would always remain a mystery to me. The weird ask of humans for things and possessions we did not have. We rarely valued what we have got - at the moment - at present.

While I sat there on the rooftop thinking of foraying out, many already took that flight. Every single time I would log in to my Facebook or Instagram handle, there was always this one or the other couple, or a family or a bunch of friends who continued to travel. There were a lot of promotions to encourage tourism and travel. With intra-country travel norms being relaxed, the public was surely motivated to travel and get out of the rut, life had become. But the ultimate choice was ours. Isn't it?

And that is what scared me the most.

That when it came to making choices and decisions, we could not refrain ourselves. We could not contain the wanderlust within us. We went into a state of oblivion. We behaved as if there was no pandemic. The pandemic and the coronavirus were things of the past but in reality, they weren't. They were very much here. And all the liberties we took were at the cost of someone's life or our own life. Was it so tough to value our lives?

People thronged in huge numbers to their favorite destinations. *Srinagar, Pahalgam, Simla, Manali, Mawsynram, Darjeeling, Rishikesh, Dehradun, Dalhousie, Goa, Gokarna, Coorg, Ooty, Kodaikanal, Chikmagalur.* And to the nearby local tourist spots for a day's outing. There were headlines of tourist destinations becoming hotspots. And when these people came back from these hotspots, they became the carriers of the coronavirus bringing the disease back to the cities that had just recovered. This behavior continued having suffered the horrors of the first and the second wave of the pandemic.

This made me think, "*Were we so quick in forgetting the miseries of the past? Did we forget that when the coronavirus hit the world, the first thing to be banned was traveling? Did we forget that the first thing nature expected us to do during the pandemic was to curtail our mobility? Did we not think once that what would happen if we get infected again?*" But still, the moment we got a chance, we traveled. And even when we traveled, we flouted all the health protocols. We didn't maintain any social distance. We gave masks a miss. Did we think that coronavirus would be kind to us in the mountains and near the sea? Rather, it would be lethal amidst the swarm of people that surrounded these destinations.

The same behavior could be observed in the markets, public places such as parks, religious institutions, shops, and even worse at public gatherings. And in general as well. This however was a short-term concern. As soon as the world would get vaccinated, maybe these would not even be concerns anymore. What should have bothered all of us was our expected behavior in the long term! What got us here won't get us far ahead in the future and that was important for each one of us to realize. The Sooner we did, the better it would be. But we were far from it. And this was the biggest fear I cupped in my head.

The pandemic didn't happen just like that. And it was very important for the entire human race to know and realize that an event that happened once in 100 years must have had a purpose to serve. But a few thoughts do not come so naturally as one would love to believe. Just like the thought of death and anticipation of the end. Human suffering could not be the only objective. That was just a by-product of the entire process. It would be foolish if we turned a blind eye to how nature reacted to the pandemic. It walked all over the world in aplomb and ambushed our existence. All the while we stayed locked inside the four walls of our homes, the wildlife - birds, animals, all kinds of species - walked freely on the roads and the streets. They came out all in the open. They invaded what we have been invading for years and centuries now - the earth! They showed their presence in all their might. The earth breathed more comfortably while we suffocated inside our homes. We could not be in oblivion anymore about all that conspired with the onset of the pandemic. That would be the most foolish state to be in.

During those two years, there were wildfires in the US, Australia, and Uttarakhand in India, red sandstorms in California, cyclones that hit

Bangladesh and India, and flooded cities in China. There were parts of the world that recorded the highest temperatures in centuries and those that recorded the highest rainfall in the preceding decades. The mountains crackled. The glaciers burst. *Kinnaur* and *Chamoli* in Uttarakhand, *Kishtwar* in J&K were recent incidents of such natural disasters. Nature continued to wreak havoc and shoo away the humans from it. It screamed loud and clear, "*Stay Away, you humans!*" This was something that we all needed to be worried about. We could not be in oblivion about that.

These phenomena were not new. They have been happening for years now but since humans were devoid of their so-called busy lives, more and more people took notice of these environmental hazards and natural disasters. With these recurring phenomena, our ways could not be old. We needed to stop wading nature on our whims and fancies. We needed to stop loitering the beautiful mountain trails and beaches with chips and chocolate wrappers, polythene bags, cola, and Pepsi bottles, cans of juices and other drinks, and all kinds of junk. We needed to stop throwing our convenience wrapped in ignorance (read oblivion) out in the open. We needed to stop polluting the places we visited to escape from the pollution of the cities. The forest cover where we discovered ourselves and found that solace needed to be protected. The wildlife that gave us the most mesmerizing sights needed to be protected as well. The animals, birds - all flora and fauna - needed to feel safe, feel at home where they belonged to and places which belonged to them. We were just visitors and we needed to remain one - the conscious visitors. The projects of creating artificial bio-parks and reserves and constructing dams to divert the natural flow of the rivers had to stop immediately. The expansion of the road network in the name of religion to take the public closer to their Gods was a sham and it needed to stop. God manifests itself in nature and nature is God's greatest bounty. Taking care of nature would be the tribute of the highest order to our *Gods and Goddesses.* We needed to stop intervening with nature and its course.

"But how on this earth could we curb the temptations of humans?" This question kept bothering me.

During one of the opportune moments, I also took that flight beyond my rooftop. I gave in to my temptation as well and started on my guilt trip. The driver kept showing us the areas around unaware that I belonged to that place. We were headed to a nearby hill station known as *Patnitop* followed by *Pahalgam* and *Srinagar.* I was visiting Patnitop after 18 years and the other two cities after almost a decade. None of the places looked similar to what memories I had of those places. None of them was in a better condition, as I would have loved to experience them. The places had deteriorated. The parks had shrunk - losing the land to man-made recreational activities. The mountains - the Shivalik range - were stripped of the dense forest cover they used to be covered with back in those days. There were more shops and pit-stops to cater to the hungry humans. The mountains lay naked reflecting the shamelessness of the humans. The widening of the roads had pushed all the debris into the river bed of the river Chenab. The blasting of the fragile mountains to construct tunnels had caused mountains to collapse into the river thereby lifting the level of the river bed. Eventually leading the rivers to overflow and cause devastating floods. For the convenience of the humans, the entire ecosystem had been put in danger. And the most dangerous part was we didn't see any wrong in it. This was called *development.*

There were more air-conditioned cars and houses in Srinagar. Only if someone could tell them, these ACs brought heat waves rather than comfort. But we humans are too short-sighted to comfort ourselves. Isn't it? The top of the mountains and sources of the rivers that flowed from mountains to the plains were contaminated by all kinds of waste. Not only tourists, but even locals at certain places also created garbage dumps near rivers and waterfalls. The rains happened, the flow of the rivers became stronger, and waterfalls cascaded all the dirt into the streams and then rivers taking them back to the cities and finally into the oceans.

I came back home and thought it was better to sit on the rooftop and stare at the sky. I could draw anything on the blank blue canvas without even polluting it. That way I could part myself from the sins of doing all the harm to nature and bringing curses upon humanity.

Have you also felt the same - disappointed in a place - you so thoughtfully planned a trip to? The interesting part of this saddening story is that we are *disappointed*. No one else.

My heart kept wondering, "*What could I do to make others feel the same pain I was going through? What could I do to convey my insecurities and fear of demolishing nature and not taking enough care of it? Because I strongly believed that at the end of the day, our karma was going to come back and haunt us. The remnant effect of our doings was our extinction, not nature's deterioration. That deterioration was just temporary and an illusion to make us feel strong and supreme about ourselves.*"

This reminds me of one of the most epic conversations between *Lord Krishna* and his consort Queen *Rukmani*. She asked her husband, "*Oh Lord! If you have already decided the fate of the ill-doers, the egotists, the harbingers of corruption, and all those who cannot maintain the sanctity of either their dharma or karma, why do you let them flourish and allow them to reach the pinnacle of the paths they have chosen for themselves?*" To this question, Sri Krishna gives a modest smile and replies, "*Oh my dear Rukmani, the greater the magnitude of his fallacies, the greater the effect of the fall from that pinnacle. That seeming ingenuity is tantamount to the suffering his ill-doings are going to bring to him.*"

There was a similar relationship between our accomplishments and us!

All this while in the past years and centuries we have thought it to be perfectly fine to not consider nature in our development plan. It would be ok to not consider nature as a part of the ecosystem and still feel supreme about our existence. What we didn't know was that we were plainly at the mercy of nature. The pandemic was just a teaser. We would cease to exist the moment nature decided to vanquish us from the planet earth. It was just a matter of time and nature's threshold to tolerate our atrocities. Nature would claim what truly belongs to it. I could not emphasize enough that we needed nature for our existence and not the other way round. The pandemic, irrespective of how it happened, was a hint to mankind to be mindful of our activities.

From our day-to-day activities at home to our exorbitant travel plans, we will have to do all we could to keep the environment clean and green. We have to do all that it takes to maintain the sanctity of nature and protect it. We could not behave as if nothing has/had happened and nothing worse can happen in the future. We could not afford to be in a *state of Oblivion. Not anymore.* We could not be reckless about the situation. Surely not after the pandemic which was an alarm struck for the entire world to be considerate of nature and watchful of our very actions. Nature and us would have to coexist if we wished to live and survive.

Would it be too tough?

As the world got on its way to recovering from the pandemic, my fear of slipping into oblivion grew stronger. There is no denying the fact that we all have been impacted by the virus and its repercussions and we all wanted to be out of this situation as soon as we could. And this scared me even more. We might as well just slip into normalcy forgetting the lessons from the pandemic. We might as well choose ignorance over wisdom. We might as well choose to be in oblivion than being consciously, collectively aware as a society - as a race. Hopefully not!

I wished, I prayed!

Chapter29: Khichdi

Among all the things I prayed for during those times, I also wished for *Khichdi* for all of us.

It must have been a few months before the pandemic had hit us. I was not feeling good for quite some days. There was this constant restlessness that occupied me. A weird kind of heaviness captivated me. I could not explain my discomfort to anyone. Not even to myself. There are a few sufferings that are beyond any rational explanation. Only you could sense and feel it.

I came back home early from work. I told my wife how I felt. I went on to blabber my condition to my sister as well. When I realized that nothing got the better side of me, I picked up my phone and called Mom. I thought maybe I was missing home. But none of it worked. My condition remained the same without any improvement.

Not that there were any disturbing thoughts. I just felt sluggish and pessimistic about everything. As if I had given up on all the hope. I continued to perform my duties not because I wanted to but because I thought I was supposed to.

Everything was amazing at the work front. All my deliverables were completed in time. I had got the promotion that was long due. There were a lot of activities to engage me during the weekends. The evenings meant some wonderful retreats to the choicest cafes and restaurants. Catching up with friends and colleagues outside work was fun. And the weekend rituals continued. I did a lot of what I enjoyed doing the most - watching a lot of cinema and web series. Life was exactly how it was supposed to be. Wasn't it?

Then, what kept me restless all this while?

Everybody seemed happy with me except for myself. Life was sailing through at a comfortable pace in the fast-paced rat race. Yet, there was something that was bothering me inside and made me feel tired forever. Have you also felt the same about yourself? Everything seems perfect at the periphery yet everything is so distorted within you. I felt like that.

To overcome that sullen feeling, I gave up everything for a few days. I canceled my evening outings. I told my friends about my unavailability for the coming weekend and gave that house party a miss. I didn't go out for any entertainment - food or movies. I planned to stay at home. I even stayed away from the television and to my surprise, I convinced myself to tap fewer clicks on my phone. I planned to chew less than I wanted to.

Then what did I do while I gave all the action a miss? I was back to my routine of getting up early. I practiced *yoga* and *meditation.* I treated myself to a cup of *chai.* I continued going to work like I used to. I clocked in a total of nine hours every day without being absent for any day during the week. I came back home, freshened up, picked up a book, and read for an hour. I made myself another cup of tea. I spent some time towards the end of the day writing - a passion that I had carried in my heart since I was twelve. I resorted to simple food during those days. No outside food. For a change, I asked our cook to make us *Khichdi* for dinner. This routine continued for a week. Yes, even the routine of eating *khichdi* every evening continued.

Khichdi - is a simple preparation made of rice and lentils. You can add salt and spices to your taste. It is accompanied by curd and pickles. It is also the first of solid foods given to newly born babies. It is so easy to digest. This is very similar to what my *Tamil* and *Telugu* friends know as Pongal and my *Kannadiga* friends call *bisi bele bath.* This is also known by some other popular names in respective regions such as *khichdi* in Odisha, *Khichuri* in Bengal, and *Khichiri* in Assam. My mother loves calling it rolling-rice. My grandfather used to tell me that the so-*desi* dish was called *hotchpotch* in English. That name always amused me. It still does - if not the name but its effect on me.

I enjoyed having this hotchpotch - *khichdi* - every single day. This made me feel better. I started feeling light. That unknown heavy weight on my chest, as if I was relieved of it with each passing day of my newfound routine. That restlessness receded. *Khichdi* and the new routine played their magic on me.

Sometimes we try to have much more than we need. Food, luxury, comfort, and even thoughts. We go on to think much more than is needed. From anticipating others' actions to reactions, to how somebody would have behaved or acted if in a particular situation to what could have been a better reaction on my part - we go on to think of situations and scenarios that are either in the past or are yet to reveal themselves to us. At times, we try to absorb more in our lives - much more than our lives need, much more than we could assimilate.

There is an abundance of everything in our lives. Even entertainment, activities, and opportunities. That abundance of everything - glorifies our existence and our being. Then we try to gather more of everything. One abundance leads to an abundance of other hundred things and possessions. We go on to have more things filling our houses. Then when we have more things filling up our houses, we go on to have bigger houses to accommodate all those things. To ensure 24x7 conveyance availability, a family of four decides to own four cars. With more cars come more houses as well. We watch more series and cinema to be more aware than the others. We want to come across as up-to-date. We are always in this needless need to catch up with peers who would have already watched the latest releases. But how does it matter? A new cafe or a bar opens and we want to experience it first. To catch up and enjoy these experiences - it then becomes imperative to clock in these activities over social media too. Otherwise, how would you establish and glorify the abundance of things in your life? And for that, you need more outfits and accessories to go with. Interestingly you don't even have to call people to your home to present your abundance. Social media does all the work for you. And you realize that this cycle never ends.

To establish your grandeur and mark your projection, you and I continue to latch on to this process of accumulating abundance however deprecating it might be for ourselves. But we all tried hard at it back then.

Interestingly, we are products of what we consume. From thoughts to food to things, we have been consuming each of them just a little more than what we needed. The heaviness was bound to happen. With so many things distracting us, the restlessness then seemed to be an obvious outcome.

I realized that we humans had complicated our lives way too much. It seemed to me that we all were caught in a web of facades, which we had to dutifully maintain. We were caught in a vicious cycle of accumulating abundant yet unwanted possessions. This process kept us engaged always, leaving us tired forever. Our tired bodies and restless souls were thus a result of an intricate lifestyle we had built for ourselves.

Khichdi broke that monotony for me. Having *khichdi* after ages felt good. I could not fathom the fact that something as simple as khichdi could be so fulfilling as well. We all were made to believe that only all things big and bold, glitz and glamour, in abundance, and more could satiate us. The idea of having khichdi was a mere thought in my head to cleanse my body. Didn't I know that it would clear the clutter in my head as well? Simple things could be comforting and satiating too, I wondered.

Khichdi brought that dash of simplicity that was much needed in my life. Probably in yours too. Sometimes, it is important to break free from the clutches of our so-called busy and taxing lives so that we can take pleasure in the simple joys of life. Life was meant to be enjoyed but somehow we turned that life into a race. We got into this whimsical arbitration of extracting more out of our lives. We burdened our lives with milestones and possessions. This left all of us with happy faces but sad eyes, a full stomach but a hungry soul, a possessions-filled life yet empty us.

We had forgotten that a simple cup of chai every evening after work could be boring yet comforting. A stroll on the road could also become the most pleasant memory. Staring at the sky could be soothing. Holding hands with your partner on a cold winter night could be the warmest feeling. Looking at the moonlit star-studded sky could make you feel ecstatic. Hugging your children after a tiring day could be the most relaxing therapy. Planting a tree could feel like the biggest achievement. Having conversations with family over the dinner table could be the best entertainment. And friends could turn the worst of days into more tolerable ones. Watching the birds fly in the sky could set you free. Dancing in the rain could give you exhilarating joy. Looking at the photographs from the past could feel like cherishing the most valuable treasures of life. Waking up every day to watch the sunrise could give you the biggest kick. A simple meal could be satisfying too. There could be unfathomable joys in the simplest of things that no money could buy. Unfortunately, we had forgotten to enjoy these little things in life. *Khichdi* brought back that realization - to find joy and fulfillment in the simplest of things.

That day, I wished for *Khichdi* to spell its magic on all of us. I wished for *Khichdi* to unravel that simplicity in our lives. I didn't know that the wish would come in handy to heal all of us from the vagaries of the times that were yet to come.

"*Couldn't we all have that simplicity of Khichdi in our lives?*", I asked myself.

Chapter30: The World Needs to Heal

4.2 million people lost their lives to the coronavirus during the times of pandemic. The world lost somewhere around 1.2 lakh healthcare workers, medical staff, and doctors in this battle against the pandemic. COVID took away so much from us. There were parents without children. There were children left orphaned. The partners went too soon, leaving their better halves in the middle of the journey called life. The COVID bereaved us of our families and loved ones. We lost friends and relatives. We lost neighbors and people we knew forever. We lost people we used to wave hello at gyms, bars, clubs, and parks. We lost people we became acquainted with at the nearby temple or the *kiryana* shop. We lost people we used to crosstalk across our rooftops and balconies. We lost people we were so used to, people who had become an inextricable part of our lives. In a whiff, our world was turned upside down.

There was abysmal sadness that gripped us. The economies crumbled. The governments stumbled. The nations panicked. All the hope was lost. The humans fumbled. We lost our freedom. We lost our sanity as well. So much so that we started questioning our existence. Everything seemed broken. We were broken physically, emotionally, and financially. Anyone who had contacted COVID-19 took months to recover and still did not feel good about their health. The bodies were weak beyond repair. There were post-covid symptoms and complications too. Those who managed to stay indoors and safe were depressed and emotionally wrecked. And the financial repercussions could be felt across strata of the society. No one was left untouched by the wrath of COVID-19. The COVID hit all of us in one way or the other. The world was left bruised and scarred.

But *chalti ka naam zindagi.* We could not be in that bruised state for long if we wished to overcome the horrors of the pandemic. We had to find ways to overcome the injuries inflicted upon us and sail through our newfound life. We all needed to heal. We all needed to heal from all that we had succumbed to in those two years. We needed to heal from the pain and suffering that the pandemic caused us.

It mustn't be easy to heal from so much that we had gone through in those two years. We could just get used to our new state and continue, in oblivion. Or probably we could have chosen to gather the pieces of us left by the storm, try to make some sense of it, and continue wiser than before.

There was a lot that we could learn from nature. Nature is magical in its way and existence. One can only be amused by the way it operates and transcends. It keeps teaching and guiding us through its esoteric ways. 800 years ago, there was supposedly a little ice age but humans survived the fierce weather conditions. Humans, in their responsiveness to change, have survived many changing kinds of weather and catastrophes of the past. The scientific studies predict that if humans are vanquished today, trees and plants grow out of control in just 1 year. In another 60 years, oceans will completely recover from overfishing done by humans. It would just take 200 years for rivers to get back to their original course and for extra carbon dioxide produced by humans to be eliminated from the environment. In another 500 years, the whole forest cover would be back as it was 10,000 years ago. That in short would be the healing period of nature if humans disappeared today.

This makes me wonder if we were so toxic for nature to heal. Were we the virus for nature as Sars-CoV-2 was for us?

Interestingly, nature could heal without us. But unfortunately, we could not heal without nature. And healing was a must. Luckily we were still alive and nature still healed intermittently with events like a pandemic that pushed humans behind the four walls of their homes. And we needed to heal from the repercussions of the pandemic.

Hence, what we needed to ensure was that all of us healed together in unison. That was the only hope remaining for our survival.

If countries had to thrive, economies needed to revive. If economies needed to revive, people needed to go back to their business as usual. But were we ready yet? With the ongoing pandemic and the fear of virus being amidst us, and the world that was still wounded from the attacks of it - the world was surely not ready to get back to its feet anytime sooner.

So that we could have stronger financial strides than pre-pandemic times and accelerate our GDP, it was first important that the human race was physically and emotionally fit to carry the strains of the moving world. We needed to ensure that we had spent enough time seeking ourselves as we have spent seeking the truth. We needed to be more sure about ourselves than ever before. We needed to ensure that as soon as the world opened up we didn't slide into our old ways of living. We had to explore and settle for new ways of sailing through life where nature was very much a part of the plan. Simplicity needed to be at the core of our newfound life and freedom. It was even more important that we had overcome the fear and insecurities of those 2 years. We needed to ensure that we were fully prepared before we took that leap of faith - before we could start all over again.

But first, we all needed to heal.

I remember, a few years ago, I walked into my lawn and spotted a sparrow lying upside down on the ground. It was half-conscious, appearing to be almost dead. I gently cupped it in my hands. The wings fluttered. I sensed that it was alive but incapacitated. I tried to locate the injury but I could not spot anything. I dug a hole - not so deep or steep - in the mud and left the bird in that cup-shaped surface. I started pouring water little by little. The bird slurped the water. But then suddenly the bird became extremely silent. I thought we lost the bird but in my last attempt, I poured some more water and the wings fluttered once again. I realized that the bird was alive but had gone to sleep. It needed some rest. I kept checking on the bird every thirty minutes or so. The bird remained there comfortably cushioned in mud and water. After four to five hours, the bird started moving its wings fiercely. I stood there looking at the birdie. It wanted to take the flight. Though I wanted to lift the bird and show it the way to the sky, I resisted myself from doing so. I didn't want the bird to lose confidence in itself and the strength of its wings. In another fifteen-twenty minute, the bird took a small leap. It flew towards me as if telling me that it was fit and fine, ready to take a flight. It took the final flight towards the sky. In a few seconds, the bird was gone high up in the sky enjoying its flight.

I learned two important lessons that day. One that healing was a must before the bird could try to fly. Second, the bird had to feel confident about its ability to take flight.

Our condition was no different in comparison to that bird. We needed to take the flight as well but we were left incapacitated by the COVID. We needed to heal from those injuries and be fully confident in our ability to take that flight.

How long would it take for us to heal and chase the dreams that have fueled us always?

Chapter31: The Dreams get you Going

Had we forgotten to dream since the pandemic hit us? If yes, it was time to dream again. Dreams were the wings we needed to take the flight.

Dreams - we all dream every time. From childhood to growing up, we had held dreams close as if they lifted the weight of the world off our chest. We would dream about anything from flying an airplane to becoming a kite one day, from becoming a magician to becoming our favorite superhero. From playing like Sachin Tendulkar or Rahul Dravid to singing like Lata Mangeshkar; from dancing like Madhuri Dixit to composing like A.R. Rehman - our dreams knew no bounds. Our dreams were not limited by our abilities to fulfill those dreams. Our dreams were like those spaceships that went too far into space to even track. As we grew up, our dreams changed but we always continued to dream. From getting a degree to getting a higher paying job, from buying the latest phone and fastest motorbike to owning a big house; our dreams changed their destination. I am only surprised by the fact that how our dreams are diminished as a part of our growing up. Our dreams start becoming more short-term than soul-serving and purposeful. In between adoring *Iron Man* to understanding and appreciating *Thanos*, our world of dreams also went under metamorphosis. But dreams did not vanish completely. Thankfully.

Dreams stuck around in one form or the other. In certain cases, we decided to live by and for our dreams. In all other cases, dreams became an alternate reality of our lives. We never stopped dwelling in our world of dreams. From extreme pain to abundant joy, dreams remained our constant companions. They helped us sail through. A few dreams got marred by circumstances of life and a few roared loud under the garb of different circumstances. In either way, dreams became an anchor point for all of us.

Dreams gave us the reason we were, we are! The fulfilled dreams gave us the reason to fly higher and the unfulfilled ones gave us the reason to fight stronger.

To me, dreams are, will always be all-pervading strong forces that move our world. To me, dreams are not what we see with our closed eyes but those that keep us going while we are wide awake. This reminds me of the famous slogan used by Indian monk *Swami Vivekananda*, "*Arise, Awake and stop not till the goal is achieved!*" during one of his speeches in 1897. These words resonate with the need of the time. These words are exactly what we needed to believe. They summarise the essence of what we needed to be to heal and overcome the pandemic.

Could we live by those words? Could we rekindle the fire within us and dream again? Could we enliven the spirit of childhood innocence and dream what was unfathomable? Could we dream that was not constrained by any restrictions or limitations?

Divided by race, caste, color, region, religion, and sex; United by dreams! The whole world needed to get together to dream big for the human race to triumph over the doomedness that pandemic thrust upon us. One big dream, for the entire world! Could we achieve that? Why not! That is the magic called dreams. Dreams are like those anchors that keep us grounded, humble, firm, and focused on our goals. They are cups of positivity that spill hope all around. And to overcome the fears of the pandemic, we needed to fuel those dreams within us.

Dreams, the powerhouses for humans!

We could not undo those lugubrious two years of our lives but we surely could dream to make this world a better place to live. We could surely dream to leave a better world for generations to come. We surely could work together towards achieving that dream. It is said that when the going gets tougher, the tough get going. The same is true for dreamers as well.

It was time to wake up and dream! Once again! It was time to spill hope!

Chapter32: Recap

There is a lot that has changed in these two years. I wake up and go stand beside the *Neem* tree standing tall and sturdy outside at the corner of the house. The leaves are green and supple because of the recent rain. The air smells and feels fresh. I look at the vegetables grown in the backyard of the house. *Lauki, Karela* and *Okra.* I look at the recently planted lemon tree. I look at the Neem tree again and realize that it has turned from an adolescent boy to a mature man. The tender branches have grown into sturdy trunks. The tree has outgrown the boundary wall and is already giving shade to areas outside on the road. I remember our neighbors telling us to cut the tree because it was spilling over to their compound. We refused. Since then the tree has not grown an inch towards their compound. It bent a little, changed its course but continued to grow. Do trees listen? I believe, Yes! There is a lot that has changed in these two years. And my mind remains stuck on that thought.

I wake up and put my phone on charging without scrolling up and down, left or right. Rather than chewing on the mindless thoughts and sensational news, I go out and enjoy the brown and green earth below, the blue sky above with not-so-the-burning sun. At times, I also water the plants. That is the closest I have ever connected to nature in the year gone by. I calm my already sleepy head and absorb nature as it is. I let it soak all my worries and frowns. I then grab my ritualistic morning cup of tea and enjoy it with my family. There are conversations mostly around what we are going to eat and what the day looks like!

Amidst all this, at times conversations are worrying about things that are totally out of our control. Like when is that cousin of mine getting married, when my uncle is going to get settled, shouldn't the other kids of the family pursue higher studies too and why are a few members have grown apart. But none of it in the wrong way, just out of concern. Sometimes we walk down memory lane only to gauge how life has changed over all these years. Nostalgia hits us strongly. In the last few months, I have changed my perspective from "no worrying at all" to " a little worrying is good". It reflects that the bond is still intact and we still care. That the concern still exists.

In that concern, we connect. And in this process, we have just grown more empathetic than before and the love kindles all over again. *"You are right, there is a lot that has changed in these two years."*, I tell myself.

Most of the day is spent working and attending calls. But in between work, we talk to each other. We share each other's routines and affection. Dad always checks on us if we need anything from the market. And Mom always ensures that she cooks something for each one of our delights and takes care of all those minutest details. My wife and I try to order stuff needed online, the best we can do to make it easy for them, which our parents seldom allow but we insist. We make social calls during the weekends. In these small little acts of kindness and sharing, love mushrooms. Life seems to have come to a complete circle. Our parents have new worries and we have newfound activities which once belonged to our parents alone. All that love and affection we all were devoid of, is back. There is a lot that has changed in these two years, I think.

Of all the newness in our lives, the toughest has been to stick to a fitness regime. The second toughest has been convincing everyone to rest. Though after we were *tested positive*, we have gone cautious about how much we exert in a day. A fine balance between activity and rest is tough to find, I guess. But I am a strong persuader of *Rest*, *Reset*, *Refurbish*, and *Re Energise*. In the toughest of times, the sanity of our minds is most important. If there is one thing these two years have constantly taught us, it is this.

Since travel is not on the cards, I keep identifying nearby places to visit. These drives were the most sought-after thing when I was away from home all those years. All of that has happened in these two years was only sought after, we didn't imagine ourselves to be living that anytime soon. I wonder, "*Wasn't all of that a part of the retirement plan? Coming back home after we had earned enough so that we could be back to our hometowns forever.*" But it all arrived sooner than later. Our parent's love. The epiphany of our work routines to them. Us staying together. The camaraderie of the family. The commotion and comfort of staying together. The lanes of childhood. The longing of the friends over virtual hangout sessions. A relaxed mind. The calmness. The peace. Some quality time for ourselves, all of it arrived sooner than we had anticipated.

In the concrete jungle we were living in, I could only yearn for the open skies and grass beneath to walk on. The phone was my only 24x7 companion. The only thing I eagerly waited for was the cab to pick me up from different locations. My workplace was my entire world. When I was not at work, we were outside partying. The house was just a rest place for a stayover. During weekends we binge-watched - anything and everything. No one bothered what culminated in reality in our lives. Neither did they, nor did we. The entire world was in a state of apathy. Sharing was not an emotion, it was a compulsion. If any of us didn't like what was cooked, we would order food online. The idea of sitting together and spending a good time together sounded boring. The idea of being stagnant in one place was shameful. The weekend was a waste if there was no plan for that weekend. We all wanted to have a new answer every time somebody questioned us, "*Wassup?*" And every time, we fell short of delivering a perfect fresh answer, we ran the risk of *FOMO*. There were too many people and too much noise in those cities but all of us wandered lonely. I waited till eternity for the sun to shine upon us. It could not make its way to reach us in those high-rise buildings. And then COVID happened. It was time for *Ghar Waapsi*. And we were soon home. Seriously, there is a lot that has changed in these two years.

There is one more thing that has changed. We all have grown full of gratitude. Every Sunday, each one of us puts a note in what we call *Thank you Jar*, where we thank Almighty, God, or superpower as you would like to recognize it for all the goodness we are bestowed with. This has helped us count our blessings rather than suffering.

"*Andar aaja, Papa wait kar rahe hain chai ka*", calls Mom. My mind shudders. I have been immersed in my thoughts. Thinking about how life has changed for each one of us in its unique ways in these two years, I had lost track of time.

I look at the *Neem* tree again, touch its trunk and sense how it has matured with us and the changing times. Are trees good companions? I believe, Yes!

Chapter33: The Lost Track

I finish off the tea and get up to leave.

Mom: Where are you going?

Me: Going to get ready. Have to be there for the office call.

Mom: But isn't it Sunday today, she scoffs.

Me: [remains silent and sits back with a thud and a laugh]

Me: Ok. Ok, another cup of chai then?

In the cacophony of times, we all laughed it out together.

This has not been the first time that I lost track of days and weeks. A few weeks before I got ready and logged in to start the office work. Not realizing that it was an official holiday that day. It has become very common to not take notice of a landmark day or an important event at home. Since the pandemic hit us, our demarcation of hours, days, and weeks kept getting blurred. Days just went by, and weeks just merged into one another. Or at least I felt so. Our days and weeks just hushed into one another without making much noise or achieving any milestone. Time became like that stretched maze we desperately tried to find our way through. Because life was no more a retreat - no more a list of things to do. Life had become a fight for survival. And we lived only to breathe and survive, fighting for oxygen.

The pandemic came and it rendered the very core of our existence - the time - unimportant. Rather distorted. In many instances, I thought that I over-thought anything related to the pandemic but actually no. That was true. Time didn't maintain the same sanctity as before. Its meaning changed and so did its importance.

Before the pandemic, our sense of time was accomplished by notifications of all kinds. From calendar notifications to app notifications, they drove our days. From waking up in the morning to attending the first office call; from waiting for the cab pickup to waiting for the *dabbawala* to deliver the lunch at the office; from a dentist's appointment to a movie show; from hanging out with friends to date night; from the appointment at the salon to scheduling the delivery for the grocery; from making SIPs to paying monthly bills; from our next weekend getaway to the bookings and itinerary for our next vacation trip; from remembering the birthdays and anniversaries of families and friends - we lived our life amidst all kinds of notifications. All of what we enjoyed or didn't enjoy was marked on the calendar or an app to be constantly reminded of that in our busy lives.

The pandemic came and many of these notifications were not even needed anymore. Our routines became simpler, less aggressive. Our life withdrew attention from our never-ending wishlist of to-do things. While we lost track of time and were not moved by the clocks anymore, we realized that we had more time by our side. The hours seemed stretched, the days seemed longer, the weeks went on forever and the months never seemed to end. It felt as if someone had played the pause button on our otherwise so busy lives. Life became pretty normal (at times inactive as compared to our pre-pandemic standards) but more impactful. A time that was always spent in a set of activities was now spent living the very moment and cherishing it.

With the onset of the pandemic, it was tough to believe that we could lead a life devoid of so many activities. But here we were, only getting used to it. Redefining our definition and sense of time.

We once again started waking up to see the rising sun and waited the whole day to see the sunset hues. We went to the rooftop to spot the crescent or the full moon. Parents once again showed their children various constellations in the sky and how they moved their positions with time. The seasons once again became cursors of time. Summers, Monsoon, Autumn, Winters, and Spring - we cherished these seasons once again after a long hiatus. The seasons we had forgotten to enjoy in the pre-pandemic era.

That was the only good thing about losing track of time during the pandemic. We stopped living in anticipation. We started living more in the present. We started enjoying and valuing each moment of life, more than we ever did. Unlike in the pre-pandemic times where looking forward to what lay next was our only motivation to wake up the next day. We were always hooked to what was lined up next. That made our life a bloody race of skipping into the future leaving the present either unattended or dejected. We were always less excited about what that day 'today' brings in for us. We seldom thought about how we could give our best and make the best out of the present. We only dwelled in the day that was yet to come. But the pandemic taught us otherwise. We might have started losing track of days and weeks but we surely were making great strides in valuing the time we have got in our hands.

Sometimes I think, *"Just when we realized everything was coming to an end and maybe there will be no tomorrow, we changed our perspective of time. But would we continue to live in the present once the pandemic is over or was our change of behavior only a temporary reaction because we thought The End was here?"* This fear grips me.

Chapter34: The End, is it?

The End.

A thought that we all carried in our hearts all the while. A thought that we could not get rid of any time while the pandemic clutched us. Two years had gone by fighting the coronavirus and battling for our lives. Trying to find our way through these strange times. Pretending to be normal during these abnormal times. Trying to live normally like before, before 31 Dec 2019. The pandemic has had enough of us. It got to our nerves so much so that we all had that one thought hovering over our heads. *Yeh kya ho raha hai, aisa lagta hai jaise pralya hi aa gayi hai.* It was weird to make sense of what the world was going through. It seemed as if *the end* of the world was here already.

Each one of us was hooked on that thought like a spider hanging by its weight to its web. Just hanging in there waiting to be released forever. But we all resisted thinking those thoughts and uttering those inauspicious words. They say that the universe reciprocates to all that we think and speak. So powerful are our thoughts and words, they manifest. Unfortunately, we seldom are so mindful of them. But this time, we were. Or at least we tried to - to not let that thought transform into a reality.

The entire world was on tenterhooks waiting for the third wave of the pandemic to arrive. There were anticipations. The rise and fall of the COVID cases were being closely monitored across villages, towns, districts, cities, and metros. Nobody wanted to go through the horrors of the past. No one wanted to lose any more loved ones because of the pandemic. But we didn't have answers for sure. We didn't know when the third wave would arrive. We didn't know if it was already there gearing up to take us by storm once again. Meanwhile, 242 children were tested positive in Bangalore. India was on alert. "*Not children, please!*" I prayed. That is the worst the pandemic could harm us. Children are like those hopes for tomorrow, we would cling to make our way forward. They are the bearers of the 1.3 billion hopes and aspirations. Not children, please!

The pandemics are not common though. The annals of history show other pandemics such as Spanish Flu (1918-1920), Asian Flu (1957-58), Flu Pandemic (1889-1890), Russian Plague (1770-1772). The infamous Spanish flu infected the lives of 500 million people worldwide. There were pandemics in the recent past as well. The most recent ones include AIDs (1981-present), H1N1 Swine Flu (2009-2010), Ebola (2014-2016) with the latest being the Zika virus (2015-present). But none of them made enough noise or spread enough scare as COVID-19 did. This one was unique. It was universal in its spread and reached the nook and cranny of the world. It affected each one of us like no other pandemic. The repercussions of the pandemic were felt far and wide. Divided by so many *ethos* and *isms*, the world united under the sufferings and horrors of the pandemic. The impact of the COVID-19 was massive.

COVID happened at the peak of human excellence and accomplishments. The pandemic came and tumbled all that humans had built over centuries to reach where we were. The fact that the pandemic put human existence into question got us scared for our lives. This caused the fear of *The End*.

The pandemic left us clueless. We kept switching between the lockdowns and the phase of unlocking. We lived in between the night curfews and weekend extended curfews. We breathed between the masks on our noses and masks on our chin. We celebrated between relaxed guidelines for public gatherings and a complete ban. We survived between the announcements of opening up and shutting down. We see-sawed between hope and despair. We juggled between staying indoors and incessant desire to be outdoors. Our hearts pulsated between being caged and roaming out wild and free. Our stomachs grumbled between eating home food and craving outside food. We hopped out and hopped in. We trespassed between life and death. We maneuvered between living life to the fullest and surviving each day as it was the last day of our lives. We were, as if on a constant toggle. Impermanence was our constant state for those two years. And we were not sure how long this state would continue. Uncertainty was a unique trait of the pandemic. The pandemic brought more uncertainty with it than what humans could handle.

It dwindled our moral compass. It made us revisit the fundamentals of Survival of the fittest. Survival is what we lived for - fought for - all those days. Amidst that fight, we rediscovered survival - our survival.

With all this uncertainty and fear gripping our minds, *All of Humanity* wondered if what was the way forward? Where did all of this leave us?

Was the pandemic just a one-off event - once in 100 years - like other pandemics? Was it here just for us to take a pause in our otherwise busy lives and continue as is once it was over? Did it happen to pause our lives and make us reflect upon our actions and ways of living and course-correct it before we returned to our "normal"? Or was it here to prepare us for the larger and tougher wars that remained to be fought in the times to come?

Not once, not twice but these thoughts crossed my head multiple times. The entire world was left in suspense lurking to find the meaning behind the occurrence of the pandemic.

Scared. Clueless. Uncertain. Either we learned our lessons and made a way forward or waited for *The End* to arrive.

Eventually, most of us had started to believe that there was no end to the ill effects of the coronavirus. It was here to stay. Though most of us wanted to get back to "our normal", that seemed like a far-fetched reality. The scientific communities predicted that the pandemic would eventually turn into an endemic rather than completely vanishing from our planet.

Nobody talked about the afterlife having been bugged by the daily nuisance of the pandemic. But deep down everybody remained bothered by these thoughts. We could only latch to that hope of "our normal" to come back. Or *all of us* could work together towards making *the new normal* a seamless possibility - ushering the world to a new beginning.

A new chapter awaited us in all our lives.

Chapter35:
A New Beginning

2030.

I am sitting at my work desk looking outside the window. It has just stopped raining heavily. The sun shines brightly from behind the clouds. The sky plays its charm in the myriad hues. A flock of birds sits in a straight line in front of me. I start counting them. There are ten birds out there. "*It's been ten years since the pandemic hit the world*", that reminds me. And suddenly I am disturbed in the middle of my thoughts.

"Dad, what happened in 2020? Will you tell me, please!"

[Aah, what a coincidence. I was just thinking about the same. I tell myself.]

"Oh dear, come here!" (We hug each other and sit together in our bean bags.)

"What makes you ask that today, all of a sudden?", I ask.

"I was watching it on the news. I asked Mom. She says I will let Dad answer that for you."

[My wife and I exchange glances across the rooms and laugh.]

"Sure, why not. I will tell you but you will have to be a very good listener. Hear carefully and be patient.", I reply.

2020 was a life-changing event for all of us. There came an invisible monster. We all were absolutely scared of it. It killed people without letting anyone know. We were so scared that we stopped going outside our homes. We hid so that the monster couldn't find us. In the entire history of mankind, it was for the first time that humans felt defeated at the hand of something so small yet so monstrous. This monster was called coronavirus.

But you know what, how did the virus come, what happened in 2020 is no more important. Really. But what the virus did to all of us and how the world changed for the better is much more magnificent and impactful. Those were dark times, for sure. But we did overcome them.

I love to remember 2020 as *The Year of Great Realisations.*

There is no doubt that the pandemic was cruel to us. But it is also true that if I subtract the pandemic from those times, we were also not building a wonderful world for us to live in the times to come. Rather we lived in a state of complete apathy and oblivion. The pandemic came and it was too harsh on us. It was quick and ruthless in exposing the devastation we had been causing on this earth. And we would have not stopped if not for the pandemic. It came like a big speed breaker in our otherwise smooth lives. It interrupted us. We might have just gone with the flow but the pandemic just made us feel the reality. It hit us hard. So, I love to believe that it was a blessing in disguise.

"But Dad, can a monster be a blessing as well?"

"Yes dear, at times. It is."

Because of that monster, we all became more considerate towards each other. Humans started taking care of each other better. Once the pandemic started retreating, there was less violence and bloodshed. The corrupt thoughts and ideas found no place in society. There was more equality and equanimity everywhere around. From villages to towns, cities to metros - all our friends lived happily. Everybody lived a fulfilling life. We all were content with what we had. We all tried to make the best use of the resources available to us. There was no fight for resources. Instead everybody tried to share the resources and use them judicially so that no one was devoid of them. Not even the coming generations. Sharing became a virtue everybody religiously practiced. Humans stopped harming other humans. All of us became like one large family. The idea of *Vasudhaiva Kutumbakkam* (The earth is one family) came to life in the darkest of hours.

We recalibrated our moral compass to navigate our ways in the times to come.

We started living simpler lives. Your uncles and aunts - my friends, sisters and brothers, and their friends and their friends of friends - all of us, we realized that simplicity could be a way of living as well. We lived in simple houses. We bought less stuff. We only bought what we needed. The idea of building huge palatial houses didn't exist anymore post-pandemic. Everybody realized that one day all of us would be gone forever. And none of it - what we accumulate in our lifetime - would go along. All will be left behind. A simpler life meant a happier life. So, all of us dwelled in that thought. That is how a family of four now has just one car instead of four cars previously.

"You see trees outside the house?"

"Yes, Dad. I do."

"A lot of them?"

"Yes, Dadda."

Right, so once the pandemic started getting over, everybody thought that nature was at the core of our existence. If we had to survive, we needed to take care of nature. Because nature always took care of us. So, we planted more trees and plants in our compounds and surroundings. We ensured that we did not litter our surroundings anymore. Nobody could throw any garbage on the road, not even your chocolate wrapper. We stopped wasting any water. Every house now has a small rainwater harvesting system set up. It is said that when we value something, it is showered in abundance upon us. So, all of us started valuing nature and natural resources much more than we ever did in our lifetimes. Also, we needed to save nature for you - the future generation.

"Thanks, Dad"

[I laugh and say nothing]

Yes, we realized that the world was not meant for us alone. It was a legacy that was to be passed onto future generations. You and your friends, all across the globe. Anyone who intends to or harms nature, cut trees and indulge in deforestation, pollutes water and other natural resources - is severely penalized and punished. The world is a box of treasures that we need to enrich - not exploit it all - before we pass it on to you.

"Dad, where was I when all of this happened?"

"You were born at the cusp of this metamorphosis. You were born in a world that had just started to transform. A world that was new and fresh in its existence."

With the pandemic, we left our old bad habits. We listened to our intrinsic voices. We listened to what nature had to tell us. We realized that only someone responsive to change is going to survive. He alone is the fittest to survive in the toughest of times and transformations. The process of unlearning and learning had to continue forever. It does. And that is why we are here!

"Dad, you also had bad habits?"

"Hahaha. Yes, I did."

"Did Daadu-Daadi also scold you?"

"Yes, they did, very much. They still do."

To that, your Mom and I made a deal. To take better care of our health and fitness. Your Mom and I decided to spend more time with your grandparents and the family. We worked hard with honesty but at the same time, spare enough time for the family you have. We have. The family, we are. This is one good thing that the monster did. It made us realize that being busy all the time was not good enough. We needed to spare some time for our health, for our loved ones, for ourselves, and most importantly - for you!

We needed to be healthy so we could be happy. And we ought to be happy if we wish to be healthy. So now you know what you need to be if you wish to grow into a healthy and happy individual. You do, right?

"Yes, I need to be healthy and happy both."

"That's correct!"

Those were strange times, dear. The whole world had started to believe that the monster was here to vanish us. Everybody felt so distressed and scared. We had started losing hope. But we didn't give up. We mustered courage, and more importantly, we tried to undo the wrong we have been doing. We didn't shy away from learning what was good for us and for the generations that were yet to come and witness the world. We shook ourselves from the long slumber. We filled our hearts with courage and hope. We convinced ourselves that something better awaited us. We pushed ourselves into believing that not all ends are meant to be painful. Some just result in lessons learned the hard way. We picked ourselves from whatever remained of the pandemic that we had survived. And we took a pledge to build a world that was a safe, healthy, and happy place for future generations. We constantly reminded ourselves that a few ends mark the onset of a new beginning. A new chapter in our lives. And that we could defeat any monster if we could win over ourselves.

"Dad, can this monster come back?"

"Hmmm... Maybe, maybe not."

"So, can this monster harm me?"

"No. I just told you that whenever any monster comes in front of you, hold all the goodness and light in your heart. That will be enough to dispel the monster away from you. That will be your guiding light in the darkest of times."

"Always remember, that the biggest monster is us - ourselves. The day we can defeat the monster within us, no other monster can harm us ever. Will you remember that?"

"Yes Dadda, I will. I love you."

"I love you too."

And the world today is a better place. A reflection of a better version of what we have become post-pandemic.

The Optimistic Me

The world stood aghast
and so did I,
thinking about what
the pandemic did to us
and the world
and all that's left behind
of immobile people
and conversations paralysed
the mass migration
the loners, the departed
orphans, and
a generation that went
berserk, broken, bare
left with a massive void
the missing physical presence
over which the virtual world preside

The world stood aghast
and so did I,
counting the miseries
the pandemic left us to fight
the immense darkness that surrounded us
we wondered, will there ever be light?

Was it all over
not yet, not so soon
only when you think
of an endless autumn
comes spring
in its full bloom

There will be a new normal
towards we all shall move
together we would craft
a world that will be all new
made in peace
with hearts full of joy
simplicity-clad humans
and have less to consume
in the hope, we all shall dwell

and dare to dream again

but before

the world needs to heal, and

recover from all the pain

that the pandemic

has bestowed.

The world stands hopeful

and so do I

that tomorrow the sun will shine

bright upon us

over a clear blue sky

and the world be full of

bees and butterflies

And maybe with time

we all shall realise, that

not all The Ends are painful

some just arrive

shaking us from the slumber

giving a reality check

as a blessing in disguise

course correct our actions

in due course of time

saving us the grace of being known
as the most eloquent of species
of all times.

The world stands in that hope
and so do I
that it will be a better tomorrow
with better versions of ours,
let us live again
for we are indomitable spirits
let us give another chance to life
The Optimistic Me
The Optimistic Me
drinks from that cup o' positivity.

About Author

Karanvir is a marketer by profession and author by passion. He loves to introspect and contemplate life. His characters and stories are inspired by the intricacies of today's life. He is extremely moved by the emptiness of the times we live in. He strongly believes that life is not to be rushed but to be breathed in slowly and the world needs to connect for real with each other. He believes in the power of words for they can cause a rebellion and yet heal at the same time. He also enjoys writing poetry while sipping his cup of chai. He feels for nature quite passionately.

CPSIA information can be obtained
at www.ICGtesting.com
Printed in the USA
LVHW031740111221
705948LV00005B/164

9 789354 724213